DESIGNING 21st CENTURY HEALTHCARE

leadership in hospitals and healthcare systems

DESIGNING 21st CENTURY HEALTHCARE

leadership in hospitals and healthcare systems

John R. Griffith

Health Administration Press
Chicago, Illinois

02 01 00 99 98 5 4 3 2 1

Library of Congress Cataloging-in-Publication Data

Griffith, John R.

Designing 21st century healthcare : leadership in hospitals and healthcare systems / John R. Griffith.

p. cm.

Includes index.

ISBN 1-56793-087-5

1. Integrated delivery of health care. 2. Health services administration. I. Title.

[DNLM: 1. Delivery of Health Care, Integrated—organization & administration—United States. 2. Community Health Planning—United States. 3. Managed Care Programs—organization & administration—United States.

W 84 AA1 G816d 1998]

RA971.G737 1998

DNLM/DLC

for Library of Congress

98-17721

CIP

The paper used in this publication meets the minimum requirements of American National Standards for Information Sciences—Permanente of Paper for Printed Library Materials, ANSI Z39.48–1984.™

Health Administration Press

A division of the Foundation of the

American College of Healthcare Executives

One North Franklin Street

Chicago, IL 60606

312/424-2800

TABLE OF CONTENTS

CHAPTER

1

THE ISSUES OF 21ST CENTURY HEALTHCARE

Winners and Losers in Healthcare

Most Americans know that their healthcare is expensive, and that even if it's not good, it's certainly fancy. However, they may not grasp just how expensive it is—costing almost $9,000 per family, the price of a new car every two years. They also probably don't realize how much the actual cost varies across the country—from about $6,500 per family per year to about $12,500, depending on what city one lives in. Finally, Americans are not likely to understand how all this money affects their health, for example, in terms of disability or premature death. In a few fortunate communities, hospital trustees, physicians, and executives have understood these matters, and have acted on their insights. The results have been striking. Insurance premiums are cut, people's satisfaction with service improves, and efforts turn to improving health itself.

Managed care, the revolution that is sweeping the health insurance industry, is also acting as a stimulus to a much more complex response to change in these communities. The new forms of health insurance themselves are not simple. Health maintenance organizations (HMOs) represent the most fundamental changes by working deliberately with a selected panel of physicians and hospitals to improve the care process and make it more efficient. Preferred provider organizations (PPOs) achieve economy by relying on a panel of physicians with whom they negotiate price discounts. The success of these two health insurance forms has led to "hybrids," more complex forms of insurance that balance price reduction, improve efficiency, and offer greater patient choice. The point-of-service plan

(POS) is one hybrid; it allows an HMO patient to pay extra to visit a physician who is not a member of the selected panel. Other hybrids incorporate devices to improve efficiency in the simpler PPOs.

Successful communities are supporting these activities in ways that often pay off, not only for HMO and PPO buyers but for all patients and all members of the community. They reorganize priorities for the healthcare dollar, change how physicians and other health professionals approach the entire process of care, and meet patient needs for convenience and reassurance. Costs fall and quality rises as a result of these efforts, rather than from the HMOs alone, and the benefits are available to all, not just those who subscribe to HMOs. Not surprisingly, such broad changes take time, and the path to success is sometimes twisted and tedious.

In this book, leaders from three communities describe their achievements. Trustees, doctors, and managers explain their philosophy of managing healthcare institutions and go on to describe their goals and their current agendas. The communities—picked to reflect different histories, sizes, and states of evolution—all can demonstrate substantial progress along paths indicated by their local histories. Although the details differ, several common themes stand out.

Greensboro, North Carolina, with a population of 350,000, is part of a metropolitan area of just over one million. Healthcare costs and overall measures of health are similar to the national averages and can apply to dozens of other cities. HMOs are just getting to Greensboro, but they are expected to grow rapidly. Greensboro has faced two key issues for smaller cities in providing health services. By its own choice, it will have only one healthcare organization, Moses Cone Health System, and will rely on regional partners to support the sale of cost-effective health insurance. Second, it will use its healthcare system to reduce costs and to address pressing issues of access for the disadvantaged.

Portland, Oregon, has had managed care for 50 years. It is one of the lowest health cost cities in the country, and its residents enjoy good, but not excellent, health. A metropolitan area of a million and a half, it is large enough to have competing healthcare providers. Legacy Health System competes with Providence Health System and Kaiser-Permanente. All are admirable. Legacy has done particularly well in this decade and has ambitious plans for the future.

Detroit, Michigan, faces the problems of many eastern cities, combining high healthcare costs and serious health risks for many of its citizens. Henry Ford Health System, the largest and fastest-growing of six systems serving a metropolitan area of four and a half million, is also the owner of Detroit's largest HMO. The Ford System is using its influence to extend high-quality healthcare throughout the metropolitan area, cut health insurance premiums, and improve community health.

Five Common Strategic Dimensions

Although their starting points differ, Legacy, Moses Cone, and Ford must each deal with the same five strategic dimensions. *Value* has to do with the cost, quality, and service of the care actually delivered. *Clinical improvement* arises out of the search for value; high-quality, economical healthcare depends on fitting diagnostic tests and treatments to each patient's needs and on integrating them effectively with one another. New *physician organizations* become necessary to support clinical improvement and value. *Diversification and community outreach* means providing care at new sites, including the home, and reaching out into the community to people who often are not yet patients with the explicit goal of keeping them from becoming seriously ill. Finally, *strategy* is a deliberate plan for enhancing overall effectiveness—for actually delivering on clinical improvement, physician organization, and community outreach, and maximizing value. Strategy includes collaboration and cooperation, that is, making decisions about partnerships with other organizations and setting priorities among competing opportunities.

Value

Value, that is, price and quality delivered to the customer, is high on everyone's agenda. But, unfortunately, neither price nor quality is easy to measure in healthcare. The most meaningful prices are insurance premiums, usually expressed in dollars per member per month. Charges for individual services, such as doctors' fees and hospital bills, tell an incomplete and often misleading story. They are incomplete because they omit utilization, the numbers of hospitalizations, doctor visits, and other services involved. They are misleading because as insurers and other payors have striven to cut costs, they have negotiated substantial discounts, so that charges are numbers nobody pays, no more meaningful than the sticker price for an automobile. The true costs are much harder to get at, even for the providers themselves. So leading communities are reporting and studying insurance premiums, provider costs, and utilization to understand the price they pay for healthcare.

Quality of healthcare is a complex subject, but it has a simple core. From a customer perspective it consists of good outcomes, easy access, and acceptable service. All three are now measured systematically. While there are inevitable gaps in the measures and arguments over the detail, leading provider institutions can document their achievements over time and against national standards or "benchmarks." Because good quality depends on satisfied physicians and employees, it is common to measure their satisfaction as well.

Value is improved by rethinking how things are done, particularly how the care of various professionals is selected and integrated. The process called total quality management (TQM) is a tool for improving value used by all three systems. (Legacy calls its TQM process "continuous quality improvement," or CQI.) Achieving value begins with setting goals. Capable institutions set realistic targets for all of the value measures for a year or two in advance, get governing board approval, and then achieve their goals in all but a very small number of situations. The governing board has three roles in this process: insisting on the measurement of all elements of value and continuous improvement of these measures, making sure the goals are both realistic and the best the organization can achieve in terms of community need, and correcting the situation (often by replacing the CEO) if progress does not occur. TQM and similar programs are comprehensive efforts to improve value, including enhancing the motivation of workers at all levels.

Most communities can improve value relatively quickly, seeing tangible improvements in a year or two. Being able to manage value is the starting point for the other dimensions.

Clinical Improvement

The core of healthcare is clinical work: face-to-face, hands-on interaction between patient and caregiver. What surprises many people is the amount of untested and even unquestioned activity that underlies these actions. It is safe to say that the specifications for wiring a home or grading vegetables are considerably better tested than what goes on in a routine doctor visit, although the electrician and the produce manager admittedly have much simpler tasks than the doctor. The clinical actions themselves are carried out by specialists, and the parts are better understood than the whole. Many of the opportunities for improvement arise at the interfaces, or "hand-offs," that are inevitable in medical care. Two processes, say, good nutrition and laboratory testing, may make perfect sense by themselves. Carelessly combined, they lead to serious errors and rapidly mounting costs. Given that modern healthcare comprises hundreds of examinations, tests, treatments, and instructions for each patient, improving both the individual processes and their interactions is a major opportunity to improve all dimensions of value.

Work in the last decade has clarified how processes are studied and improved. There are three well-tested approaches. *Protocols*, also called *pathways* or *guidelines*, are consensus statements of best practice—what will be done routinely for typical patients. Writing protocols down reduces errors and omissions, discourages unnecessary steps, and helps identify the areas needing further study. *Profiling* is the collection of data about clinical processes. Like protocols, profiles are made around carefully identified clinical entities, such as normal pregnancy or adult asthma. They describe the components that went into the care, the costs, differences among patients, and differences in the ways that doctors or institutions treated the entities. They can describe how often, why, and by whom protocols were not followed. They can be the basis for incentives to encourage closer compliance or simply less extravagant practices.

Finally, *case management* identifies high-risk patients and bolsters the processes for their care. A relatively few very sick people, less than 5 percent of the population, consume almost two-thirds of the healthcare costs. Many of these people don't fit the protocols. They have catastrophic illness, like a birth defect or spinal injury, or they have several disease processes interacting in complex ways. Profiles for high-risk patients show mainly that each patient is different. So case managers, specially trained caregivers, design special assistance for these patients as soon as they are identified. They work with individual patients to identify goals, address needs, and overcome difficulties. A number of impressive gains have been made in maximizing recovery and reducing patient discomfort by assigning specially trained teams to manage groups of high-risk patients.

The leading institutions are developing all three of these approaches systematically, in an ongoing search for improved outcomes, patient satisfaction, and cost.

Physician Organization

One of the myths of medicine is that it is a transaction between one patient and one doctor. The modern reality is much more complicated. Even a routine visit for an annual physical, for example, will require at least four different professionals. Something serious, like heart surgery, will involve more than 20. The chances for confusion, delay, waste, and error mount exponentially. Traditional organization has clung tightly to the myth. Most physicians work alone (solo practice) or in small single-specialty groups. The support services that doctors and patients need are partly organized in the traditional hospital, and partly available from a variety of small industries—drug stores, labs, home care agencies, and so forth—for ambulatory patients.

Physician organization coordinates these entities, beginning with the doctors themselves. It provides communication, shared goals and resources, and conflict resolution between the caregivers. The organization is necessary to implement the incentives for increased value; build the support for using profiles, protocols, and case management; and find consensus among differing perspectives. Physician organizations build bridges between primary care physicians—those that tend to see the patient first—referral physicians—those who spend most of the money—and hospitals. The organizations have a number of names and even more styles or approaches. Physician-hospital organization, or PHO, is probably the most common label.

PHOs negotiate the contracts between payors and providers. They establish and manage incentive programs aimed at improving value. They take the concepts from quality management and clinical improvement to the outpatient setting. They support information systems that allow all caregivers access to the complete patient record. They coordinate the purchase of everything from paper goods to surgery and use aggregate purchasing power to hold down prices. They recruit and train support staff. But the value of these contributions is variable, and to some extent controversial. More than most people, doctors hate bureaucracy. It is not always clear to the doctor who has been practicing successfully for years by himself that all of this organization is really a good thing.

The other issue is that no particular form of the physician organization has dominated. The hospital extension approach may be too specialist oriented and high-cost. The multi-specialty group may be too inflexible. The national publicly held corporation may draw off funds for stockholders and add little local value. The insurance company may be insufficiently sensitive to quality and patient satisfaction needs. And the hospital-doctor partnership, the PHO, may be too clumsy and slow to respond. Although there are successful examples of each of these models somewhere (and all will come up in the case studies), none has emerged as the model for the future.

Part of organizing physicians is devising new methods of compensation. The traditional fee-for-service option encourages doctors to do more than is necessary, and it is proven that some doctors yield to this temptation. Capitation, a fixed annual payment for each patient, does exactly the opposite. Too little medical care and too much are both vexing and dangerous. Various intermediate approaches have been tried. The proposals quickly get numbingly complex, like trying to simplify the tax code, but the solution still evades us. All three sites discussed in this book will describe their experiments and their hopes, but none can offer a proven solution. Neither can anybody else. Designing the winning variant of physician organization and compensation is the challenge of the next decade.

Diversification and Community Outreach

The transition from hospital to health system demands efforts on two interrelated fronts. First, alternatives to the inpatient hospital must be developed to make care less complicated, easier to access, cheaper, and more closely tailored to patient and family needs. Second, the organization must reach out to get to people who often are not "patients" but either have silent disease or are at risk of getting it. Outreach includes early testing and prevention.

Diversification arises from the cost and inflexibility of the inpatient acute hospital. Under the impact of technology, it has changed from a place of rest to a place of intervention, like surgery or a heart catheter. Much of its activity is intensive and critical, and the costs parallel that. As this transition has occurred, specialized, less costly sites have developed for the other needs of the sick. The alternatives include outpatient sites, ranging from adult day care to surgical and treatment centers that are almost hospitals, and inpatient services for rehabilitation and for several levels of long-term care. They also include care and support delivered to the home, through home care programs, hospices, and respite care facilities to assist families providing chronic care.

Community outreach has many targets. Smoking, unprotected sex, domestic violence, immunization failures, drug and alcohol abuse, and the deferral of necessary care are the main culprits causing disease. Preventable illness and lack of access are known to cost America more than 20 percent of the healthcare budget in avoidable healthcare, disability, and premature death. The cost of all this is divided among several sources and is effectively buried from public view. Medicare, Medicaid, and local governments may bear the largest burden, but employers and health insurance buyers are not far behind. Charitable organizations and individuals also contribute. The dispersion of responsibility has made the problem everyone's and no one's. Under capitation payment, the providers accept the responsibility. Each illness prevented reduces the total cost of care, and the savings are shared between the providers and the people who pay the premiums.

But while some forms of community outreach are cost effective, others can be very wasteful. The key to success is targeting population groups at special risk and devising low-cost methods to reduce those risks. The nature of disease and disability is such that the persons at risk are often nearer the margins than the center of society. Poverty and lack of education are powerful predictors of a huge fraction of preventable healthcare. So community outreach is a set of programs targeted at various high-risk populations, helping them through education and motivation to eat better; stop smoking; get more exercise; practice safe sex; make their homes, cars, and workplaces safer; and help their children learn. Outreach can also address environmental hazards by cleaning playgrounds, repairing housing, and reducing legal and illegal drug use. Our case study sites will report examples covering all these issues.

Effective community outreach assesses the health needs of the community by analyzing existing data on mortality and morbidity, and developing additional insight through local surveys and marketing assessments. Using community input together with objective data, it identifies risk and promotes a broad consensus on priorities. Then it identifies who is at risk, what population groups most need assistance, and only last develops programs aimed at local high-priority needs.

Effective programs go to the high-risk groups and use advertising and promotional devices to attract them. They experiment with alternative designs and rigorously test the outcomes. They monitor the underlying hazard and look for improvement in the overall community performance as well as in the target population. Because so many of the hazards are associated with social and economic deprivation, successful programs often collaborate with other agencies striving to reach the same groups. Public health departments, United Ways, religious organizations, schools, welfare departments, and police departments become part of the health outreach team. Such collaboration requires sensitivity and flexibility.

Outreach that skips some of the steps tends to be ineffective, to hit low-priority targets, or, worse yet, to fail to reach the people who need the service. When these things occur, outreach becomes window dressing, rather than value enhancing.

Strategy

Healthcare organizations that pursue value, clinical improvement, physician organization, diversification, and community outreach are more complicated than hospitals, with more at stake for a more diverse array of constituents. Such organizations must handle an increased flow of decisions affecting large numbers of people, including patients, doctors, other caregivers, at-risk populations, collaborating community agencies, health insurance companies, employers, and taxpayers. Strategy, the effort to integrate all of this into a coherent whole, is as important as the first four dimensions described. Given the amount of money involved, the variety of perspectives that must be accommodated, and the seriousness of good health, the discussions are not always tranquil.

For healthcare systems that have progressed on the first four dimensions, the core of strategy is managing relationships. Who is represented in our decision forums? Who are our partners, and how do we accommodate their needs? What is our competitive posture, and how do we convey it to our competitors? Strategy is the ability to answer these questions, using general philosophies that help large numbers understand, and specific decisions that convince individuals. The answers quickly become complex. Never has the maxim, "Competition is a form of collaboration," been more realistic. Yesterday's competitors are today's partners and tomorrow's mergers. Collaborations often occur on specifics, while the general relationship stays competitive.

Strategy has become the management of relations with groups. The governing board and executive office of the modern healthcare organization must relate to physician organizations, competitors, payors, and social agencies. The number of contracts, joint ventures, acquisitions, and mergers to be evaluated and implemented has grown to a major task. When it is not performed effectively, outreach becomes enmeshed in turf disputes, physician organizations fail, improvements don't happen, and value isn't delivered.

In the next chapters, we will hear how each of these communities wrestles with the problem of cost-effective healthcare in terms of the five strategic dimensions. Trustees, doctors, and managers of the study institutions will explain what they are doing and why they think it will work. We will start with the smallest and least complicated community. The path is not easy to follow: science and economics have combined to make a tangled web of acronyms, professions, and actions that is hard to comprehend when it works—and mind-boggling when it fails. To the best of my ability, I will be your guide over this path. The final chapter will draw the lessons—what clearly works, what is still problematic, and where to start. It, too, will follow the framework of value, clinical improvement, physician organization, diversification, and outreach, and it will suggest a strategy useful for many communities.

CHAPTER

2

MOSES CONE HEALTH SYSTEM, GREENSBORO, NORTH CAROLINA

The Metropolitan Area

The Greensboro–High Point–Winston-Salem metropolitan area includes five counties. With a population just over one million, it is the second-largest metropolitan area in North Carolina and has 80 percent of the population of a 12-county region called the Piedmont Triad.

The lower end of the Blue Ridge Mountains runs through the Triad, a temperate, upland plateau with a long history of farming, particularly of tobacco. Textiles and furniture were important industries. The Triad is part of the New South, aggressively seeking new industry, and it describes itself as a place "Where Business Is Better and Living Is Great," with more than half the nation's population within a two-day truck haul. Plastics, automotive parts, food products, fiber optics, and financial distribution centers are growing industries. The area has one of the highest levels of manufacturing employment. "Healthcare is another dynamic industry emerging to the forefront of the region's economy," the chamber of commerce publications say.

The metropolitan area also includes Winston-Salem and High Point. The three cities are about 30 minutes apart. The area is close to U.S. medians on most statistics, although it has a high percentage of nonwhites. Guilford County, the largest in the Triad, has a population of 347,000. Household incomes and education levels are in the top 20 percent of all U.S. counties. The proportion of poor people is low, but still near 20 percent. Guilford County has high levels of crime and homelessness, not only relative to the metropolitan area but also compared to the nation as a whole. Despite these problems, the area is clearly a favored setting (Table 2.1).

Health and Healthcare

Like many American cities, the Greensboro metropolitan area is changing its health insurance. Six HMOs operate in the metropolitan area, and by 1996 they had enrolled 29 percent of the population. Partners, owned by Carolina Medicorp (CMI, formerly Forsyth Hospital of Winston-Salem), had more than 100,000 lives, and Physicians Health Plan (PHP), recently purchased by United Healthcare, a national insurance company, had about 90,000 lives. Four other HMOs had a total of 70,000 lives. HMOs did not begin to penetrate the Medicare market until 1997. PPOs have largely replaced traditional commercial insurance, and some of these have been hybrid plans with improved cost containment. Much of the HMO enrollment is in other parts of the metropolitan area; Greensboro itself has less than 10 percent penetration. However, the leadership of Greensboro feels that HMO growth is imminent, and many leaders consider it desirable.

Health insurance premiums in Greensboro are near national averages. The plans set premiums based on prior years' expenditures, resulting in a wide variation among employers. Partners reported the highest rate in the state, \$137.30 per member per month. PHP, at \$131.07, is the third-highest in the state.

Table 2.1 Moses Cone Strategic Quality Goals

	FY 96 Results	FY 96 Goal	FY 98 Goal
(A) Best Value to Our Customers 1. Patients			
Patient Satisfaction (average rating)			
Inpatient	87.2	89.1	*90.7*
Outpatient	88.7	91.4	*93.3*
Emergency Department	77.5	81.7	*85.0*
Quality Measures	See Attached Clinical Outcome Measures		
Percent of Charges Below Comparison Group	77.3	78.0	*75.0*
Market Share by County			
Guilford	49.68	52.0	*53.0*
Rockingham	20.79	21.9	*22.5*
Randolph	21.66	21.9	*22.5*
Alamance	7.15	7.2	*7.5*

(continued)

Table 2.1 (continued) Moses Cone Strategic Quality Goals

	FY 96 Results	FY 96 Goal	FY 98 Goal
2. Medical Staff			
Percent Medical Staff Very Satisfied	84.0	N/A	N/A
Number of "Active User" Physicians	414	390	*401*
Percent Members of PHO	50.0	50.0	*29.0*
3. Employees			
Percent of Employees Satisfied	80.0	N/A	N/A
Turnover	12.0	13.0	*15.46*
Internal Customer Satisfaction	95.0	92.5	*92.3*
(B) Improved Community Health Status			
Measures to Be Defined		2 projects begun	
(C) Financial Viability			
Consolidated Fund Balance Growth (per year)	7.50	7.50	*15.87*
Net Operating Margin (per year)	4.0	5.76	*9.21*
Credit Rating	AA	AA	*AA*

Indicator	FY 96 Results	FY 97 Results	FY 97 Goal
Cesarean sections as percentage of deliveries	21%	21.5%	*21.0%*
Primary C-sections for failure to progress (%)	32%	28%	*41%*
Mortality of infants 500–1,500 grams	20.0%	14.7%	*16%*
Mortality of newborns >2,500 grams	.045%	.05%	*0.05%*
Post op. deep sternal infection, CABG*	0	0	*<.5%*
Post op. stroke within 30 days of CABG	2.26%	2.23%	*2%*
Post op. renal failure, after CABG	2.26%	2.93%	*2%*
Post op. CABG mortality, as ratio to national guideline	3.1%	3.5%	*3.5%*
Emergency CABG due to complication of PCTA**	1.59%	1.22%	*2%*
Mortality post elective PCTA	1.1%	1.8%	*2%*
Average mobility change in rehabilitation	42.5	43.2	*46.4*
Mortality following anesthesia	.19%	.10%	*.18%*
Breast cancer 5-year survival	78%	80%	*81%*
Prostate cancer 5-year survival	74%	84%	*69%*
Lung cancer 5-year survival	12.4%	14.9%	*13%*
Colorectal cancer 5-year survival	61%	55%	*53%*
Breast cancer with breast conserving radiation	N/A	55%	*57%*
Breast cancer detected at Stage 1	N/A	60%	*62%*
Mortality of severe trauma patients	25	N/A	*19.5%*
Average stay in days, severe trauma	9.0	N/A	*9.5*

*CABG: Cardiac artery bypass graft

**PCTA: Percutaneous transluminal angiography (cardiac catheterization and treatment)

Intense price competition has not yet come to Greensboro, but it seems likely that it will. Partners has a substantial market share in Winston-Salem, only about 30 minutes to the west. Preferred has been sold to United Healthcare, a for-profit national HMO with growth intentions. As HMOs become more sophisticated competitors for people under 65, and as they attract more Medicare and Medicaid beneficiaries, they will force price reductions. The Medicare premium, established by federal regulation, was $373 in 1996, just over the national median, but was relatively low for metropolitan areas. The low premium will slow but not stop the growth of Medicare HMOs in Greensboro. North Carolina has a demonstration project moving Medicaid to an HMO style of payment and may adopt it statewide. The combined effort could shift about 10 percent of healthcare expenditures in the next few months.

Public Health and Indigent Care

Guilford County enjoys average to better-than-average health compared to the nation. It is in the lowest quartile of metropolitan areas in heart disease deaths, and near the median in cancer. The most serious health problems are stroke, infant mortality, and low-birthweight babies. AIDS is substantially less prevalent in Guilford County than in the nation at large, but other sexually transmitted diseases are more prevalent (Table 2.2). The Community Health Partnership survey suggests that county residents need encouragement on exercise, smoking, well-child care, and condom use. Alcohol abuse and depression may also be problems. The survey suggests that all but 8 percent of households have health insurance, but a more specific question on coverage indicates that 17 percent have no coverage for hospital bills. Moses Cone Health System will not turn these people away. A substantial part of its agenda involves financing care for the uninsured.

Guilford County has had public health clinics for many years. In 1996, those clinics provided services to over 10,000 adults with communicable diseases and 4,000 people seeking family planning and maternity services, and an array of screening, immunization, and treatment services reaching about one-third of the school-age children and a large fraction of the needy infants. In total, the public health services are about the same size as the community outreach program developing at Moses Cone, but the combined impact reaches only roughly half the likely needs of the poor.

Table 2.2 Guilford County Scores on Available Measures of Health and Healthcare Quality

	Guilford County	Nation
Health		
Age-adjusted mortality (per 100,000 population)		
Cardiovascular	249	281
Cerebrovascular	74.9	56.4
Cancer	204	204
Accidents		29.4
All Causes	877.2	871.57
Decline in mortality, 1985–1992	63.3	71.18
Low birth weight*	8.5%	1.49%
Persons reporting fair or poor health status	16%	13.39%
Health Insurance		
Households reporting:		
HMO coverage	32%	22%
PPO coverage	48%	11%
Fee-for-service coverage	12%	39%
Uninsured	8%	15%
Patient Perceptions		
Percentage of adults who smoke	19%	30%
Percentage who consider healthcare too expensive	19.9%	N/A
Percentage of households with children who did not get an annual checkup	20	N/A

*Percent of live births weighing less than 1,500 grams.

Source: Household Survey of Guilford County by Tripp, Umbach & Assoc., 1995; National Center for Health Statistics.

Healthcare Provider Organizations

Care in the Greensboro area still follows the traditional pattern of independent medical practitioners and competing hospitals. The Moses Cone Health System defines its service area to include three of the five counties in the metropolitan area. Greensboro, with a population of 183,000, and High Point, population 69,000, are the principal cities of the service area, and both are in Guilford County. Randolph County, population 106,000, and Rockingham County, with 86,000 people, have their own hospitals, but they rely on Moses Cone and High Point for referral care. Moses Cone is clearly in a position to lead the market: it has arranged a merger with Wesley Long, the only other hospital in Greensboro, and has a strategic alliance with Randolph Hospital, the only one in Randolph County.

Most physicians in the Greensboro area practice in small single-specialty groups. Neither Moses Cone nor High Point has purchased practices on a large scale. The Greensboro HealthCare Network (GHN) is a physician hospital organization jointly developed in 1996 by Moses Cone and Eagle Physicians and Associates. Eagle is the largest organized practice in the area, but it has only about a third of the primary care doctors.

Moses Cone Health System

Moses Cone Health System began in 1953 as a small (51-bed) hospital, and it grew steadily through the next three decades. For its size, it placed unusual emphasis on education. It accepted medical residents in 1954, and by 1960 it had nursing school affiliations with both the University of North Carolina at Greensboro and the local public schools. Moses Cone became an Area Health Education Center (AHEC) affiliated with the University of North Carolina Medical School in 1974. (The AHEC coordinates physician education.) Dennis Barry, the current chief executive, joined Moses Cone in 1979. In the 1980s, Moses Cone established a day care center and a family practice center, a trauma center, and a rehabilitation center. It acquired a competing for-profit hospital that it reopened in 1990 as the Women's Hospital of Greensboro. It began a regional cancer center in 1990.

In 1991, Moses Cone adopted four strategic goals, which have guided its actions in the last six years:

1. **Community Service.** [To make] a major rededication and commitment to our mission of providing service to the community.
    - A primary care model of service to the indigent
    - Programs [that] focus especially on the needs of women and children
    - A community corporation, including other community constituencies, structured to get to work
    - A geriatric day care program
    - Outpatient drug abuse programs
    - An AIDS program
    - School-based health—"We should do what we are allowed to do and . . . support the general needs of the school system to focus on a better educated and more self reliant community."
    - Advocate appropriate care and equitable financing

2. **Increasing Scale.** [To] serve our community by successfully competing and increasing scale.
   - Centers of excellence and [other activities that] enhance our role as a regional referral center
   - A Piedmont Regional Healthcare System [that] would include High Point and North Carolina Baptist Hospitals
   - A satellite strategy for hospital and physician services
   - Prudent support of new services
   - Interest in smaller, regional hospitals
3. **Value to Stakeholders.** [To be] indispensable to our constituents . . . compete on price and quality.
   - Clinical and administrative decision making linked further down the organization and closer to patients
   - Protocols and information to influence resource consumption and quality
   - Clinical technology [that] supports our regional referral role
   - Ethical medical care a visible and formal part of the Moses Cone community
   - Education within our organization at several different levels
   - Broadcasting our comparative advantage in cost and outcome
4. **Physician Relationships.** [To] boldly and imaginatively define and evolve a new, closer, and more productive relationship with our physicians.
   - Seek out proactively those physicians who will work with us
   - Pursue managed care contracts
   - Work with physicians who express an interest in cooperative practice
   - Prepare for outpatient DRG mechanisms and experiment with global fees in selected services
   - Continue to identify joint venture opportunities [that] would benefit us and our physicians

This list of objectives was unusually visionary for the time and place. HMOs had less than 5 percent of the market. Attention was just beginning to turn to "managed competition," and the national discussion of Clinton health reform was still two years away. Also unusual is the rigor with which Moses Cone followed its vision. Major steps were made on each of the four issues, although it was not until 1996 that tangible progress emerged.

Moses Cone Implements Its Vision

Value to Stakeholders

Moses Cone has mounted several strategies to reduce its costs and improve its services in the traditional inpatient and outpatient programs. It has developed a total quality management (TQM) program, and provides basic quality management instruction to all employees. It has established goals for quality of care and has begun routine reporting of a "dashboard" covering several measures of cost and quality. It has established a rigorous operating and capital budgeting system and has undertaken strategic process reengineering. As a result, the medical center has held cost increases to near zero over the last six years, and has kept prices constant. In 1996, it decreased prices. Compared to 14 other large North Carolina hospitals, Moses Cone's charges per case were lowest for 11 of the 30 most common DRGs (reasons for hospitalization) and were never above the median. ("Charges" are only a rough guide to what was actually paid to the hospitals, but the performance is commendable.) Financially, the hospital has an exceptional record (Table 2.3).

Moses Cone and many other institutions are using multiple measures of service that they monitor at the governing board level. Moses Cone's dashboard includes patient satisfaction, market share, physician and employee satisfaction, financial performance, and some clinical outcomes (Table 2.3). The table shows that Moses Cone set ambitious goals for all of its dashboard measures. Although it has shown continued improvement on almost all measures, it has so far been unable to meet many of its goals, with the exception of the financial performance measures. It has substantially exceeded its fund balance growth and net operating margin goals, and met its goal of a AA bond rating. Its financial performance has generally stayed close to that of its largest competitor, High Point.

The trustee role in value

Charles Reid, trustee and former board chair, talks about how the Moses Cone board of trustees evolved:

> "I've been around for 15 years, almost as long as Dennis Barry has been here. A lot of the current philosophy about being a not-for-profit and achieving a positive operating margin was sorted out in the early years when I was on the board. Moses Cone garners more and more respect as a preeminent high-quality, fairly priced hospital system. When I joined the board,

Table 2.3 Moses Cone Health System Key Financial Indicators

	FY 1995	FY 1996
	(Amounts in Thousands)	
Net Patient Revenue	$232,755	$255,453
Other Revenue	9,344	10,632
Total Revenue	242,099	266,085
Expenses	$225,581	$240,239
Income from Operations	16,518	25,846
Non-Operating Gains (Losses)	8,658	21,733
Net Income	$25,048	$47,388
Operating Margin	6.82%	9.71%
Total Margin	10.30%	17.80%
Long-Term Debt to Equity	26.70%	20.60%

> the perception was that Moses Cone was a good hospital, the largest in the county, that must have wealth behind it because the Cone family endowed it. It did not have the Centers of Excellence that we've built since.
>
> "Healthcare wasn't that big an issue in the early 1980s. The business community expressed concern about the skyrocketing costs of employee health programs, but never made a well-organized, proactive, get-your-arms-around it effort. We had two fine hospitals in Greensboro, and if you wanted specialty work you would go to Duke or Bowman Gray. You wouldn't consider Moses Cone for open heart surgery or something that complex. The simple matter is that Moses Cone developed much of this tertiary capability over the last dozen years. People don't have to go out of town to get specialty care."

As Charlie Reid sees it, the landmark change was an acceptance of the need to earn a profit and to assure financial stability in an environment where revenue would be harder to come by:

> "Before 1980, the board was dedicated and sophisticated, but the feeling was that there was no need to achieve a margin. You set your prices and your business plans to break even. As we began to realize there were some storm clouds—Medicare reform, the cost-plus bonanza was probably not going to last, the county's lack of indigent care—that's when we started the process of agreeing to some operating philosophy."

And Cone's board also needed to look beyond the conventional activities of the hospital:

> "I think our original goal was rather than break even, we should manage the hospital to achieve a 4 percent margin. That way we could build some additional financial resources and be prepared to expand into an integrated hospital system. We would not stay focused as we had on one campus and an acute care hospital. We decided that that mission was too narrow, and we accepted a much broader challenge. Dennis helped facilitate understanding and appreciation for the challenge we might be facing. It was very emotional. There were great trustees who loved this hospital and this community who were asking themselves and us, 'Is this an ego trip we want to take? What's wrong with restricting ourselves to an acute care hospital? Will we simply be capturing turf of competing entities?' We always had two trustees who were physicians, and the elected president of the medical staff attended the meetings. Some of the physicians were nervous that Moses Cone would try to build an empire, becoming too powerful in the community.
>
> "It took us months and months to sort through that. We went off on retreats. We had facilitators. The board took psychological tests to get an appreciation of ourselves, where we were coming from, and the diversity of styles among a very impressive board. Buddy Weill, who was board chairman at that time, made it happen. He was a very successful local real estate broker. He had no personal stake, but he thought it was important to come to a conclusion. Dennis proposed the change, and the board wrestled with it. We agreed to it, but we were a little more conservative than Dennis preferred."

With a solid consensus on a sound financial position, Moses Cone Health System began to move in 1991 to curtail costs and increase its competitiveness. There was reaction from the physicians, and Charlie Reid explains the board's response:

> "The issues from 1991 [community service, scale, value, physician organization] hadn't been settled when I took the chair. A lot of our physicians said, 'Greensboro is one of the most desirable places to practice medicine because the physicians have a collegial relationship. We don't get enthused about some kind of alliance with one hospital.' It goes back to the concern Cone might become too powerful, too dominant. It wasn't difficult

> for our board to understand that Greensboro had been sheltered from the change, and it would not be permanent.
>
> "We just kept saying to the physicians, 'The world's going to be different. Let's do it as partners, together, rather than having for-profit entities come in here and start making physicians choose sides and face off with each other.' It wasn't all that difficult to see from models out there like California and others that if we didn't prepare ourselves in a constructive way with the physician community, together, we'd find ourselves in conflict and chaos when the sea change emerge[d] in Greensboro."

Finally, Charlie talks about the pressure to control costs, and the board's response, which was to emphasize quality and value:

> "Some of the major employers offer PHP, some Partners. Many offer a choice, with premium sharing. That started around the same time. The CEOs began to look for more cost-effective programs for health insurance. When we were going through this sorting-out process to determine our priorities, there never was any question in my mind about the quality of patient care nor price. The board and management were totally committed to top quality. We were also committed to a good financial value for the patient. We wanted to offer price that was conservative and competitive with anything in this region.
>
> "Management put together business plans that said here's what we can do if we leave prices flat, raise them 2 percent, or 4 percent. We said, 'Leave them as is.' We felt we could still accomplish everything we needed to do and not raise prices. There was not a basis to raise prices just because there was an opportunity to do so. Once again, we were going to offer top quality, and we want to offer a bargain on prices to the patient. The idea that we should be economical goes way back in Greensboro. A good word for it is 'Good Value.'
>
> "We decreased our prices last year. The finance committee of the board and management initiated that decision. They ran their models. After giving management its opportunity, the committee makes its recommendation. Lanty Smith, Carole Bruce, and Dennis recommended the decrease. The feeling was, 'Change has started to come to Greensboro. We need to put the pressure on ourselves to find ways to be productive and effective without compromising quality in any way.' It raises the bar for management."

Charlie's thoughts are echoed by Lanty Smith, J.D., chair of the board of trustees:

> "The budget process at this hospital starts with what we think the costs are going to be. Then we look at what our pricing needs to be in order to achieve a positive net margin. We don't want that margin to be very high. We view this hospital as having one shareholder, and that shareholder is the broad community. It's certainly not a group of for-profit shareholders, and it's not the doctors, who are stakeholders but not shareholders.
>
> "There was no decision to freeze prices. It was on the other side, that we are committed to reengineering the hospital, drive down costs, restructure it in the same fashion as has been happening in the manufacturing industries throughout this region, and also in the same fashion that has been shown to be possible in the healthcare industry elsewhere in the country. We ought to work tenaciously on quality measures and cost reduction, and the outcome of that was that we didn't need to raise prices."

Bob Newton, vice president of financial services, talks about the kind of trustees who, like Charlie Reid and Lanty Smith, make value happen. He also refers briefly to one way to make sure it *doesn't*:

> "Somewhere in the early '70s, the board membership rules were changed, putting a limit on any individual's length of service. That triggered turnover, which brought people like Buddy Weill and Charles Reid to the board—people who were cognizant of what it took to run a business over the long haul. They were less influenced by the historical perspective that was deeply rooted in the Cone family. They looked at the operation in a more objective way and recognized the need for change. They were hands-on operating managers.
>
> "Prior to that time, Caesar Cone and others had been on the board for many years. Mr. Cone had been chairman, and the board was less involved. When he left, a group of managers began to emerge, with a much more collective judgment. This transition was not always smooth, but overall it was positive."

Carole Bruce is a trustee on Cone's board and chairs the finance committee. Carole notes that she has served on many of the board committees. (She has also chaired the United Way and the hospice board, and has engaged in other community activities):

"I think among the volunteer leadership, Moses Cone is perceived as a real contributor to Greensboro and a great community asset. Most people realize we don't have a county-funded hospital, and [that] Moses Cone stands in those shoes. There is some perception that we are very large, and powerful, but not necessarily in a negative way. Size brings strength and stability, some good things. My perception, having been on the inside, is of an institution dedicated to community health and community welfare. I've been asked to serve on the new merged board.

"I think the whole point of the merger with Wesley Long is to carry on those goals, to provide the best healthcare at the lowest possible price. The merger enables us to do that better. I personally know every person on the Wesley Long board very well. I think their objectives are the same as ours. We are in this for community welfare, and no other reason."

As chair of the finance committee, Carole considers the hospital's charges from both the hospital's perspective and that of the impact of price rates on the community:

"I'm proud of what we've done. We studied those financial statements three or four years ago, and I said, 'We ought to cut some rates.' The other business people on the committee said, 'Cut rates?' I said, 'But it's the right thing to do. We can cut rates.' We kept rates level for a couple years, but we actually cut rates last year. I realize our first requirement is a bottom-line addition to our capital, but we've done that. We try to hit an operating margin of at least 4 or 5 percent, and keep our debt down.

"How to know when you've spent enough is a much harder question. That really comes more from the medical leadership. We have analyzed every capital request, and we certainly feel we have met all reasonable requests. You protect the downside and build on the upside as you see the opportunity. Even if you have money, you don't want to spend it foolishly."

Dennis Barry, CEO, explains how that strategy paid off with community support for Moses Cone:

"Many of the big companies in Guilford County understood the cost of healthcare here compared to other areas. They thought Greensboro was a really good buy. The trustees knew that, and wanted to preserve it. Historically, the board's number one interest is serving the community. They feel Moses Cone plays a very important role in the infrastructure of the community, and they want to see that continued and enhanced over time. Secondly, they want us to continue to focus on quality, and third on cost. They understand very well the transition the field is going through today. In a very real way, the 1991 work was preparing the board for what we are doing today. We tried to put together a plan that contained a framework for the future, as opposed to a more definitive layout, because we knew the field was in for a lot of change.

"By 1987/88, when we began to make some good solid margins, we began to not raise rates. We did that very judiciously. Even though we had a lot of outlay in terms of capital requirement, we continued to build the endowment. We continued to borrow from tax exempt funds, and arbitrage the earnings on our investments. The organization now generates about $60 million a year in cash. We have been investing most of that recently."

David McCombs, executive vice president, expands on the value strategy as it translates to operations:

"The issue is not charging what the market will bear. Some of our physician colleagues, up until recently, had that perspective. I fought up until recently many battles over charging what the market will bear versus charging enough to maintain our operation. I've never heard articulated, 'Keep charges flat.' As we have succeeded and exceeded our financial targets year after year, the conclusion is, 'Well, we don't need to raise charges. In fact, isn't there an opportunity to turn back some of this money to the community?'

"As operating officer, I think the board of trustees would have entertained increases, if it had been necessary. But it has been a strategic goal to keep our rates low, so that this is not an attractive market for alternative providers. We've had many opportunities to justify rate increases, but we chose not to because the long-term strategy is to prevent this from being an attractive market to Kaiser, or Prudential, or Aetna. We want to make our prices so low they could not make a profit. We don't want to be one of those communities that inadvertently becomes a target for those initiatives.

"I think the strategy is the vision of Dennis Barry, but the board has been supportive of it. The board's view is of a community asset. We should only take out of the community that amount which is necessary to have a viable, first class health system. We would rather that those moneys be used for something else, and keep the cost of health insurance down for our employers."

As chief operating officer, David led the team that got the results. He knows how they were achieved:

"Over the last four years, we have reduced cost per admission 2.5 to 3.0 percent per year. The other part of the strategy is growth. The admissions per year have grown 3 to 6 percent per year, and outpatient activity has grown 5 to 10 percent per year. Most of that has been through market share growth. In the initial phase, it was the local market. In the last four or five years, it has been growth in our secondary markets.

"The focus has been on both management controlled costs and clinical utilization. If all we did was add volume without changing the length of stay, number of x-rays, et cetera, we would not have made the gains we did. Particularly over the last three to four years, there has been a concerted effort with our physicians to cut the utilization of services per patient."

Measured performance and continuous improvement

A value strategy like Moses Cone's requires more than simply a top management consensus. It requires measured performance, so that specific goals can be evaluated and attained; an annual goal-setting exercise selecting realistic targets for the coming year or two; and a program of training and incentives to motivate members of the organization. Continuous improvement arises because people—caregivers, clerks, cleaning and maintenance personnel—are convinced that they can change processes, invent new methods, and rely on their teammates to make it work. The "360 degree evaluation" that both Dennis and Ken mention in this section is a deliberate survey of team confidence. The usual reviews are duplicated in reverse. Workers evaluate their supervisors, and suppliers their buyers, and the internal users of service are included as well as outside customers.

Dennis Barry, CEO, explains the evolution of TQM, measurement, and incentives. These tools strengthen the ability of operating personnel to change:

"There's no question that TQM has changed this organization. People now have a much better understanding, and much

> more focus on quality, and a genuine belief that one can improve quality and reduce costs at the same time. We are beginning to move into 360 [degree] evaluation. Wesley Long has done a good job with their program, too. Their recent employee attitude survey, in March, shows better results than we've ever done. When we announced the merger, we spent a lot of time explaining and reassuring people.
>
> "We always use house organs and announcements to focus people on annual goals. We have employee councils at both hospitals. I personally meet a random group of employees every month; I have since I came here. I'm not as close to the employees as I used to be. More recently, I did a series of four town meetings talking about the changes associated with managed care, the things we as an organization need to do in order to be successful.
>
> "We've had no layoffs. We maintained merit pay increases every year. I think people feel relatively well served. Our problem today is that Greensboro has such a low unemployment rate—around 2½ percent—that our turnover rate is going up. We used to run 13 or 14 percent; we are now up to 20 percent. I'm very concerned about it. We are starting a whole initiative to look at the off-shift, part-time, and weekend jobs, to restructure them or introduce a set of premium pay levels. We have to do a better job of recruiting and retaining, and we can't under the traditional ways."

Middle managers are a key to success in continuous improvement. They must answer workers' questions, learn new methods, and debug new systems. Many have trouble making the transition. Dennis says:

> "We went through a whole process of changing middle management, but the new group has been stable. The managers are more and more in a matrix kind of situation. We have training programs that include a basic management program and an individual assessment and development plan. The program is four years old. TQM is still part, but we are more focused now on quality assessment. We had a program of reengineering last year. It's been interesting, because a number of the things they thought they could do got into quality problems they hadn't anticipated. It engaged the organization at a different level.
>
> "We have had some management attrition, and some flattening of the management structure. It's been done little by

little. We will have some turnover with the merger. This has been the most stable management team I've ever had, but there are a number of people who are at a position where they need to get on with their career, and others who are getting to the end of their career. We are about to start a new period with a new management team. I want to keep and develop the really good people, and help the others on with their career."

Ken Boggs, vice president for quality and resource management, expands on the evolution of TQM:

"Historically our departments had individual monitors that they were chasing. It was hard to see action coming out of those measures. We would periodically debate whether any of them were worthwhile. Meanwhile, the medical staff was doing standard peer review, looking at chart after chart on an individual basis. Their criteria were generally on target, but not a whole lot came out of that process. We had no general corporate measures, and a much stronger tendency to sort of name a problem and then name a solution, without understanding or tracking through the relationship between the two.

"In 1991/92, we all got training under a formal quality improvement program. We trained on the difference between quality control and quality improvement and quality planning. Then we focused on quality, customer satisfaction and customer focus, teamwork, and empowerment. Empowerment was a struggle for us as a concept. [Empowerment is the concept that the person closest to the job should have the authority to do it right, changing the process or, in an emergency, stopping it.] It still is. We want folks involved, but we tend toward a top-down decision process. But by 1993 we had given all staff 8 hours of training, and management 16 hours.

"We adopted a dashboard of indicators that tried to focus on three areas. Service includes patient, physician, employee satisfaction from formal surveys and performance, such as admissions per physician and market share. Cost measures include comparing our top 30 DRGs to other North Carolina hospitals. Finally, we have some measures of outcomes. We asked each of our major clinical programs to tell us the two or three measures by which we can watch what they are doing. We have comparisons to a national database in each case. We set 1993 goals and 1998 goals for all three types of measures.

The 1998 goals have been somewhat beyond our grasp, but the corporate scorecard has allowed us to stay focused at the corporate level."

Training and incentives for value

Once performance is measured and goals are set, training—so that hundreds of people know why change is necessary and how to do it—and incentives to reward success are essential to sustain the program. Although the incentives go well beyond financial rewards, all three sites use financial rewards.

Boggs continues, discussing how satisfaction surveys and 360-degree reviews become incentives:

> "We train new employees in TQM principles 90 days after arrival. Related concepts are covered in other management courses. We recently did a program called 'Walk the Talk' for all the management personnel, which tied well to TQM.
>
> "Out of our employee satisfaction survey, we learned that employees felt that their suggestions were being sidetracked or ignored. So we started a suggestion program run out of my office. The commitments are, 'You will hear back,' and 'We will at least give it to the right manager to evaluate.' Part of the value is to get an answer back quickly. We told our managers that they didn't need to accept every suggestion.
>
> "We have an interdepartmental satisfaction survey that we have done for four years, where each department surveys its internal customers, department to department. So if nursing is dependent on pharmacy's getting the right meds into the cart, pharmacy should be asking nursing, 'How are we doing?' That's been real helpful. We've had some real contests, where people said, 'You are not meeting my needs at all.' That sort of forced the issue in some of the departments that really do have a problem. We want to push satisfaction up to 95 percent. We are now at 92. We think if our internal customers are satisfied, it rolls on to the patients."

David McCombs, executive vice president, on incentive compensation for management:

> "Our system has been in place over ten years. Department heads may earn up to 12 percent over base pay. Executives can earn up to 18 percent over base pay. It covers 20 some executives and about 180 department heads. The base salary

> is a competitive market salary. The objectives are in three tiers. There is a set of strategic goals for the entire organization, including value to our customers, improving health status, and maintaining financial viability. Most of those are quantified with specific measures that have annual and five-year goals. Second, there are annual divisional objectives such as improving physician participation in our utilization strategy, expanding the care management program, adding new primary care practices, and so forth. Third, individual objectives track the divisionals.
>
> "There are defined measures and quantitative goals. For department heads, 70 percent of the incentive is based on their individual goals, and the balance on division and system. For executives, 50 percent, and for senior executives only 30 percent. You get 50 percent of the incentive if the goal is achieved, and the rest as it is exceeded."

The combination of training, measured performance, and financial incentives provides strong motivation to the top management at Moses Cone. Keeping all of the goals in perspective requires a dedicated team, a strategy, and a measurement system:

> "When we tied them to the incentive payment, that was very powerful. In the last four years, the strategic and divisional goals have been met, and your actual bonus depends upon your personal performance. In 1991, there was no bonus, because we elected to bring in premium priced nurses to deal with a shortage, and we failed to make the strategic financial goals. In the last ten years, the average bonus has been 12 to 14 percent, with the last four at the full level.
>
> "It has not triggered decisions that favor financial goals over quality. It's had a very favorable effect on our team environment, because everyone shares the strategic goals. I think the only drawback is that it's only one year at a time. A longer term would be useful. We might change the weight between financial, patient satisfaction, and employee satisfaction. We measure performance every six months. It's a focused management model, where everyone has a good understanding of their role in the total enterprise goals and [of] their individual accountability."

David describes why Moses Cone does not extend its compensation system to a larger group of employees:

"We have been discussing gainsharing for the entire staff for about five years. We've explored various models pretty seriously, but we've not been convinced that gainsharing is a sustained compensation policy. Last December we gave every employee $250, after taxes. That was a one-time recognition of an outstanding year. It was unbudgeted. It will affect our bonuses. The response of the employees was extremely positive. We remain somewhat skeptical of gainsharing as a long-term compensation strategy."

Marketing for value

The final element in achieving value is a continued protection and expansion of market share. Marketing is important to gain revenue, but its impact on profits is even greater. Most parts of most hospitals have excess capacity that is already paid for. Additional patients come in at much less cost than those already there.

Marketing depends heavily on quality. It ties to patient and physician satisfaction, two of the closely monitored nonfinancial measures. It also depends on strategy. The institution's scope of services, competitive posture, and alliances with others have a direct impact on market share. And of course, in a managed care market, share depends on having a competitive price.

David McCombs, executive vice president, discusses some ways in which Moses Cone has worked to make itself attractive in the marketplace:

"The operating managers are accountable for identifying ways to increase market share and implementing them. As an organization we have invested infinitesimal money in advertising. Up until recently, the way we gained market share has been to work with our physicians, understand needs of the secondary market setting, and deliver to those demands. It's been around service, around meeting the community needs, like our satellite programs.

"We have implemented two very successful programs. One is CareLink, a ground transport program, using two dedicated ambulances whose sole purpose is to transfer patients between care sites. We do about 150 transports per month, mostly in heart, trauma, and neurology. We don't need a helicopter. Our patients are within 50 miles and we can get them here fast enough. The ambulance is a full critical care unit with a nurse and equipment to stabilize the patient.

"The other is StatLine, a single telephone number that doctors can call. We find the doctor, the bed, give the initial orders, and arrange transportation in one call. The same number is used for CareLink and for noncritical patients. We educate doctors and ERs in outlying communities about our clinical pathways. Before the patient hits our door, we have verified the initial condition, orders, tests, and completed the initial steps of the pathway. The patient does not stop in our ER, but goes straight to the ICU. That's a benefit we didn't foresee in our planning. Patients brought in on CareLink have a length of stay two or three days less than patients who arrive by other means.

"We are recruiting an executive for Triad Health Alliance who can market managed care contracts for the seven-county region. The idea is to have single signature contracts for employers with care sites throughout the region. Many of our employers have multiple plant sites in the region, and their employees may live anywhere in a 100-mile radius. Moses Cone [alone] could not serve all their needs. With the Alliance, which includes High Point and Carolina Medicorp in Winston-Salem, we can offer a single price for service across 250 miles. We think we can get some leverage in dealing with large managed care companies."

Clinical Improvement

Moses Cone started a clinical pathway program in 1992. As in most communities, the program began with hospital inpatients because the organization is stronger there, the patients' needs are most clearly differentiated, and large amounts of money are spent. It was very successful for its first three years, resulting in a 25 percent reduction in length of stay and a 16 percent reduction in cost per case for covered diagnoses. Sixty percent of inpatient admissions had pathways by July 1996, but no substantial improvements occurred in cost or stay during that fiscal year. Kenneth Boggs, vice president for quality and resource management, noted that only 40 percent of the 1996 pathways met "moderate" guidelines promulgated by a nationally known consulting company, and only 13 percent met "well-managed" levels. Ken identified 9,300 days of care that failed to meet moderate levels. The DRGs contributing most significantly to those 9,300 days are the focus of goals for 1997 and 1998. The improved effort resulted in almost 5 percent cost savings and an additional 14 percent reduction in length of stay.

A study of 38 likely diagnoses for case management—those where pathways don't work very well—indicated that Moses Cone was losing nearly $8 million per year. Management decided to pursue both pathways and case management. Case management programs in other institutions were visited and evaluated, and a model appropriate to Moses Cone was proposed. A pilot program was begun in 1995 and expanded in 1996. For case management patients, those not included in the pathway program, lengths of stay declined 13 percent and costs were reduced 12 percent in 1996. Results for the 1997 fiscal year were promising.

Finding improvements

Jim Whiting, CEO of Women's Hospital, describes a comprehensive program of clinical improvement for obstetrics. He begins with attractiveness in the marketplace, and the way goals are set around the various elements of performance:

> "Admissions to Women's Hospital are still growing, because it captured local market share and expanded in secondary markets. Volume has increased over 20 percent since 1990. Between 1994 and 1995 we actually reduced our cost per stay, and we expect to do so again in 1997. We are in the 99th percentile in patient satisfaction among hospitals of less than 150 beds, significantly above the average.
>
> "Our approach is what industry calls a 'focused factory,' where we look at a very few lines of business, but try to do those extremely efficiently and continually improve our quality. All of our efforts are focused on improving service, costs, and outcomes. We had the opportunity to focus the entire institution, lab, nutrition, pharmacy, and so on, on a few DRGs—deliveries, women's reproductive needs, gynecological surgery, and neonatal care.
>
> "We have independent goals for finance, clinical outcomes, patient satisfaction, physician satisfaction, and employee satisfaction. Financially, we have met or exceeded our goals for the last four years. We set ambitious five-year quality goals from comparative databases for low birth weights, total cesarean sections, c-sections for failure to progress, and neonatal mortality. We are improving in all areas. We used the Maryland Quality Program for comparison. More recently, we've used data from the National Perinatal Information Center, or from a group of eight women's hospitals across the country that shares information."

With a solid operating team, the Women's Hospital is prepared to go to clinical protocols. Jim continues:

> "We have clinical pathways that cover 90 percent of our patients, and we have very high compliance with those protocols. We use our peer review committee to approve the pathways before they go to the full medical staff, and we've had virtually no problem getting physician approval and support. We developed our pathways after review of what has been done elsewhere. We revise them regularly, getting physician input regularly."

Not every concept is a winner. Jim describes one that failed, and how they dealt with it:

> "We had spent two years preparing for LDRP [labor, delivery, recovery, and postpartum care delivered to most mothers in the same room]. Under it, nurses have to be cross-trained, in delivery and mother–baby care. Our physicians had to buy into that approach. I spent a lot of time with the doctors on an individual basis, discussing the program we were about to initiate and getting their advice on what they liked and what they were concerned about. When LDRP started, we realized within three months that we had such a high number of high-risk deliveries, who stay much longer, that the room turnover wasn't working out. So we moved labor, delivery, and recovery to one end, and postpartum to the other. It wasn't difficult because all the rooms were designed for deliveries. The most difficult part was getting the physicians confident that we could make the change work.
>
> "The other challenge was that our nursing staff felt that they had failed. The nursing director and I spent many nights in the hospital, letting our nurses know it wasn't them that failed, it was our planning process. We learned later that to that date, no institution our size had successfully implemented LDRP. We kept the capability of LDRP if a mother specifically requests it, but most of our people are trained to be either a labor and delivery nurse or a mother–baby nurse."

But other projects worked out better. Jim describes some of the successes:

> "People walked into a building they had helped design but they'd never seen before. Half our people came from Moses Cone, a quarter were already there, and a quarter were new hires. We had people who referred to a given department by

different names. For the first two years we had 25 to 30 percent turnover. What some people didn't realize was that a third of our beds are critical care. The lab, for example, was one of the units that had been on site. They had never experienced the need for fast turnaround that comes with supporting intensive neonatal care. Wherever it made sense to establish a separate department at Women's we did. We have our own social service and our own respiratory service, and we get most other services by arrangement with Moses Cone. Our turnover is now very low, about 10 percent.

"Our customer service training programs are mandatory. We developed our own customer satisfaction goals, and a training program that all our employees attend once a year. In a previous position, I had been trained as a trainer by PSA Airlines, so I started the internal program. We saw that when you concentrate on providing service, efficiency improves, and you can transform that into profitability. We focused the entire institution on quality and service. We cannot be seen as anything but caring and quality. We actually hired extra people when we first opened to make sure our patients and physicians were well served.

"We changed our organization two years ago. I had a vice president of nursing, a vice president of support services, and a controller who reported to me. When our vice president of support services left, to show the rest of the organization we were serious about cost containment, we decided not to replace that position. We now have a patient care division including nursing and several clinical support services. Our controller has the hotel support services.

"We have a maternity admissions unit to reduce the number of admissions for false labor. The incoming patients are evaluated by our in-house physicians and nurse practitioners. The length of stay averages about three hours, and about two-thirds are discharged. The first year, the unit avoided 800 admissions. The physicians see the service as valuable.

"We had women driving to Duke or Chapel Hill for oncology care. When Duke realized we were recruiting an oncologist of our own, they offered an extension of their service for our community. What we ended up negotiating was a contract that provides for all but the most demanding surgeries to be done in our hospital. In the past year-and-half, only one patient has had to leave Greensboro."

Successful obstetrics depends on a healthy mother. When the mother fails to get prenatal care, problems go unrecognized. As Jim notes, the problems create almost inestimable expense. The step that's emerging now at Women's is prevention:

> "North Carolina is 47th among the 50 states in infant mortality. If you adjust for white and nonwhite populations, our rate is 17 per thousand for nonwhite and 8 for white. We have about twice as many NICU admissions, babies under 1,000 grams, as we had two years ago, because we can now bring these babies successfully to discharge. Those infants stay an average of 55 days. Our costs are relatively low, but still that's expensive. We have improved our ability to save babies under 1,000 grams, but we have not reduced the number of these babies born. It has been documented nationally that many of these infants have serious problems later on. We're struggling now with what we ought to tell the parents about these babies. The parents tend to think that since the baby is discharged it will eventually be okay. The fact is it may never be okay. We have a group of neonatologists, perinatologists, and pediatricians studying what these outcomes are, and what it means to our institution and our community.
>
> "We've made significant progress in reaching the mothers at risk. When we opened there were 150 to 200 mothers a year who showed up at our door ready to deliver, without any prenatal care. Now it's down to 30 to 40, but there are a number of women who don't seek care until the second trimester. And every trimester that you miss, the chances of a low-birthweight baby double. We now have workers in the community through our public health department and a Coalition on Infant Viability, trying to identify mothers in early pregnancy and get them into a high-risk program. We've established an 'Adopt a Mom' program, in which we provide prenatal care, and rides to the clinic or office are provided by volunteers from local churches. We provide free or discounted care for the moms who earn too much for Medicaid. We've taken over 150 mothers through that program.
>
> "The more difficult issue is the mothers who know they are pregnant but don't take good care of themselves during their pregnancy. Mostly it's driven by issues that face lower socio-economic groups, like substance abuse. We've focused on geography, and have tried to pinpoint geographic areas [at

risk]. I'm meeting with the county health officer Wednesday, because our statistics show a blip upward. We will explore the reasons for that by matching birth data with other health measures. A small committee of our doctors, the chiefs of peds and OB and neonatology, is working with us.

> "We now have over half our patients on negotiated PPO or HMO contracts, and a third on Medicaid. Medicaid in North Carolina pays on a per case basis. Medicaid now pays 58 percent of our charges. We never refuse a patient. We have been able to reduce our costs and increase our volumes, so that we have not had to raise charges but once in the past six years. The merger will improve our costs another 10 percent. Right now our charges are lowest or next to lowest in almost all our charges compared to our group of eight."

David McCombs describes the program in the larger and more diverse Moses Cone Hospital, describing efforts in protocols, case management, and moving to patient-focused care:

> "We purposefully chose an education model for clinical pathways, not a mandated change. We've had the luxury of taking that approach. We started slowly. We started with education and profiling, and we focused on key benefits and outcomes. A big part of our success has been external benchmarking. We've made the most headway when we brought outside consultants who brought external data. We've had a few successes just with internal comparisons. Some of our surgeons were keeping mastectomy patients five days post-op and another group three, with the exact same results. Everyone converted to three days within a few months. We found the five-day group was not ordering ambulation until the written lab report was received, while the three-day group went ahead based on the frozen section. [The frozen section is done while the patient is in surgery. The written report is a second check for the spread of cancer which is more thorough, but not often different.]
>
> "Up until this year, the pathways were pieces of paper on the front of the record and thrown away on discharge. Now they are a part of the permanent medical record. The pathway was supplemental, not fundamental to care. Most of the pathway benefit has been from nursing, which is able to undertake many steps under the protocols that previously required individual orders—ambulating the patient, managing the IVs,

reducing the frequency of lab tests, starting discharge planning. The next stage is physicians challenging their clinical process. That really hasn't occurred yet. That's where we need a physician to lead the dialogue.

"We've gathered a lot of the low-hanging fruit, but our comparative data still show that our lengths of stay are higher in our top 30 DRGs. The missing piece has been physician ownership of the pathways. Where we could make a strong case of physician benefit, we have done well. Cardiology, where we have a global fee contract including the physicians, is one example. A full-time or near-full-time physician leader would help."

Protocols are more than just paper. They involve new ways of doing things that sometimes get quite complicated. David describes two programs that developed:

"We have a dedicated, in-house, critical care service of four pulmonologists. They manage patients directly or consult with the attending physician. We're learning physician thinking in critical care, what risk models they use to make decisions, how long they wait for indications of progress before moving the patient, for example. That all requires a high physician comfort level. We formed a task force headed by the chief pulmonologist. We have benchmarked using the APACHE data [physiological data used to classify immediate risk of death] from 70 other medical centers on ICU days, ventilator hours, portable x-ray, renal dialysis, and so forth. The task force identified a whole set of targets around those clinical components. A current target is the low-risk patient who is being monitored. These range from 25 and 45 percent of our patients, across our four ICUs. Best practice is 15 percent. We have a real opportunity if we can monitor the risk in a less expensive setting. Last September we started five clinical protocols to guide decisions around these issues. What for the first four or five years has been a nursing-led educational model is moving toward a physician-led integral part of the care process. The next real gain is to integrate the protocols, and make them physician-owned.

"Two-and-a-half years ago, my director of nursing came to me and said she'd like to dedicate an individual to studying how to do a community case management program. I said it wasn't clear to me how it would be beneficial under fee-for-service, but I did understand how it would help under managed care, so I encouraged her. We took one nurse off her assignment for a year and sent her to visit five or six sites. She proposed a nursing-driven community case management model. I said that was good, but that the program still had to have an economic benefit under fee-for-service. If it doesn't, we probably wouldn't be able to continue it. One way to do that is to take patients who are net losers for Moses Cone. A second is to identify diseases that have very high readmission rates. Third, identify heavy emergency room users that don't pay us adequately. Finally, let's look at patients that cost the community.

> "Out of those criteria we identified 27 DRGs where we lost money, we had high readmissions, and there were community costs. Not unexpectedly, these are chronically ill medical patients, primarily Medicare and Medicaid. Next we set up outcome measures for each of the four criteria. We piloted this for one year with our teaching service and two private practice groups. After one year, we turned an average loss of $1,200 per case to an average margin of $800. The readmission rate was reduced 60 to 70 percent, and the ER use was reduced 70 to 80 percent. We don't have a good measure of community costs, but anecdotal information tells us that these people's general health status has measurably improved. There are a lot of requests to use community case management for other purposes, but we keep it focused on those criteria. I think that's critical, at least in this environment. We probably won't broaden from those 27 DRGs until we have a larger percentage of capitation payment."

The protocols are patient-oriented, and they cut across the traditional service organization. David describes how a dual accountability is developing for many professionals, answering both to patient-oriented teams and their traditional functional superiors:

> "We have not spent a lot of time on patient-focused care in the sense of redesigning units, bringing all the ancillaries to the patients, and that sort of thing. We have defined centers of excellence, which focuses management and physician leadership around those centers. We knew we needed to be competitive in those areas. Rehab, oncology, and behavioral are true product lines, with their own physician managers. Pulmonary, neurosciences, cardiology, and trauma are more of a matrix structure, with an administrator, director of nursing, and one or more physician leaders who form a triad or a

council that manages the activity. In a few instances, such as oncology, the accountability is spelled out. Pharmacy, nutritional services and one or two other support services have written contracts. More commonly, there is a multidisciplinary program with a set of objectives and goals and [we] indicate one or two services with leading accountability. The group is almost self-policing, but we may take a critical goal and incorporate it into the service's objectives for the year. The accountability would be for the service manager as an individual to see that the goal is met.

"We have a patient assignment plan that identifies the preferred unit for each patient. Our goal is to have 80 percent of our patients on that unit. We have a designated secondary assignment where the people have similar training. We actually get about 85 percent on their primary unit.

"We have been very aggressive in developing alternative sources of care. We expanded day surgery and added overnight capability. We beefed up the case management model, substantially increased our home health and durable medical equipment services, and added infusion services and other options for home treatment. We created several day treatment settings for rehabilitation and behavioral needs. That's been the other side of the coin to the protocols and pathways. We will continue to work on that."

The agenda for the future

Ken Boggs describes the frontiers of using protocols. His list is pretty typical of the evolution from the old way to the new. There are old, less-effective systems to dismantle, and differing rates of transition among individuals and specialties:

"Our medical staff quality improvement stays mired where it was. We haven't hit on the right way to get them away from chart review into a more quality improvement mode. Our physicians are more involved in multidisciplinary quality improvement, but it comes in bringing data related to specific problems and developing a protocol. The cardiac surgeons are probably furthest along. They have some pretty clear practice changes that came from the literature and from talking through the data with our staff.

"Cardiology and OB have also done well. General medicine and general surgery have talked about it, but there's really not much going on. Both would love to disband their peer review in favor of something better, if they could figure out what it is. When I've tried to talk about that, they can't figure out what I'm talking about. Getting the mainstream of surgery and medicine more active in quality activities is a current issue. Their financial incentives are not yet aligned to this, and it costs them their own time to sit in meetings talking about getting patients out more quickly.

"OB and cardiology have done some interesting things integrating their nurses and physicians. Most of our units still don't have a common vision between our nursing and medical staffs that says, 'Here is where we are headed; here are the measures that will track how we get there; here is the structure that will get us there.' A product line structure might help, and we might get there after the merger. We don't have accountability at the program level in a lot of areas. We are looking for employed physician directors in some of our programs, but mostly we work with volunteers. We profile our physicians against each other, but not against California. We have a lot of physician input, but not a lot of physician leadership directed at quality improvement."

And beyond those issues are the questions of keeping up-to-date, moving to outpatient care, and matching national benchmarks in each disease group:

"Ninety percent of our protocols are complied with, but they are written around today's practice. The challenge is to move it to more effective levels. Everybody knows about the California levels, but they wonder if those levels are ever coming here. We have no way to reward them for further effort.

"Eagle Physicians Associates [an organization of primary care physicians] has a different perspective. They were formed to get ahead of the game, and they've stayed on track. They are beginning to manage not just the hospital stay, but whether the patient can be kept out of the hospital. They are working on office protocols.

"For many of the major programs our quality measures are near benchmark, but we are not the leader. The chief of oncology has said he doesn't see getting our doctors excited about the cost side, but the quality side might be different. We have measures in mortality, frequency of various clinical events, frequency of compliance with major protocol steps.

We have not used functional outcome measures yet. We struggle with internal quality measures, such as drug reactions, on accuracy and data collection issues. We are not trying to do original research. If we pursued those measures it would be in terms of compliance with professional standards.

"We are considering whether an employed physician would assist in clinical improvement and cost reduction. We are still some time away from a decision."

Physician Organization

The strategy at Moses Cone is to work with its physicians and systematically minimize conflict. Pursuing this in 1985, with a radiology center, the organization began a series of collaborative ventures with physicians. It has since then expanded rehab, formed a heart institute, and developed centers for cancer, neurosciences, and behavioral health. In the 1990s, its strategy is to encourage closer alliance, pursue managed care contracts, and develop joint ventures with mutual value. It formed the Greensboro HealthCare Network (GHN), a physician-hospital organization formed to share risk, and it has formed a partnership with Eagle Physicians and Associates, a physician organization representing 38 primary and 116 specialist physicians. In 1996, two new managed care contracts with capitation payment arrangements were signed, one with Partners and the other with Wellpath, a joint venture between Duke and NYLCare. Together they cover only about 5 percent of physicians' incomes, not enough to cause more than minor economic inconvenience for most doctors.

Understanding medical organization

Lanty Smith, J.D., chair of the board of trustees, talks about how trustees can assist the physicians in moving from solo practice and small groups to more collaborative arrangements:

"It's been very difficult to organize the medical profession in Greensboro. Herding them is like herding butterflies. They are late in recognizing what's occurring. Some of them do not like the options that are realistically available, and as they get older they want to keep checking the box, 'None of the above.'

"We have a very fine medical community. This is one of the best places in the country to practice medicine—low cost of living, high incomes, wonderful facilities, and not that much competition, particularly for specialists. The hospitals, particularly

> this one, have been good at changing without a crisis. That's the hallmark of good management, being able to adapt and make significant change without a crisis. It speaks as well for management as anything I know of.
>
> "We have had no crisis, but we have a healthy balance sheet and have held down rate increases for many years. As a result, there hasn't been a tremendous amount of pressure for change from the employer community. We haven't had the kind of catalysts you've seen in other parts of the country. Fortunately, we have been able to get strong physician support for merging the two hospitals, and we are slowly, slowly creeping up on a more comprehensive, integrated delivery system. My dream is that we can put that system in place on a regional and a statewide basis. Certainly we'll see growth in managed care, but I'd like to see that growth come without some of the more negative things associated with the HMOs."

The hospital must stimulate the formation of physician organizations, but not be too intrusive. As an employer, Lanty recognizes aspects of the regional economy that few doctors in Greensboro would imagine:

> "We are trying to build our relationship with the Greensboro Health Network. We want to put a regional effort in place, and Dennis is chair of a committee trying to put something in place on a state level. Moses Cone can go in a lot of different directions strategically. We sat down three or four years ago and set out the sequence of events that we think must occur to best position Moses Cone and our community for the longer term. The merger has to come first. Second is a provider network within Greensboro. The third is increasing risk-sharing, and the fourth and fifth are regional and state expansion.
>
> "The hospital has to lead the development of an integrated delivery system. It is important to put some reasonable constraints on what the doctor does with his fountain pen. There is nobody else to lead that effort within the community other than the hospital, defined as the people who work here and the people on the board. When I say the people who work here, that's not just the administrators, it has to be physician leadership as well. We are well along the path within these four walls. The reengineering we have done, the cost structures and quality measures we have put in place, the use of statistical process quality control, all of those kinds of methodologies

that the for-profit world has had to use to survive have been applied here reasonably well, and our rate structure reflects that."

Lanty relies heavily on the CEO to carry out the vision.

> "Dennis [Barry, CEO] and the board are good partners. He enjoys exceedingly strong support from his board. Part of that is simply the quality of individual he is, part because he's been in the post for a long time, and part of it is the support that the board leaders have given him. Board leaders have been outspoken in supporting him in the initiatives and in being proactive. I'd like to think we've given him a stronger platform to work off of. Almost without exception, the individual board members do not undercut Dennis with the medical community.
>
> "I think that if we are ever going to put this integrated system together community-wide, the hospital has to lead it and the greatest visionary is Dennis. The strongest community leader we have on healthcare is Dennis. We will affect some physician incomes as we do it, so it will be controversial. But change will occur with or without the hospital and the physicians working together. It is far preferable to be partners in leading that change. We have to educate the physician community that they can't check the box that says, 'None of the above.'"

Dennis Barry, CEO, on efforts to build a physician-hospital organization with emphasis on primary care, says:

> "This is a medical community that has pretty much been together over the years. Changes have started to occur. There's been a lot of fractionating, between specialist and primary, and between specialist and specialist. Rather than focusing on managed care and how to manage care effectively in the future, and bringing more modern management to practice, most of them have hunkered down and taken a defensive position. Specialists have not been hurt yet.
>
> "The medical teaching programs at Moses Cone have always focused on primary care. We've always had a program in general internal medicine. Because we've had such a strong family practice residency program, we continue to have good relationships. Over the last three years we have helped them recruit additional doctors and have developed our practice management services for those doctors who want them."

Dennis spells out a strategy that is flexible, encourages primary care, minimizes the hospital's capital investment, and tolerates considerable physician autonomy:

> "We have had a number of opportunities to purchase primary care practices, but we have developed relationships rather than acquiring the practices. The only practice that we have acquired is a large oncology group, which made strategic sense for our cancer program and which prevented them from being bought by a national group. We have developed relationships with outlying sites. For example, we helped build a practice in Kernersville that now has four doctors in it and we are arranging specialist visits. In Madison, we built the doctors a new building and leased their old one, which we will convert to an outpatient rehab center and medical specialty services.
>
> "We had spent about two years working with the medical staff on managed care and its implications. We took a strong pro–primary care attitude throughout, and developed a framework which gave the PCPs a majority say in the PHO structure, much to the chagrin of the specialists, as you might imagine.
>
> "One of the major primary care groups, an internal medicine group, was providing a lot of leadership. They were invited to join in with a group of family practitioners who had been trying to collaborate. They decided to sit in to see if there was any common ground. After about six months they decided they would have to form a single group if they were going to be a significant player for the future. One of the large pediatric groups joined them. They formed Eagle Physician Associates. We are working with them to develop satellites, and there are another 15 doctors in the community who are likely to merge with them. We have about 150 specialists associated with Eagle. We hope to expand that and get them an ownership position in the PHO.
>
> "There is a loose coalition of other primary care practices, mainly family practices, which appears to be developing a relationship with a physician management company. A countervailing group of specialists has also emerged, formed into an IPA, which has some primary care doctors. They have not established a contact with the hospital so far. There are still a number of physicians who did not want to collaborate either with the hospital or the specialists. Some groups . . . feel that their day has come, and they are into retribution in one sense

or another. They don't make good partners for anybody now, but maybe their attitude will change given a little time."

Income is the magnet that holds physician organizations together. Dennis describes new contracts that will eventually strengthen the organization and resolve some of the conflicts:

"Partners [the leading HMO in the region, owned by a Winston-Salem hospital, CMI] has a Medicare license, and is seeking a risk contract with us. United [the second-largest HMO] has applied. They have given us a case-based payment [a fixed amount for each case treated, allowing the hospital and the specialists to control costs within that amount], because we have all the specialties, and because we can give them competitive prices. They have become more aggressive in the last year, but we have continued to insist on case-based reimbursement."

Developing the strength of primary care

A pecking order established in medicine has up until recently emphasized the specialist and particularly the interventionists, doctors who do something dramatic with their hands. Surgeons not only have received very high incomes, but they also have tended to dominate the hospital medical staff. Under managed care, the primary care doctor has emerged as the most important, the doctor who sees the patient most often, and the doctor who can guide the patient through the expensive maze of specialty care. Dale Dreiling, M.D., describes what this shift means from a primary care physician's perspective:

"I have been in family practice in Greensboro since 1984. When I came to town, I needed to inform people what family practice entailed. The medical community had been specialist-oriented. A study several years ago showed a shortage for internal medicine physicians, but a more predominant one for pediatricians and family practice.

"In the past, Moses Cone has not had a primary care focus. Family practice does not admit many patients to the hospital. When I admitted patients, people didn't even know who I was. Now, Moses Cone is an access to the future. I think you see hospitals as partners, but if I work with the hospital, I need to look out for myself."

One of the first issues in building medical organization is dealing with the history, which in part means convincing primary care physicians that they do have authority and can make a difference, avoiding retribution and getting the specialists to accept the change constructively. Dale continues:

> "Managed care has caused significant changes in the medical environment. In the past, someone could hang out their shingle and build a practice. Now we are much more dependent on working together. We can't be as parochial as we were. There's not a bone to pick now. There's not a score to settle. Some specialties act like they have a corner on the market. I don't think they have woken up to the fact that those patients could easily go to Winston-Salem. That's not going to take long to occur. When managed care really starts moving, those things will straighten themselves out."

Yet another issue is to have physician organizations that form a stable whole. The physicians themselves may be comfortable with several organizations competing for managed care contracts, even though such an arrangement creates problems for the health system that must deal with them all. It also may turn out to be unsatisfactory to the customers. People selling managed care insurance find that small physician panels do not sell as well as larger ones. Dale Dreiling describes the situation:

> "There are four physician associations in Greensboro. Eagle is one. Eagle has more than a third of the primary care doctors in the area. The Guilford Primary Care Alliance is a primary care association that will be signing a contract with [a national for-profit physicians' organization] soon. There is a large group of medical specialists that has been aggressively recruiting primary care doctors. The fourth is Piedmont Physicians Network, a multi-specialty group of approximately 350 physicians with limited primary care. This group evolved from loose affiliations into a single large physicians' association. They have hired an executive director who has coordinated their efforts and is attempting to obtain insurance contracts."

Dreiling goes on to describe the organization he is trying to build. Eagle Physicians Association will have a strong group of primary care physicians; each Eagle primary care member will provide care to about 2,000 people:

> "One major impetus for Eagle was that we could see discounted fee-for-service coming and the cost of practicing medicine going up. The question was 'How are we going to

survive? How can we help each other? We're spending all these hours and getting burned out; what can we do together?' Eagle is a way of stabilizing our income and having a voice at the table as our environment is changing.

"There's some sentiment that primary care had been the lowest on the payment totem pole, and we deserved being on top for a change. We don't agree. We feel the pendulum is going to swing back, and we will have to work together to achieve common goals. We would like to see primary care, specialists, and the hospital working to provide the best care. You do it as a group. When you put your protocols together, you are not just saying, 'Primary care, what's the best way to treat low back pain?' You get everybody in the room to look for the best protocol. 'Let's look at outcomes and see what really is the best protocol.'

"Eagle started as a merged group with three family practice units, one general internist, one pediatrics. We now have two satellites open, and a third opening this fall, a total of 40 physicians, with a majority in primary care."

Eagle will coordinate with specialists through a larger organization, the Greensboro HealthCare Network. Dale notes that the network has a full array of affiliated specialists, some risk management contracts, and a plan to manage the risks. In short, Eagle is about to fly:

"Through the Greensboro HealthCare Network, we've been able to put together approximately 160 specialists and the hospitals. We have started to contract for 'at risk' products, and we've put together a risk model that aligns incentives. We have 8,000 globally capitated lives through GHN, but the majority of our business is through Eagle contracts with Blue Cross/ Blue Shield, United Healthcare, and various PPO products."

Once a physician organization is formed, it faces two major challenges. One is to get some contracts for real patients; the other is to actually manage the patients' care effectively. Dale discusses how Eagle will manage care, beginning with the information system necessary to develop statistical profiles of care. Eagle used direct education of individual practitioners and moved rather quickly to protocols for common, expensive diseases:

"Eagle picked an information system that is also used by the residency programs at Moses Cone and made available to all Moses Cone doctors. We feel we have good physicians in our organization, but we will be tracking information to verify this. We have two medical directors who started about a year ago, one in internal medicine and the other in family practice. We plan on using them to talk to doctors one to one. Both are part-time. We feel the medical directors should continue to see patients; that helps their credibility.

"When Eagle started we had a Quality Assurance Utilization Review committee, but it was slow getting started. Now the group is putting out one protocol a month. The protocols are evidence based, using protocols from other systems and standards in our own community. We want to meet HEDIS goals, although we see ourselves trying to perform beyond what HEDIS has requested. Now that we are on a common information system, tracking this information will be much easier."

One way to economize in medicine, and to save the patient time and trouble, is to keep care that might be referred to a specialist under the primary physician. Superficial surgery, done under local anesthetic, is one example. Evaluating chronic heart disease using a treadmill is another. The tradition of family practice was to undertake these routinely. The tradition of internal medicine was to avoid all forms of surgery, but pursue chronic disease care. An internist might keep a diabetic that a family practitioner would refer. Dale Dreiling comments on the Greensboro situation:

"Family practitioners repair lacerations and perform minor surgery. There are unique opportunities with the different practices, including culposcopies, [examination and biopsy of the cervix], treadmills [for heart testing], and vasectomies. In the past, internists might send sprained ankles to orthopedists, but on most occasions we can manage these problems within our own organization. This has been a great learning process within our physician group.

"We will have a 'hospitalist' [one physician who will manage all the family practice admissions in the hospital] join us in September. Several years ago this might have been rejected as out of line, but now we have found this improves our productivity, and improves our cost-effectiveness and patient satisfaction in the hospitals."

Next, the group has to get some contracts for insured patients. They will continue to see patients under traditional commercial insurance, PPOs, and Medicare. These patients often do not have insurance for office care. Dale describes the gains Eagle has made to date. "Gainsharing" is an incentive payment on top of a fee for services, based on achievement of specified quality and cost goals. Primary care doctors earn their gainsharing by keeping their patients as healthy as possible. The episodes of severe illness—heart attacks, diabetic comas, complicated pregnancies, and preventable childhood diseases—are 100 to 1,000 times as expensive as an office visit. So, given a fairly distributed population (as usual, a serious caveat), primary doctors are rewarded for their skill:

> "We have two gainsharing arrangements. The gainsharing is based on the savings accomplished by the companies. There are also quality standards. We are hoping to get more."

The ultimate primary care incentive is global capitation, where the primary physician is paid the premium from the patient, less an administrative fee called retention. He or she pays the specialist and the hospital, and keeps what is left. Global capitation is also called the "gatekeeper model." It is known to be very effective in reducing premiums rapidly. Dale describes GHN's early experiments with it and Eagle's business strategy:

> "Before we started Eagle, we saw our business change from fee-for-service to discounted fee-for-service. GHN allowed us to move directly to global capitation. Our thought is not to be overwhelmed with numbers initially, but to learn how to manage care well in this environment. Our contract of 8,000 is a good number to develop our systems and to learn. That number will be important in our primary care offices, but it will have little impact on the specialists.
>
> "Eagle's business strategy is to be proactive in acquiring good-quality managed care contracts, because we feel that's where the market's going, and where we want to be. Our feelings are that the premium may go down, or it may go down only a little bit and costs will rise, so there will be a crunch. The payors are starting to push down. There will be a lot more pressure. You know your income is going down. The question is, 'How can you fare best?' The answer is through taking risk.
>
> "I'm president of several organizations, including Eagle, GHN, and Triad Medical Care Organization. Eagle is built on a joint effort. There have been a number of physicians willing to step forward as administrative personnel. Eagle

and Moses Cone have developed a very strong working relationship.

"GHN has been the most proactive force in our market. We have been willing to step forward and take global capitation. Other surrounding communities are starting to do the same thing. We decided not to take an enormous amount of risk initially, in order to develop an infrastructure and a medical management system. We realize that as we are proactive there will be criticism. Nevertheless, we realize we need to step forward and gain experience."

Dale notes three problems that Eagle would have serious trouble with without a strong hospital partner:

"One of the problems we foresee is the need for capital. We have a desire to expand, but all this takes money. This may become a more significant issue down the road.

"Another problem is competition. Competition is not just with physician groups, but also there is a significant consolidation within the insurance industry and hospitals. National physician management companies are also a concern.

"We will have to align with other groups in the Triad. The three communities within the Triad are growing together. Each physician community in the Triad evolved differently. Through the Triad Medical Care Organization we are developing relationships with the other PHOs and physician organizations."

Rebuilding the referral specialist capability

Robert Gay, M.D., chief of pathology and president of the medical staff, discusses some of the hospital/specialist organizational issues. By tradition, his job is to make sure the doctors' views are heard by management and the governing board:

"We have been fortunate not to have the divisiveness and competitiveness that many communities have had. Whether we will continue not to have it remains to be seen. The orthopedists are going through some problems right now, because a capitation contract has been put out. It's a take-it-or-leave-it situation. If one group takes it and the other is left out, that will be one of the first waves. I don't know what will happen. I think the smart thing might be for them to all stand firm and say, 'We don't want that contract.' I can't see patients in this town who want to march out of Greensboro to wherever to have their orthopedic work done.

"I think it's unfortunate that we did not form the physicians' organization [PO] and the PHO back when we had the opportunity. That would have prevented or significantly retarded a situation where physician groups could be played one against another. Piedmont Physicians Network [PPN] has not been successful at talking with the Eagle group. So we are going to have these two camps, plus another group of non-Eagle primary care physicians who do not appear to know who they want to associate with. There is certainly a point there for us all to become more competitive and less collegial. I wish I knew how it would play out down the road.

"Forming PPN gave the specialists opportunities to decrease their costs of doing business. Doctors got some really fine cuts in their malpractice costs. I was talking to a gynecologist who said he saved on the order of $12,000 a year. Talking to people, you get the idea that many offices are pretty inefficient. There are some management sorts of things, using a medical services organization, that could reduce practice costs. I think we'll see more groups and larger groups. A couple of general surgeon groups have come together already, and a group of OBs. We will see more of that. If they carry it out well, they'll get along."

All of these problems are tougher when there are more doctors in a given specialty than the community needs. Bob discusses how difficult this question is:

"I have been concerned that we have too many doctors. It's a little hard to believe that there aren't more of some specialties than we need, but on the other hand, I haven't heard that any of them are starving. I don't know, off the top of my head, one doctor has left town. Years ago, my friends said a new orthopedist could come into town and have a full practice within six months. I know at least one group considered taking in an associate and didn't.

"We haven't done systematic studies of the need for specialists, and I don't see the hospital administration doing that. If we had an overabundance of cardiovascular surgeons that would limit the number of cases each could do per year [so that quality of care is endangered], then maybe they would."

Dennis Barry, CEO, on retaining a relationship with referral specialists:

"The Moses Cone–physician joint venture in radiology has been very successful. It demonstrates that doctors and hospitals can work together. It's been going over ten years. The

North Carolina Heart Institute is a management–medical staff effort. We've done some global pricing and used it as a vehicle to work on both cost and quality issues, and have had major success over the past four years. Our price is the lowest in open heart surgery and cardiac catheterization. The rehabilitation program started in 1983, and has grown since. We have a major day hospital program and two other ambulatory sites planned. We have been working with High Point and Forsyth hospitals, looking at expansion of the rehab program in the Triad. We're looking at bringing in a full-time trauma surgeon. Neurosciences has a facility with its own operating rooms and intensive care unit. We work with two large independent physician groups, one in neurosurgery and one in neurology. At the Women's Hospital, we have a core group of employed obstetricians and a neonatologist who take care of indigent patients and manage the intensive neonatal care unit."

Peter Young, M.D., trustee and surgeon:

"This hospital in the past has responded to the need. Sometimes Dennis anticipates the need and is ahead of us on it. If the technology changes, the hospital has responded. If it views itself as a tertiary center, it can't afford to back off. As long as the administration stays, we all feel okay. When Dennis retires, you just have to hope that whoever succeeds him will do as well. The doctors will have four positions on the merged board, which, to me, is plenty. I think four positions can easily represent the medical community. The board frequently turns to its doctors to find out how doctors will feel. When we have said that the physician community would look negatively upon it, they have backed down. Socially, these people are all friends.

"Cohesiveness has been one of the attractions of the town. I'm concerned that the big medical group and the Eagle group and the other primary care group are going to be at odds. The specialists are all hoping we don't have to pick sides."

Learning to share financial risk

All payment systems have incentives built in them. No one knows the best design, but it clearly will not be simple. Risk-sharing incentives, from gainsharing to global capitation, must involve "pools," essentially the aggregate experience of many patients. Although any single patient might have widely varying needs, sets of 100 patients with the same disease will be almost identical, so long as the patients are aggregated in an unbiased manner.

Dale Dreiling describes a new risk-sharing model that is designed to be stronger than gainsharing but that avoids some of the problems of a total capitation or gatekeeper model. His model is based on "shared risk," where individual physicians and the hospital are paid only part of their fees as the work is performed, and the unpaid portion is a "withhold." The providers get an incentive to earn back their withholds by avoiding unnecessary care. If the expenses for one group are more than expected, the loss is covered first from the withhold of that group and then from the withholds of other groups. Overall, the system hopes to give doctors a reward for meeting goals, a protection against failure, and an incentive to cooperate with each other and the hospital:

> "GHN put together a risk model with a national consulting organization that we all seem to be comfortable with. We have not had much experience with it yet, but it does an excellent job of aligning incentives. The insurance company takes 20 percent of the premium. Eighty percent comes to GHN, which takes 8 percent for operations and contingency. The rest is split among four pools—hospital, specialist, primary care, and miscellaneous. Miscellaneous includes out-of-plan services, home care, and medical equipment. Pharmacy and mental health are carved out [that is, excluded from the pools and handled separately by the insurance company]. The fees are drawn from each pool."

The 28 percent taken for administration is one reason why Lanty Smith says he'd like to eliminate the insurance organization. In Dale's model, if the hospital payments at year end have exceeded budget, the overage is met first from any surplus in the specialist pool, and vice versa. This makes the hospital and the specialist share a common incentive. Remaining deficits, if any, are charged first against the group's own withhold, and then against the withhold of others. Finally, any remaining surplus in the hospital account is divided by all three, and the specialist pool surplus is divided by both specialists and primary physicians. Dale says:

> "The essence of this risk model is that we are all winners or all losers, aligning incentives. We see our risk model evolving, and we also see the specialists being more active and having a seat at Greensboro HealthCare Network in the near future."

Diversification and Community Outreach

Moses Cone has cutting-edge programs in diversification, that is, in providing alternatives to acute inpatient care, and in community outreach, prevention, and health promotion aimed at high-risk groups. Both diversification and outreach require a positive trustee perspective. Carole Bruce, trustee and chair, finance committee, brings a solid community background to the board:

> "Four or five years ago, I sent Dennis some things I had read about community health and outreach. I chaired the building campaign for Hospice. We raised over $2 million. The hospital contributed $150,000. The rest came from the community in a matter of months. The HealthServe Ministry support hasn't been quite that strong, but it has been solid. It's amazing what the community will do."

Diversification

A broad spectrum of nonacute services is important in reducing unnecessary reliance on the acute hospital. A healthcare system does not need to own the nonacute services, but it should assure availability, price, and quality for its patients. Tim Rice, executive vice president, Health Services Division, describes how Moses Cone is using collaboration to diversify Greensboro services:

> "We have a group of nonacute services that we call the Health Services Division. Hospice and our Medical Office Building are joint ventures, one with a community group and the other with the physicians using it. Our joint venture with the radiologists is operated through this division. Our nursing home and a geriatric assessment center are wholly owned, but we contract with other long-term care institutions for respiratory and physical therapy. We hope to contract manage a second nursing home, and we encourage our physicians to provide coverage to a lot of homes. We have a home care/durable medical equipment company that is a joint venture with three other hospitals in the area. Guilford Child Health is a joint venture with the other hospitals to privatize the Health Department pediatric clinics. We operate a Nutrition Management Center for diabetics and for cardiac and hyperlipidemia patients. Our Developmental and Psychological Center started out with a developmental focus, and now sees kids for all psychological reasons. Our Greensboro Occupational Medicine Center is a joint venture with our emergency physicians and

an occupational medicine network that we are starting next month. Call-A-Nurse, nurse triage for physicians' practices, is also a joint venture with another hospital system. We hope it will evolve into some other services."

A day hospital, with "customer-focused outpatient services for convenient care," opened in 1996. Moses Cone founded a hospice in 1988 and launched "Decisions Near the End of Life," an ethics program, in 1994. It opened an extended care center on its main campus in 1991. Tim continues:

"These efforts have really grown in the four-and-a-half years I've been with the division, and we expect them to continue to expand. Overall, we make a modest margin, but the activities involve almost 500,000 patient contacts and provide $54 million worth of care. Almost half of the patient contacts are through the home care program, which serves over 500 people a day. The extended care center has a census of 147, and the hospice supports an average of 120 patients a day. Call-A-Nurse handles almost 200 calls a day.

"We started with home care, because there was no good home care program in Greensboro. The community-based hospice program was kind of struggling, and Moses Cone got involved to infuse some capital and management assistance. Then we spun off the durable medical equipment. So we have gotten to a strategy. If you ask Dennis if he had a grand vision back in 1984, when the home care venture started, I don't think he would say we had a grand strategy. But we did recognize that we needed to be more than a hospital. It was very tough. Some of our board members really questioned the diversification functions.

"We spend a lot of time with Eagle and the Greensboro Health Network. We are doing a satellite for the largest group practice in town that is not an Eagle activity. We don't want to be associated only with Eagle. Our MSO serves some other non-Eagle groups as well. A lot of our work in the past few years has been managing real estate—finding sites, negotiating purchases, and managing properties."

Tim notes that Moses Cone is flexible in the kinds of arrangements it accepts for diversified services:

"I wouldn't say we emphasize joint ventures. What we try to do is look at the best way to get the job accomplished. We do not have total control. We do have a mentality saying, 'We don't know how to do everything ourselves.' It's natural for us to look for partners who know how to do what we want. For example, in the Wendover Medical Center, a large physician office building, we teamed up with one of the area's largest developers. An excellent example has been our diagnostic and imaging center, with our radiologists. Call-A-Nurse—we established a relationship with a lady in the community who had developed a similar program in Winston-Salem.

"Most of the joint ventures have their own boards and their own very strong executives. The executives handle the day-to-day management, and my involvement is not that great. For instance, Advanced Home Care has an excellent team, and I have a fairly arm's length relationship: I meet them once every two months at a board meeting. In between, I'll probably talk to the CEO once a week or so.

"Hospice is a separate corporation, with its own policies, human resources, and so forth. Half the board is appointed by Moses Cone, and half is elected by the public. Home Care is a joint venture with Wesley Long Hospital, High Point, and Forsyth Memorial Hospital in Winston-Salem."

Some of Tim's programs include both diversification and outreach. He describes a child care collaboration across the county, aimed at poor children:

"Guilford Child Health was formed not even a year ago. The county came to us, and we discussed their inability to run their child health clinics efficiently. We formed a task group; hired some consultants, which Moses Cone paid for; and talked to High Point and Wesley Long. After the study, we agreed the clinics would be more efficient under hospital management. The new entity is owned three-sixths by Moses Cone, one-sixth by Wesley Long, and two-sixths by High Point. The county was spending approximately $1.6 million. We asked them for a seven-year commitment for no less than $1 million per year. We are at risk for the remainder. Our goal is to break even; the contract forbids us from making money. We think the county was serving about 10,000 children, but there are about 20,000 children who are eligible. What we are not seeing are healthy kids or kids whose parents might have thought they weren't eligible because they have a job. So we expect to increase the number of visits.

"We committed to new salary and benefit structures, a practice management system and trained managers, and new hours. We have said we will take all Medicaid-eligible patients and other children whose parents do not have real health insurance. Greensboro churches bring in a number of immigrant children from Bosnia and places like that, and we serve those children. We collect from Medicaid, and we have a sliding fee scale, and we ask those who can afford to pay to do so. We are trying not to take the commercially insured patients and compete with our own pediatricians.

"One of the reasons I don't sleep at night is that it isn't going as well as we wanted it to. We are plagued with a number of operational issues that aren't working as they should—throughput, information systems, billing, and financial reporting. Our first executive just didn't work out. We are actively recruiting an executive, so we are leading it as board members and spending too much time [on it].

"This will work if it continues to be a true partnership with the county. It can't be an opportunity for the county to wash their hands of any social obligation. Our current county commissioners are very much into privatization. They are very excited about the concept. There may be a lot of opportunities to work with the county down the road."

Community outreach

In 1995, Moses Cone contributed $17,690,700 to the Greensboro area in charity care, patient education, professional education, community outreach, donations, and contributions of services (Table 2.5). This was 7.3 percent of its net operating revenue.

Table 2.5 Contibutions by Moses Cone Health System to Special Community Needs

	1995	1996
Charity Care		
Free care and bad debt	$10,069,000	$11,282,000
Area Health Education Center	3,473,000	3,802,500
Other Education and Training of Health Professionals	675,200	807,000
Donations to Community Charities	598,000	510,400
Community Health Education/Outreach	228,900	335,800
Employee Donations through MCHS	267,300	309,100
Contributions of MCHS Volunteers	75,300	84,000
Total	$15,386,700	$17,130,800

Moses Cone began its outreach services in 1993, when HealthServe Ministry was founded as a joint venture with the Greensboro Urban Ministry to provide preventive and primary services to the uninsured.

The total Moses Cone community outreach program has three major parts. The HealthServe Ministry is one. In 1996, the clinic provided about 19,000 visits to 11,000 contacts. Moses Cone screening programs reached about 1,000. Health fairs reached 2,000. One thousand used emergency phone lines. About 7,500 attended various educational events, including 3,500 school children. The HealthServe Ministry is not a trivial effort, but it falls short of the need. Guilford County has about 75,000 people with low incomes and about 40,000 uninsured. That population would generate 5,000 to 10,000 hospital admissions and 200,000 to 300,000 office visits a year. Fred Levick, president of HealthServe Ministry, describes the clinic:

> "Dennis Barry suggested the feasibility study for HealthServe, a new model that would provide primary access, combining the hospital's skills with volunteer services and broad community support. HealthServe opened in December 1993.
>
> "HealthServe has institutional members who commit to helping in some tangible way. We started out with a board of 12, 4 from Moses Cone, 4 from the Urban Ministry, and 4 elected by the membership association. Since then we have added Wesley Long and the Junior League, with one seat each. The Urban Ministry is supported by over 200 congregations representing the Protestant, Catholic, and Jewish faiths.
>
> "When we started out, we hoped we could eventually get the county to be a partner. We've spent four years trying to get commitment from them. We now receive some funding on a year-to-year basis, but no long-term support. We also seek corporate support. When we speak with business leaders, they say, 'This is an important program, but why isn't the county doing more?'"

Fred describes how the ministry is staffed. Part of his job is to make sure this combination of paid and volunteer service maintains high quality and meets patient needs:

> "We have about 340 volunteers, including about 70 physicians (of whom about 30 come regularly) and 125 nurses. We have 30 dentists. All told, our volunteers provide over 7,000 hours of care a year. Specialist care is provided free of charge by many specialists. The radiology group at Moses Cone reads the films on a volunteer basis. We get medication samples

from drug companies and physicians' offices. Volunteers repackage the samples for us. We will dispense about 36,000 prescriptions, of which 7,200 will come from sample supplies.

"Our volunteers come because it makes them feel good. They have a sense of civic duty; they want to give something back. They enjoy it. We have a lot of people in the helping professions. HealthServe is an easy program to understand. People understand what it does for the whole fabric of community life.

"We have 33 paid FTEs. We've recruited our paid physicians on our own. We were able to qualify as an urban physician shortage area; that status supports medical school loan repayment. The state helped us with loan repayment. Our physicians are paid less than they might earn in private practice, but there are no inpatient responsibilities."

The ministry, like any other healthcare operation, must assure that it continues to attract a substantial volume of patients and to get financing for them. Fred describes their plan:

"The hospital ER refers patients here for follow-up. We also work with the Health Department, Social Service, and United Way agencies to have them refer patients. We talk to the churches and participate in community activities to let people know we are here. We have sent some doctors to the schools. Now we are about to expand. The long-term concept is to have clinics spaced around town. Our plan was to start with one and see how it works.

"Our entry criteria include income limits and lack of an existing primary care provider. We accept Medicare and Medicaid patients. When we opened, there was a big problem with uninsured, Medicaid, and low-income Medicare patients getting access to care. Medicaid patients could not get into primary physicians' offices. The copays and deductibles were a financial barrier for Medicare patients. A couple of years ago there was a problem with any Medicare patients getting into a practice. The hospital worked with the physicians to deal with that.

"We have to operate like a managed care organization. Our providers are very judicious in making referrals, but at the same time we work hard to expedite the referral process. We have a goal this year to improve to over 95 percent referrals within 24 hours. We also have to arrange transportation so the patient can get there. A local church gives us funds to pay for cabs.

> "We have health education programs. Our weekly diabetic education program has outgrown the Center, and we had to move it to a church up the street. We have a trained diabetes nurse and volunteer nutritionists who come from the hospital.
>
> "We are open 8:30 to 6:00—to 8:30 on Tuesday and Thursday. On Tuesday and Thursday evenings we have a walk-in clinic, staffed by volunteers. By 5 o'clock there are 30 people waiting. When we open the new clinic, we will have expanded hours to be more attractive to the working poor."

The other two parts of the total community outreach program are the collaborative effort with many different Greensboro agencies, and the Health Improvement Fund, which awards grants to community agencies and is the predecessor of the Community Health Foundation planned after the merger. Kate Ahlport, vice president, Community Health, describes the survey to establish needs, Moses Cone's systematic response to the needs, the deliberate bridge-building to other community agencies, and finally a plan to measure performance. This is not, she insists, a "feel good" program:

> "The Moses Cone Community Health Program was established for a very specific purpose, to address unmet and undermet health-related needs with programs that focus on prevention, produce measurable outcomes, and that ideally are developed in collaboration with other agencies in the community.
>
> "At Moses Cone we do not view our community programs as 'soft marketing.' Our programs are developed to achieve a measurable improvement in health status, not to promote use of services. Some of our competitors do patient and health education classes and mall walks. We do those things, but they are through the hospitals, not the community health programs."

In 1994, Moses Cone sponsored an initiative with other community organizations to "address the unmet and undermet health needs of greater Greensboro residents." The Greater Greensboro Community Health Partnership was formed, bringing together 11 community leaders, 5 representatives of health and social agencies, and 5 representatives of government, public health, and education. High Point Regional Hospital began a similar initiative, and the two collaborated on a survey of health needs completed in 1995. Moses Cone contributed $95,500 to survey costs. The survey included both household sampling and focus groups around identified risks. After reviewing survey results, the partnership voted on the importance of identified needs and the ease with which they could be addressed. Kate describes the program to build community consensus on priorities:

> "One of the first activities of the Community Health Program was to conduct a community health needs assessment. The job of the 21-member community advisory committee was to come to consensus on a short list of the most important unmet health-related needs in the greater Greensboro community. The top one was to improve access to preventive and primary care. The other three were health education for school-age children, prenatal and postpartum care for special populations, and parenting education as a way to decrease stress on the family unit.
>
> "After the report, we did a little more research on the access issue. We conducted a community interview process to identify who was most in need. We convened a community task group to develop a vision of primary care that would meet the needs of the underserved in greater Greensboro. The task group had representatives from the medical community, from HealthServe Ministry, the African-American community, the Health Department, small business. It wasn't just to get buy-in. We did not have a preconceived mission. It really was to develop a vision of what needed to be done.
>
> "We went through an elaborate planning process. Our community interviews, which we had done previously, identified the group most in need of access as the working poor—low-income workers. We have about 40,000 uninsured in the county. Moses Cone Hospital is always available to them on an acute care basis. We still have a fair number of Medicaid patients who have trouble finding a provider, particularly in the southern part of the county. We found through our surveys that these people delay seeking care. They end up seeking care at a more acute stage, needing to use our ER and inpatient resources when their problem could have been taken care of earlier, more efficiently, and with a better-quality outcome.
>
> "The task force agreed on a network of four clinics, specified by geographic area and prioritized assuming a gradual development over a period of years. The HealthServe Ministry was asked to bring forward a proposal to start the first of the four. The task force developed the vision, and our board and the HealthServe board have both approved the proposal. Our

board has provided startup and first-year funding to get the first clinic off the ground."

In 1996, the Community Health Program Committee of the Moses Cone board began work to develop intervention strategies and measures of performance. A Primary Care Planning Group identified unmet needs and expected primary care visits by section of the county. It reviewed project descriptions of the Robert Wood Johnson Foundation "Reach Out" initiative, and studied the structure of four existing programs for the uninsured (in Florida, Texas, and Minnesota). The planning group developed specific proposals for eligibility, scope of benefits, clinic location, and source of personnel, but stopped short of a specific budget to implement the program.

Kate Ahlport continues on the task force's second priority, school health:

"We have several efforts under way related to school health. Greensboro and High Point are served by separate health systems but by a common school system and public health department. In 1996, Moses Cone and High Point Regional Health System each approached the county school system separately, seeking ways to work with the schools to improve student access to primary care and health education. The school superintendent expressed a strong preference for administrative simplicity. Rather than deal with the health department and two separate health systems, he wanted one coordinated administrative structure.

"The initial discussions led to a countywide planning process to develop a comprehensive vision of school health services that would meet the needs of elementary, middle, and high school students. I don't think anyone in this community has conducted as comprehensive an analysis of health services as we are doing in this planning process. We are also looking at different school health models across the country, and we will make recommendations this summer. The recommendations will go to the two health systems, the superintendent of schools, and the director of the health department.

"We received a grant from the Duke Endowment to plan the expansion of school-based health centers in the county. The planning group submitted an application to the Endowment for implementation funding, and we are waiting to hear if it will be funded."

Kate discusses the third community goal, improved birth outcomes:

> "The county health department operates family planning and maternity clinics. Moses Cone runs the high-risk maternity clinic for them. One area we are particularly interested in, because it came out of our community needs assessment, is the need for prenatal and postpartum care for substance-abusing women and their children. There already is a community-based group working on the issue, and we want to be careful not to step in and take over. I heard Moses Cone referred to as an 800-pound gorilla. We have to be careful of that. We have made our offers of support to the community group, and we will be watching their progress. They want to establish a halfway house for these women and their children, and that is one of the services that is needed.
>
> "We haven't done anything ourselves on the family stress goals, other than the educational programs offered through Women's Hospital, but we have funded five different community projects through the Community Health Improvement Fund."

Moses Cone also established a $100,000 Community Health Improvement Fund that the United Way of Greensboro administered according to the partnership priorities. Six agencies' projects were selected from among the 23 agencies that applied. Kate describes how the agencies integrate project activity with the community needs assessment and coordinate with other agencies:

> "The four needs that were identified by the Community Health Program provide the framework for Moses Cone activities. One of the key things we have done is to develop a community grant program, the Moses Cone Health System Community Health Improvement Fund, to encourage local health and human service organizations to develop projects in the four priority areas. We have funded four projects on access through the Health Improvement Fund—medical transportation, a half-time dentist and dental assistant, a health screening program run by the Salvation Army in their boys and girls after-school day care program, and a sickle cell disease monitoring and education program. We have funded some other projects as well. United Way administers the fund on our behalf. We work closely with them.

"We will create a new foundation as part of the Wesley Long merger. Its new board has met once. The work of the Community Health Program will be merged into the foundation. I think the board will embrace a very proactive approach. They will probably set aside some funds for reactive grant making, but I think they will help develop or act as a catalyst for needed services. It will be a challenge, but we have several projects in the pipeline already.

"Greater Greensboro is resource rich and cooperation poor. We're trying to have an impact on that. We are moving in our role as convener and catalyst to get everybody to sing off the same page. We are working with the health department and High Point Regional Health System to apply for a Healthy Carolinians task force that would focus on Healthy People 2000 objectives. Healthy Carolinians is a process for working through priorities in a community. The task forces in other communities have shown a wide range of results. Some of them have developed impressive programs."

The commitment to meeting recognized needs does not rule out accepting some interesting (and highly newsworthy) targets of opportunity. Moses Cone has a literacy program for its employees and a child sexual abuse clinic. It has sponsored two Habitat for Humanity houses. Kate describes some other Moses Cone efforts:

- A comprehensive gang tattoo removal program, called "DeTag," where the children are brought in and paired with a mentor, and complete a community service requirement. The kids are then bussed over to an academic medical center for special laser removal treatments. Those who have not completed their community service requirement cannot receive treatments.
- Wrap-around services for Medicaid-eligible kids, a program with the Salvation Army Boys and Girls Club that provides medical transportation and assistance with referrals and follow-through.
- Assisting with two comprehensive domestic violence projects coordinated by Family and Children's Services.
- A health education program for at-risk adolescents. The agency proposing the program, Triad Health Agency, had a proven curriculum with proven outcomes, a great idea. But they did not have access to the kids. We put them together with Greensboro Parks and Recreation and other agencies that deal with at-risk youths.

And finally, Kate says, the foundation and its programs must continue to assess how well they are doing in community outreach:

> "You need to measure outcomes to make sure you are using your resources most effectively. We have always had a strong emphasis at Moses Cone on effective use of resources. There are a lot of programs out there that are 'feel good' programs. They might make people very happy when they are participating, but they don't produce behavior change. They don't improve health. When you invest in programs like that, you are not using resources effectively. That's why we want to invest our funds only in programs that have been proven effective. That's not to say we won't take risks, but the program has got to stand a good chance of achieving good outcomes.
>
> "We participated in a needs assessment this spring that is based on the CDC Behavioral Risk Factor Assessment Surveillance System. The Health Department knew of our interest, so they asked Moses Cone, Wesley Long, and High Point Regional if they would assist in funding. We will get the results shortly.
>
> "United Way has been proactive in measuring outcomes. They are implementing a measurement system in all their agencies. I think that will help people understand that an outcome is not the number of people you serve, it is the change in behavior you produce."

Carole Bruce, trustee and chair of finance, adds:

> "I think one of the most positive outcomes of the merger is the $100 million Community Foundation. I see Greensboro coming up with a model for the country on the healthiest a community can be. I'm truly excited about what a community foundation with $100 million can do. Five million dollars a year of new money for health is a lot of money in Greensboro. Our United Way campaign raises about $12 million a year. This foundation will grow that by 50 percent. It has the potential for truly improving the health of the community."

Lanty Smith, J.D., chair of the board of trustees, concludes:

> "The foundation is being created for community health initiatives, with emphasis on wellness, children, and the disadvantaged. The foundation's charter provides very specifically that

the foundation's work is not in lieu of the indigent care this hospital has always provided. There's a significant advantage that can come to the community as a whole from spending money on those objectives."

Strategy

Moses Cone has a strategy of increasing scale, which means consolidating its market share in Greensboro, reaching out to nearby communities, and developing affiliations throughout the region and the state. It was able to increase its market share and its annual discharges throughout the '80s, ending with a 33 percent share of the three counties and a 42 percent share of Guilford County. Moses Cone's Centers of Excellence continue to thrive. The number of obstetrical deliveries increased 13 percent from 1990 to 1995, and integration with Wesley Long will raise the market share to almost 75 percent. Emergency visits have remained stable at Moses Cone, but the merger with Wesley Long will raise market share to two-thirds. The North Carolina Heart Institute was opened in 1992, and by 1996 dominated invasive cardiology treatment throughout the metropolitan area.

In 1996, Moses Cone formed a strategic alliance with the Randolph Hospital and announced a merger with Wesley Long Community Hospital. Relations with the High Point Regional Health System have been cooperative. In 1995, both participated in the North Carolina Health Network, an alliance of nine systems throughout the state. In 1996, Moses Cone, High Point, and Carolina Medicorp (CMI, formerly Forsyth Hospital of Winston-Salem) formed the Triad Health Alliance, an affiliation that gives Moses Cone some access to Partners HMO, which is owned by Carolina Medicorp.

Keeping focus

Strategy begins with a goal and gets complicated from there. Not-for-profit organizations have a particular problem identifying what their goals are. The goals must be understood and endorsed by many people, and a continuing effort is necessary to do that. The goal for leading healthcare organizations has become the improvement of community health within a limited total expenditure, but spelling that out in a specific community remains a challenge.

Lanty Smith, J.D., chair of board of trustees:

"I know I spend more time on the hospital than any other business I'm in. I've been a business executive for 20 years.

> Precision Fabric Group [where Lanty is president and CEO] is an engineered textile business. We do a great deal of specialized chemical finishing for fabrics. I'm involved in a number of other things as well. Over the last ten years I've spent half my time with not-for-profits—education, healthcare, government-related, something called the Center for Creative Leadership. I probably spend 15 or 20 hours a week on healthcare and the hospital.
>
> "If a colleague said, 'I've been asked to serve on the local hospital board,' my advice to him would first be, 'Don't do it unless you are willing to make a real commitment.' There might have been a time an individual served on a hospital board for the honor of it, and membership was restricted to those who had a certain social position or whatever. That was probably never a good idea; today it's a terrible idea. You ought not be involved unless you are going to make yourself knowledgeable, and this is one of the most complex industries in our country. It's an extraordinarily important part of our economy, and it's complicated. Moses Cone is the most complicated business in Greensboro.
>
> "The other thing I'd say is, 'Don't get involved unless you are willing to represent all stakeholders and from time to time disappoint some members of the medical community.' There's a tremendous tug and pull, a love-hate relationship between physicians and hospitals. If an administrator is going to successfully run a good hospital, he can't always be the physicians' buddy."

Lanty describes how the Moses Cone board faces up to its record and uses that record to keep its focus:

> "I have served on many of the not-for-profit boards in Greensboro, and this is the best. It's one of the really fine boards in the state. We have a core of people who are willing to put in the time to be knowledgeable supporters. One of the things we've done is to go back over the last 20 years and look at the decisions that were made, at which ones were made correctly and which incorrectly. The record was really very good. For example, the purchase of Humana and the creation of the Women's Hospital were tremendously far-sighted. The board did some other brave things.
>
> "There were a couple of situations involving strategic decisions where the board did not back Dennis. In both instances,

he was right and the board was wrong. We went back and shared that with the people who made those decisions as well as with the board as it is constituted today. The first was the opportunity to invest in PHP. Wesley Long put $2 million in and got out $47 million. Moses Cone could have participated. It would not only have been a very fine financial investment, it could have been the cornerstone for developing a community-wide, risk-sharing, true managed care system. The second was a surgical center in town that the hospital had an opportunity to buy. Some of the board, looking at the balance sheet, saw almost nothing there and what they thought was a significant price being asked. So they turned it down. That was of lesser significance, but it was a mistake.

"That's a kind of humbling thing, when you take bright business people who are accustomed to running businesses and making big decisions, and you make them revisit those kinds of issues. I think that's also strengthened Dennis' hand. We have tried to make one of the real functions of the Governance Committee to look at the board itself, engage in self-evaluation, say, 'How are we doing? How am I personally doing as a trustee? How is the chair doing? And the CEO?' Put some ratings on performance, and find four or five things we are doing well and four or five things we ought to work on. That's been very helpful. I think it's an essential part of the governance process that's too often lost.

"Getting discipline in not-for-profit organizations is a tough job, and I'm worried about it. I'm a great believer in not-for-profits. I've put half my life into them. I'm getting more and more concerned, because there is so much money going to community foundations. I'm not sure we should be putting so much money into them. I'm not sure they are going to take risks, and create jobs, encourage entrepreneurship, and those kinds of things that we are going to need 25 and 50 years from now."

Dennis Barry, Moses Cone CEO:

"When I got here, I inherited a board that had been in place for a good long time. Prior to 1978, there was no requirement for turnover. When Caesar Cone retired, it gave the board an opportunity to choose new membership and new management, and to reinvent itself. I believed we needed a board with equal representation of everybody in the community, with active working committees. That's the kind of structure we put in place, and it has worked very well.

"There's no question that in 1979 this board had been very much involved in a lot of operational stuff it should not have been involved in. More importantly, the things it should have been involved in weren't being addressed, in terms of the institution's role and mission, strategies for the future, and so forth. It showed in a whole bunch of ways. It wasn't until 1983 or '84 that we got into a position where the board had backed off their involvement in operations. That's when their role really changed.

"The board has always gone on a retreat for two or three days each year. We have tried to bring in a lot of folks from outside to educate the board on what is happening in the environment. When we took a hard look in 1991, a lot of today's change was foreseen."

Dennis describes a board committee that's called "development" but is really responsible for several aspects of board operation:

"We have always had a trustee development committee responsible for nominations, new member orientation, planning the retreats, and other activities management should do to help the board. I had a lot of difficulty getting the board to do routine self-assessment. Leadership previous to Lanty did not have a great deal of desire to do that. The work over the last few years has been from Lanty. Last year we did a self-evaluation and the report was not surprising. It said that most everything that the board has done has been done darned well. They know what they are doing; they understand their role.

"One of the reasons that we have worked together is that we have a great deal of respect for each other. There is a strong commitment to the community. All of our board members work as hard as they do because they think it is the best way that they can make a contribution to the community. I have heard them say repeatedly that of all the boards they have been involved in, this is by far the best experience. They really feel good about the governance process.

"As trustees have rotated off, we have had our pick of the litter in Greensboro. We can bring people on in a very selective way. There are two social structures in Greensboro. What people call 'Old Greensboro' revolves around people who have been born and raised here and whose families have been in business here. A second group is the new leadership. Wesley Long has far more of the old leaders. A good blend is okay. Some of the old leaders had some real blinders. The new leadership doesn't. They are much more focused on the breadth of the community, much more interested in what is right for the whole community.

"In the early '90s we became much more sensitive to the need for diversity. A lot of that occurred when we bought the Humana Hospital and turned it into the Women's Hospital. It became clear that we would have to have a larger representation of women on the board, and that raised the other questions of diversity. We have had some outstanding women and minority representatives."

Dennis reviews the hospital's progress on the goals of community service, scale, value, and physician relations:

"The real key is to build an integrated system. We have a long way to go in that regard, but we're over the initial organizational stages and we are moving forward. We're making significant progress, not only in Greensboro but at a more regional level.

"On community service, this hospital has always served as the charity hospital for the greater Greensboro area. In more recent years, we have begun to understand that we must be in a position of indispensability to the community. The most appropriate way for us to get there is to do extraordinary things relative to the status of our community. That's a direction we are clearly moving in. What's interesting is the opportunity through the merger to create a new foundation, with a new board. It will initially be funded with $50 million, and 18 months after the merger it will get another $50 million, dedicated to health needs in the greater community.

"For a number of years we were working on our centers of excellence, and bringing along our Moses Cone Hospital facility. That took a significant investment. The organization now generates about $60 million a year in cash. We have been investing most of that recently. By '87–'88, when we began to make some good solid margins, we began to not raise rates. We did [the freeze on rates] very judiciously. Even though we

> had a lot of outlay in terms of capital requirement, we continued to build the endowment. We continued to borrow from tax-exempt funds and to arbitrage the earnings on our investments.
>
> "Then we got to the Women's Hospital. In 1988, we bought a former Humana hospital. We had to wait to get the price we were willing to pay. We operated it a couple years as a medical-surgical hospital, but we knew we couldn't continue to run it that way. The first question was, 'What should we do with it?' and the next was, 'What is that purpose worth to us; how much would we be willing to pay for it?' We went through a whole variety of options and gravitated to a women's and children's hospital. We actually did pro formas and understood that a women's and infants' hospital would stand on its own and be cost effective. We had also acquired a medical office building nearby, and we had to upgrade that, too. The Women's had a shaky start, but it's doing well today.
>
> "That experience did something for us. It made the Moses Cone Hospital more efficient, because of the impact of scale. Also, we had started vertical integration, with a hospice and home care and long-term care. The overhead got spread over a much larger organization, making the whole thing enormously more productive.
>
> "In a very real way, the 1991 work was preparing the board for what we are doing today. We tried to put together a plan that contained a framework for the future, as opposed to a more definitive layout, because we knew the field was in for a lot of change."

Dennis notes how the definition of community is shifting to larger perspectives:

> "We obviously play a very dominant role in healthcare in this community, and we are mindful of that. Having a board that is focused on how well we serve the community is very important. How we define community may change over time. We are serving our outlying communities more and more, and our relations with outlying hospitals are growing. We're not sure where all this is heading. We try to build alliances with the right partners in other parts of the state and here in the Triad. It may turn out that only two or three systems serve the whole state, but we are not looking at major mergers at this point; there is no need to do that. There are a lot of smaller hospitals

> around us that are struggling, and helping them is part of our agenda."

Jim Roskelly, vice president for planning, explains how his department supports the strategic focus:

> "We've had a dedicated corporate function for strategic planning for 13 or 14 years. We have a six-member committee of the board that meets bimonthly that tracks strategic projects. This is also the body that considers strategic questions and makes recommendations to the full board, from property acquisition to decisions on major capital projects. We always want a physician member and a cross section. Now it's two attorneys, a banker, a retired accountant, and an internist. The board chair also is active on the committee, ex officio. They meet on average for a couple of hours. The full board accepts their recommendations almost without exception. My department prepares the agenda and all the supporting materials, and briefs the committee chair.
>
> "The planning department also plays a big role in the annual retreat. The majority of the retreat is devoted to strategic issues. We use that time to update the full board on what's going on in our environment. This year our retreat will be almost exclusively on clinical reorganization after the Wesley Long merger. The retreats are two-and-a-half days, off site. Sometimes we invite people other than the board. Last year we had representatives from Eagle Primary Physicians. This year we plan to have the newly configured board and the task force working on the clinical services plan."

The Moses Cone board has used outside consultants about every five years to help it focus its strategic plan. The nature of the plan and the services of the consultant have changed, as Jim notes:

> "In 1990, we selected a new consulting company because of its president—very intelligent, articulate, thoughtful man. The board saw him as someone who would expand our thinking, raise our sights above facilities and services to more encompassing issues. Now we have a plan that is much less detailed, but in a different way much more substantive. It talks about some key issues. While we don't provide an annual status report on the plan itself, it has led us to a host of specific actions which we do track. Once the merger is completed, we'll probably establish a new plan for the merged institution."

Setting financial policy

The governing board makes two basic financial decisions. One, setting the level of profit, is complicated by the unique history of healthcare. The other, using the profits wisely, has become challenging as the opportunities have grown and the available funds have shrunk.

Most organizations cannot set their price; it is set for them by the marketplace. Healthcare organizations were in a unique situation for several decades, where they could dictate their price and increase it annually. The consequence was that caregivers' incomes rose, costs to insurers rose, and health insurance premiums rose until they could rise no more. In the new order, the market will set prices. Trustees must then set the amount of profit the organization requires. What is left is what management and doctors must spend for care.

Here is how they think about the question at Moses Cone. Jim Roskelly talks about setting prices before it becomes necessary from market pressure:

> "Other organizations have approached this as making hay while the sun shines—make money now because we may not in the future. This organization has said, 'Anybody can make money from raising prices.' Management is held to a strict level of accountability to return value to the community. That was a self-imposed discipline. It's becoming a market discipline. Greensboro people realize and feel pretty good that they anticipated where the market was headed. Some of those folks who were making hay while the sun shone have been trying desperately to catch up. This organization anticipated what was going to happen."

The second financial decision is what to do with the profit or, more accurately, the cash that the organization generates. There are three basic options that must be balanced: investing in more of the same, replacing and expanding the acute care technology; investing in a new concept emphasizing primary care, clinical improvement, community health, and prevention; and remaining liquid, holding funds liquid for opportunities that may arise in the future.

Moses Cone has moved dramatically to the new concept. It has also moved deliberately to increase its liquidity, but it has not neglected acute care technology. The technology investment is largely in response to medical staff requests. Doctors always want the latest and most powerful. Saying yes all the time is a path to bankruptcy, but so is always saying no. Wisdom lies in realizing that each item must be evaluated on its own and that doctors are the best people to do the evaluation.

Bob Newton, CFO:

> "The hospital has not been held hostage by the medical community. There has been some noticeable but peripheral playing off of Wesley Long against Moses Cone, but that's not been substantive. The hospital has cultivated a partnering relationship with the medical staff as long as Dennis has been here. We've been held to high standards by some parts of the medical staff, but that's not the same as a medical staff that has exhibited selfishness: 'I want lots of things for myself, and it is up to you to provide them.' I don't think we've seen that.
>
> "The trustees did not influence that dynamic in an explicit way, but by setting a very well recognized tone for the organization as being a community-based asset. To try to exploit Moses Cone for one's personal benefit would have been to exploit the community. The medical staff has understood the tone of community involvement that the trustees have set, and has accepted working within that frame of reference.
>
> "The capital budget is generally a bottom-up process. There are usually two or three items which come from long-range facility planning, but the majority of items are in equipment additions or replacement. Departments report replacement needs or new technology needs. Some years ago the budget was a wish list that was whittled down by senior management. More recently, we've worked out a rationale at the operating level so that we don't get unrealistic requests, and physicians have a greater influence on the priorities. Instead of getting an \$18 million list and whittling down to 12, we get a \$13½ million list. We usually put the million and a half in a contingency for further exploration as the year unfolds. It took about three budget cycles to build that discipline."

Robert Gay, M.D., chief of pathology and president of the medical staff:

> "I feel the medical staff positions are appropriately heard by the board. There are two physician members on the board. The ones on now are fine physicians, not afraid to speak in defense of physicians in general, not just themselves. The medical staff president and president-elect get to attend board meetings and present important things from the medical staff. We are going to try to make the physician role stronger in the new organization. We will suggest revision of the bylaws—

that the staff president actually have a vote. I believe there will be four physicians on the new board.

"I can't really identify a group of physicians who are out of joint. Doctors always want something more. There aren't that many things that they need to do that they can't do here. There have been some people that are unhappy, but I don't think it had anything to do with Moses Cone Hospital. It's more what's going on in their practice of medicine.

"I have heard very few complaints about the quality of service at the hospitals. There were some complaints at Women's Hospital, because they didn't think they had adequate staff in intensive care. They did some renovations and responded. About the only ongoing problem is in the ED. Some of the problem has inadequate facilities—too small for the amount of work. We have tried to address that. We can't merge the EDs because of the patient loads; we have already studied that."

Carole Bruce, trustee and chair of finance, talks about information systems, one of two expensive areas where the board must eventually decide the investment:

"Information services is a tough one for me. In the business world it can be a bottomless pit. We've studied the requests and have granted every request from management. I dream of an information system that would allow somebody at Hospice to recover the entire medical record for the patient. The only reason we haven't spent more is that we haven't been shown that the systems exist that will do those things. Some of our problems have been systems that haven't worked, or have been difficult to implement. The business people on our finance committee have had too many experiences with systems that don't work; they want to make sure the systems they buy will work."

And Jim Roskelly, vice president for planning, talks about the other:

"Some board members may think we have expanded specialty services to excess. One of the differences between now and before 1979 is that in the '80s we aggressively developed our specialty programs. Our invasive cardiology program is one of the most active in the state. Radiation oncology and neurosciences, rehab, those sorts of investments clearly distance Moses Cone from any other institution in the area. In 1991, the board began to view investments more closely. We've never

> been a place that invested in technology for technology's sake, or a place that worshipped at the altar of super sophistication, having the only one of something. We've always had a business dimension to any of our strategic decisions. Unless management thought the project would make sense from a business standpoint, we didn't spend a lot of time thinking about it."

Bob Newton, CFO, talks about moving away from liquidity (an unusual stance for a CFO):

> "We expect a lot [about two-thirds] of the assets to be in long-term investments by the end of the decade. We have already begun to address that in substantive ways. About four years ago, at a meeting of former trustees—whom we bring in once a year to keep them familiar with what's going on—one of them observed that the organization is getting more financially successful than it needs to be to sustain itself. He asked what we are going do about that. He argued the need to translate that financial benefit into something for the community, either give it back to the community or stop taking it from the community. Out of that grew our Community Health Program, to which we committed a substantial chunk of our annual non-operating income, subject to our ability to use that money wisely and effectively."

Bob expands on some of the investment considerations:

> "Part of [mastering finance] is not getting overwhelmed with all the things you could do just because they are out there to be done. The board has a strong banking and insurance interest. They really understand balance sheets. The board does a great deal of its day-to-day work through its committee structure. The finance committee has a good grasp, and we also have a separate investment committee. Both have been involved in any of the major balance sheet transactions, particularly the debt transactions, so we have had the benefit of their combined judgment."

One issue is the amount of debt to incur. Bob's three rules are valuable anywhere:

> "If I were going to point out one thing that I had a hand in, it is managing the balance sheet. Recognition of equity growth as a fundamental measure of long-term financial viability is

important, and the corresponding use of tax-exempt debt to lower the cost of capital. It didn't make sense to leave that tax-exempt money on the table. The real question was how much of it should we use. Early on we said several things. One, we never want creditors to own more than we own ourselves. Never more than one dollar of debt for each dollar of equity. Two, if the operation cannot support its capital needs, then we have a problem, but it is not one we will solve by borrowing more money; that just substitutes one problem for another. Three, the level of comfort we have—and actually the number dropped to $40 of debt for every $100 of equity. And really we want it down around $30, because the trustees, from a fiduciary point of view, will have no difficulty explaining that on the front page of *The News and Record*, or going to sleep at night. It will benefit the organization, and we will find a way to translate that benefit to the community."

Alliances with other institutions

As community health organizations pursue their broader goals, opportunities for collaboration grow. Physician organization is itself collaborative: closer relationships that used to be independent. Clinical improvement raises the need for alternatives to inpatient care, from ambulatory acute centers to rehab and long-term care facilities, hospices, home care, day care, and preventive activities. These exist as separate organizations in most communities, raising the question of competition or collaboration. And collaboration has many forms, from contracts to longer-term alliances, joint ventures, acquisitions, and mergers.

Moses Cone has been especially adept at managing the spectrum from competition to merger. It has a wide variety of affiliations networking it firmly into the Greensboro community. Its continuing discussions with its closest competitor have led to merger. And the possibility of affiliations across the metropolitan area has not been ignored.

Lanty Smith, J.D., chair, board of trustees, on the Wesley Long merger:

"After I joined the board, around 1990, I became more and more convinced that we needed a merger between the two hospitals in Greensboro. I started quietly lobbying within our own board six years ago. The initial reaction I got was, 'Why would you want to do that? Competition's good. It's making both institutions better. It's holding down prices.' I did not share that view. My perspective was that frequently a medical arms race will develop. I read studies that say that where you have two hospitals in one city, rates are generally higher than where you have one.

"I also saw that sometimes the physicians, who are the ones with the real power although they might not understand that fully, were playing the two hospitals off against one another. That led to higher costs, not lower costs. I also was convinced that the healthcare industry was going to be restructured. It had to be. Cost escalation was just out of control, and the nation was not going to address the basic problems of third party paying and allowing health benefits to be nontaxable income. Those issues are at the root of our structural problems, but government is not going to deal with them. So the private sector will be forced to cause some sort of restructuring.

"I thought that over time our community would be better served if we had one healthy not-for-profit system. We are very close to putting that in place.

"We really try to live our not-for-profit mission, and I think we do reasonably well, but we can do a whole lot more. After the merger, we will have the Community Foundation. Moses Cone already has a history of supporting initiatives similar to what the foundation will undertake. It got Hospice and the HealthServe Ministry started, and it is expanding the Ministry. We've teamed up with the school system to take on school health. If Moses Cone puts together the kinds of initiatives that are worthy of the support of others, like the Duke Endowment, I'm sure they will join in."

Charles Reid, trustee and former chair, describes the Wesley Long merger:

"Wesley Long will have half the seats on the board and we will have half. Even though they are less than half our size, it is in the interests of the community. We would never have offered that unless we were comfortable with the Wesley Long board members. We initiated contact when I was chair, four years ago. We put in a lot of time. When we first approached them, they said, 'We are just not interested. We plan to go it alone as an independent entity. We feel we've got a commitment to the community, a commitment to the people who built the Wesley Long Hospital as volunteers and contributed money, and the physicians, that part of the physician community that is so fond of our hospital.'

"Lanty and I thought that if we offered the suggestion of the 50/50 board, it that would be a powerful and appropriate statement that this is not an ego thing, not a power play; it's someone who is putting the two hospitals together for the benefit of the community. It was my assumption that my seat would be one of the first to be vacated, on the 50 percent going out. My intention was to retire anyway. We also said we'll give you the chair—you nominate, we approve—and Dennis will be our CEO. We felt, we were confident, that the two hospitals would go together and the community would benefit.

"Some of the people at Wesley Long nominated Dave Brown for the merged chair. He's a super guy, very successful, done a lot of things in the community. Just a conscientious, straight up, good guy. One of his hesitations was the size of the combined operation. He said to me, 'Charlie, you work for a big company, I don't.' I said, 'Trust us. Dennis is a real good CEO. He will support you. He will make it easy for you, but he won't try to dominate you, and he won't try to dominate the board. He has respect for what the board does and what management does. We've sorted that out over the years, and it works great. You'll be an outstanding chairman of the combined system.'"

Charles goes on to discuss some of the real problems of mergers:

"The Cone organization will be the surviving organization. At first, the Wesley Long people wanted a two-step process with a probationary period. Particularly, the business leaders on our board didn't want that. When you successfully merge two for-profits, you merge them. You merge the systems, you deal with the social issues. Mergers that fail are the ones that didn't deal with those things. Since we started working together, they have gotten comfortable that this was a merger, not an acquisition; we are sincere, we are going to work together, we are going to benefit the community.

"We are going to have to work hard and communicate real well to say we're one system, to be sure we don't get into 'We/They.' Gary Park, the CEO at Wesley Long, will be the COO of the merged corporation. He and Dennis are working well together. The number one priority of the merged corporation is the clinical services plan. [The arrangement of the merged medical staff, especially the selection of the department chairs: after the merger, there will be one chair for several departments currently duplicated between the two hospitals.] We have a standing committee of two nonphysician trustees from each hospital, one each as co-chairs, as well as nine physicians, and some management. The physicians will have tremendous influence, and they are very conscientious about it. The hospitals selected two consultants and brought them to the committee. The committee selected one, a firm with good experience. We committed that the Wesley Long campus would continue to offer a meaningful amount of acute care hospital services for the immediate future. There's no commitment to keep it forever, but there's no intention to close it down."

Carole Bruce, trustee and chair of finance:

"Greensboro is better off if a lot of for-profit businesses don't come in with different motives and net revenues going back to wherever instead of being reinvested here. That's definitely a pathway we would work for—retaining local control and direction. I feel that way about healthcare and education, and other services. If you are going to take profit out of this community, that's not what's best for us.

"The prime example would be the Wesley Long Hospital, when their trustees agreed to merge with Cone Hospital, instead of Columbia and getting millions of dollars they could control, with their own foundation as a continuing freestanding organization. Or even an association with Duke or Baptist that would retain their freestanding character.

"The merger is going to cause some pain. The merger will cost some of my good friends their jobs. We have realized that the biggest cost savings are in moving management people out. That is painful. Like any other business decision, it's what you've got to do to keep the institution healthy. That's the advantage of having business people on the board. They know the pain of downsizing. It helps to have people who know that you make tough decisions first thing on Monday morning and carry them out. We've got to make certain it's the right thing for the community."

Peter Young, M.D., trustee and surgeon, on physician response to the merger:

"I was president of the medical staff, and chief of surgery. Now I'm on the board of trustees, and I will be on the new board. I think the physician community in general has been for the merger, because the alternative wasn't very palatable. Given their druthers, they'd rather have two independent hospitals competing against each other for their business, but that is no longer possible. Wesley Long's conclusion was that they had to partner with somebody.

"There were a lot of political reasons not to do it with Cone, including the lack of competition. But their choices were to sell to Columbia HCA, which was not acceptable, or to deal with Duke or Bowman-Gray. The physicians looked on that as an anti-physician move, because the only reason Duke or Bowman-Gray would want Wesley Long would be to serve as a funnel for specialty patients.

"The Long board had a series of focus groups with physicians to work their way through what the physician community wanted them to do. Ninety-five percent of the physicians are privileged at both hospitals. I'm told that every physician said that if Wesley Long could not live independently, they should try to do it locally and not go to an outsider. That was a turning point for their board."

Robert Gay, president of the medical staff, on the merger:

"A lot of doctors don't really like having to go to two hospitals; it's not very efficient for them. But there are some groups established at each hospital that will have to be integrated. There are also some differences in credentialling. Can the physician who was credentialled for a procedure at one institution now do it at both? How are we going to work that out? There are some physicians at Wesley Long who were not certified, and were grandfathered in. Everybody wants the merger to go well. That means making decisions about consolidating services to meet the cost saving.

"I haven't heard any doctors indicate that they are uncomfortable with the plan. It was a way of keeping people from outside the community from coming in, with the real potential of dividing the medical community even more acutely. I can't say that Columbia is bad—it is just not the way I would want to practice medicine, by just having a group buy it, pack in an administration, and just begin telling me how to do things.

The nicer way is by consensus, agreeing that in the framework of the times that we are living in, there are some things we have got to do together."

Moses Cone is thinking about other affiliations beyond the Wesley Long merger. Jim Roskelly, vice president for planning, talks about future possibilities:

"Our regional strategy has significantly more potential, but it too took several years to work closely with High Point and CMI. The board is very well briefed on the strategy. We talk about it at every one of the Strategic Planning Committee meetings. The trustees look on it as really important, and they want to see results.

"I think we are in the somewhat tenuous position of leading the market with this Triad strategy. Our physicians are much more comfortable with a local model where each community has its own PHO. Winston-Salem has the most advanced PHO. They have been managing the risk for 75,000 covered lives for several years. High Point is a single community provider with less incentive to develop. I'm sure they ask themselves, 'Why should we fuel this development, when the best course may be to ignore it?' That's a challenge for us, to keep them engaged.

"We don't yet have any health insurance products for sale jointly. The Triad Managed Care Organization is a super PHO, composed of individual PHOs. The Triad Health Alliance is an alliance of just the hospitals that can provide capital for growth—for things like management talent, information systems, and management services. We are seeking a CEO. That step is what we need to give life to the Triad strategy."

Alliances with other provider institutions are important, but there is also the matter of alliances with insurance companies. This is a complex issue where our three sites will have very different positions. Jim Roskelly summarizes the Moses Cone position:

"We are not going to start our own managed care company. The time to do that has come and gone. We are going to contract with Partners, United, and others. We are now developing a contract with Wellpath, a joint venture between Duke and NYLCare. It is one of a number of plans that are relatively new, with low penetration in the Triad, positioned for the long haul, and very amenable to working with providers.

They see a value in developing a subscriber base quickly. We'll develop contracts with other companies like that."

Lanty Smith sees another possibility. He talks about what health insurers or intermediaries actually contribute:

"I'm a great believer today in HMOs, but I think they represent a transition. Why do you need an HMO between the provider and the patient? To change incentives and reform the current inefficiencies of the fee-for-service system. If you can accomplish that without the HMO taking a bite out of it as it goes by, that would be a much more efficient delivery system. I think the providers have to be involved in risk-sharing. A small minority of providers used to feel that way; a larger minority does now, maybe even a majority. We are signing our first contracts now. The hospital and the physicians have to stand shoulder to shoulder.

"Let me give you an analogy. I was a partner in a large corporate law firm. I love the practice of law, but I'm the first person to admit that there have been some abuses. We don't have an LMO, a legal management organization. Nobody's ever suggested that we have an industry to manage legal services. Why do we need one in health? It's because the structure is so broken, so inefficient. I believe that was true because the receiver of the service was not paying for it. I believe that over time we will make the provider more responsive to costs."

CHAPTER

3

LEGACY HEALTH SYSTEM, PORTLAND, OREGON

The Metropolitan Area

Portland, Oregon, a metropolitan area of 1.5 million people, includes three counties in Oregon and one in neighboring Washington. It ranks among the leading metropolitan areas in people with college or graduate education, and only 10 percent of its adult population lacks a high school degree. It is 90 percent white, with small populations of African Americans, Asian Americans, and Hispanic Americans. Portland has a broad-based economy with a number of multinational firms, including Nike and Intel; agricultural and forestry industries; and a large percentage of small and medium-size businesses. It is well above the U.S. medians for income, but it also ranks high in homeless people, crime, and divorce. The area has grown rapidly and is forecast to reach 1.8 million by 2000.

The metropolitan area consists of 24 separate cities, stretching over a land area of 20 by 25 miles. The central city accounts for one-third of the population. Oregon's strict land use laws have limited the size of each city through restrictions on parking, retail store size, and conversion of agricultural land. The result is a series of small communities around a dense, pedestrian-oriented downtown Portland. Transportation is aided by a successful light rail system, but the metropolitan area still ranks only average in commute time. Parks and mountains ring the metropolitan area, and the peaks are frequently visible.

The city of Portland and Multnomah County, the central county of the metropolitan area, have relatively more people of color, without a high school education, and with lower income than the metropolitan area as a whole. It also has somewhat more crime and homelessness (Table 3.1). Portland and Multnomah County have about half the

Table 3.1 Portland Metropolitan Area and Multnomah County

	Portland Metro Area	Multnomah County
Population	1,515,452	583,887
Median Age	33.7 yrs.	34.2 yrs.
White Population	92%	87.2%
Median Household Income	$31,130	$27,140
Income Below $15,000	8.7%	10.8%
Total Crime Index	121	198
Educated Families Index	142	101
Homeless Index	186	199

Source: 1990 U.S. Census. Crime, Education, and Homeless Indexes by Easy Analytic Software, Inc.; U.S. mean = 100.

percentages of minorities and of poor people compared to Greensboro and the Triad. The overall picture is of a metropolitan area with unusual resources and less severe problems than many U.S. cities.

Health and Healthcare

Unlike North Carolina's Triad, where healthcare is focused in each of the three large cities, Portland has more of a hub-and-spoke array. Tertiary care is available only in the central city, and the suburban hospitals and health centers are smaller.

Portland is one of the lowest-cost cities in America for health insurance. According to a 1995 Robert Wood Johnson survey, 43 percent of the population is under HMO managed care and 9 percent under formally organized PPOs. Portlanders themselves say that everyone not in an HMO is in a plan that at least manages prices and provider panels; essentially, there is no traditional health insurance left. The Oregon Health Plan (OHP), started in 1989, provides Medicaid eligibles, others below the federal poverty level, and small employers a choice of HMO plans at community-wide rates. A similar plan serves persons up to 200 percent of federal poverty levels in Clark County, Washington. Overall, 7 percent are uninsured, about two-thirds the national average. A plan to mandate employer-sponsored health insurance, scheduled to become effective in 1996, was abandoned by the legislature before it could take effect.

To put Portland's healthcare cost advantage in perspective, commercial health insurance is available for $95 to $110 per member per month, Medicaid (a very high-risk population) for about $120, and Medicare for $390. Each of these numbers is a quarter to a third below the national average, and as much as two-thirds below the most expensive cities. Translated to national terms, if we all had the Portland cost structure, we would spend about $250 billion less on healthcare each year, enough to wipe out the deficit and increase federal education expenditures by 30 percent. In business terms, health benefits in Portland (including taxes for Medicaid and Medicare, and Medicare supplements) amount to $1,850 per employee per year. In a typical city, they would run $2,400, and in the most expensive, $3,000.

The economical level of healthcare is the result of several decades of unusual opportunities, rather than a sudden reversal of a high-cost setting. The most critical factor seems to have been Kaiser-Permanente, which has been available to anyone as the low-price provider since 1945. The second factor has been the willingness of business and community leadership to take advantage of the Kaiser presence, insisting that private insurance be reasonably competitive. Some major employers were using "menu" benefit plans as early as 1980. A business group on health promoted the collective pricing of health insurance and encouraged companies to offer Kaiser. Around 1990, costs became an issue to more companies, and hospital board membership "became a working assignment rather than an honorary one," as one trustee put it.

As the price of health insurance continued to rise, Kaiser experienced major growth. Early misgivings about Kaiser's quality or service were overcome, and the plan grew to 100,000 members around 1966. Kaiser developed home care and dental and alcohol benefits in the 1960s. Successful experiments were begun in Medicaid (1980) and Medicare managed care (1981). Kaiser enrollment continued strong in employee coverage as well. With Kaiser as the price leader, other insurers and providers were forced to hold down prices and improve efficiency. They did. In 12 years, hospital use in Portland fell from one million days per year to 600,000.

Public Health and Indigent Care

Public health in Portland is thorough, focused, and strategic. The Multnomah County Health Department has extensive programs for teen health education, assistance to addicted and other high-risk mothers, and control of tuberculosis, AIDS, and other sexually transmitted diseases. The county has improved control of these problems, with the exception of teen pregnancy, in recent years. It has formulated a plan for teen pregnancy and recently began STARS (Students Today Aren't Ready for Sex), which is based on nationally recognized methods and begins with sixth graders. Controlled trials have shown that students at high risk for pregnancy who take part in the program change in knowledge and attitudes, and the program has been expanded to all high schools and most middle schools.

Indigent care has been important in Portland. Neighborhood health centers, established in the late '60s, continued in operation when those in other cities shrank. Project Health was a 1975 experiment in insuring the Medicaid population that led eventually to the present Oregon Health Plan (OHP), one of the best-financed Medicaid programs in the nation. The Multnomah County Health Department operates 7 clinics for indigent healthcare and 11 inner-city school-based clinics. These clinics provided 234,000 visits to 71,000 people in 1996. Much care is financed through OHP. The county participates in OHP and provides direct support as well. The county clinic program is a substantial fraction of the primary care for indigent citizens and an important contributor to Portland's overall health. It reduces private healthcare costs directly, because the cost of these operations is in the county and state budgets rather than in unpaid visits to doctor's offices and hospital emergency rooms, and indirectly, because it helps maintain the health of a high-risk population, preventing expensive illness and complications.

Portland's health is satisfactory by available measures. Multnomah County has been near the median of similar counties in metropolitan areas. It ranks among the best 20 in heart disease mortality and in the percentage of low-birthweight babies, and is near the median in stroke and pulmonary mortality. Cancer deaths are a problem: Multnomah County ranks among the highest of large urban U.S. counties. Other available measures of healthcare quality show that Portland is equal to or ahead of national averages (Table 3.2). Portland's lack of progress on mortality reduction could be a cause for concern. Its overall mortality improvement from 1985 to 1992 was 65th among similar urban counties. Salt Lake City, Hackensack, Seattle, and Grand Rapids are examples of cities with mortality rates almost 100 deaths per 100,000 persons lower in 1992 and with greater improvement in mortality since 1985.

Healthcare Provider Organizations

Portland is the archetype of the mature twenty-first century healthcare market. Most care is given by three large healthcare systems, each of which is a partner with an insurance carrier. Legacy Health System and Providence Health System each have about 30 percent of the

Table 3.2 Portland Scores on Available Measures of Health and Healthcare

	Portland (Multnomah County)	Nation
Health		
Age-adjusted mortality (per 100,000 population)		
Cardiovascular	234	281
Cerebrovascular	30.2	56.4
Cancer	229	204
Accidents	30.2	29.4
All causes	877.2	871.57
Decline in mortality, 1985–1992	63.3	71.18
Low birth weight*	0.97%	1.49%
Persons reporting fair or poor health status	16%	13.39%
Health Insurance		
Households reporting		
HMO coverage	43%	22%
PPO coverage	9%	11%
Fee-for-service coverage	30%	39%
Uninsured	7%	15%
Patient Perceptions		
Needed care in past year but could not get it	10%	12%
Think quality of medical care has improved compared to 3 years ago	47%	46%
Think family healthcare costs are under control	75%	73%
Rate reasonableness of out-of-pocket payments excellent	36%	25%†
Think trend to managed care is a good thing	63%	59%

*Percent of live births weighing less than 1,500 grams.
†Significant at $p < .05$.

Source: Louis Harris and Associates telephone survey, available from the Robert Wood Johnson Foundation, National Center for Health Statistics, and National Center for Quality Assessment.

provision of inpatient services. Kaiser-Permanente and Oregon Health Sciences University have about 15 percent each. The balance is scattered among several sources, including direct contracting with providers. The other significant providers are the Southwest Washington Medical Center in Vancouver, and the Adventist Health System. There are two small independent hospitals.

Kaiser-Permanente, strong in both the under-65 and Medicare markets, has one-third of the HMO-insured market. HMO Oregon, sponsored by Blue Cross and affiliated with Legacy Health System, has almost one-quarter. The Good Health Plans, affiliated with the

Providence Health System, have one-sixth. PacifiCare and several other commercial carriers share the remainder. Blue Cross and Providence also have a substantial PPO/traditional membership. In the combined health insurance market, they have half the market, and Kaiser, with 20 percent, is the only other large insurer.

Use of healthcare services, as indicated by hospital admissions, and outpatient visits have been stable in recent years, but only because increasing population growth has offset declines in the rates of use.

Of the three leading systems, Kaiser is the easiest to describe. It is a staff-model HMO, emphasizing the employed Permanente physicians and operating two hospitals. It has been in Portland since World War II, and it has compiled an excellent record. Kaiser is fully accredited by NCQA and is recognized as one of 13 "Benchmark Plans" by the General Motors Corporation. (GM rates all the HMOs it deals with on cost, accreditation, and HEDIS quality data.) Through the 1960s and '70s, Kaiser and Providence shared the leadership of Portland healthcare.

The Sisters of Providence, headquartered in Seattle, have hospitals from California to Alaska. For decades they have operated two in Portland, of 450 beds and 250 beds, and a third, smaller one in a southeastern suburb. With the increasing popularity of managed care, the Portland Providence hospitals founded Good Health Plan, an HMO with both employed and private practice physicians, which successfully competes with Kaiser. In the '90s, they integrated their hospitals, acquired and closed a fourth, and strengthened their insurance plan and medical staff affiliation. Although the Good Health Plan is popular in Portland, it has not yet achieved NCQA accreditation.

Legacy Health System

Legacy, the focus of this case study, is significantly more complicated. Its origins appear to be largely in response to the Kaiser and Providence successes. In 1976, Emanuel Hospital, 400 beds, and Physicians and Surgeons Hospital (since closed) in downtown Portland merged to form HealthLink, and built Meridian Park, a 100-bed suburban hospital 10 miles south of the city. By 1988 they had acquired Holladay Park Medical Center (later closed), the Visiting Nurse Association of Portland, and Mt. Hood, 100 beds in an eastern suburb. Legacy was formed when Good Samaritan, a second 400-bed downtown hospital, merged with HealthLink in 1989. John King, its current president and CEO, joined in 1991.

As of 1991, Legacy was organized around its four hospitals and the Visiting Nurse Association (VNA), operating as relatively independent units, with their own boards, executives, and trustees. According to John Warne, a trustee whose association began in 1978, "The governance system was so unwieldy it wasn't working. . . . To really manage Legacy like a business, it's absolutely essential to have central control over management and budgeting. We decided that the board should be downsized. . . . We had board members coming out of our ears. So we let some of the old members go. . . . We asked for volunteers to quit, and then we set an age limit."[1] The centralized board assumes fiduciary responsibility for all units. It has been reduced from 23 members to 16. Four community boards, including one for the central city, one for Meridian Park, one for Mount Hood, and one for the VNA, are responsible for monitoring quality of service, including credentialling, and for community relations.

1991 Reorganization

Under John King's leadership, Legacy began a centralization process and a quality improvement program. It identified five strategic pathways:

1. **Integration**. To become an integrated healthcare delivery system, linking health plans and physicians, to assure convenient access to a competitively priced comprehensive range of services;
2. **Organized Capability**. To apply continuous quality improvement principles [principles called "total quality management" at Moses Cone and Henry Ford] and techniques to all aspects of management and patient care, implement data systems to support the work of the system, and empower employees and medical staff to seek innovative approaches for achieving the vision;
3. **Market Share**. To attain market share equal to or greater than key competitors by increasing enrollment in aligned health plans, coordinating marketing and sales for the system, and offering services at competitive prices;
4. **Financial Performance**. To maintain an A bond rating, finance developmental and replacement capital expenditures with internally generated funds, and improve cost position to price services at competitive levels;
5. **Collaborative Community Relations**. To enhance geographic access through strategic alliances, cooperate with other healthcare providers to avoid unnecessary duplication of services, and improve the health status of the community.

[1]Warne, J. 1996. "Governance: The Hospital's Conscience." *Trustee* October: 26.

Legacy made two major organizational moves as it pursued its pathways. First, it emphasized clinical entities—groups of related diseases—rather than functional units like hospitals. Legacy designated seven clinical areas for systemwide integration. Program development teams (PDTs) were formed for heart/pulmonary, cancer, women's, pediatric, rehabilitation, behavioral services, and laboratory services. The teams were broadly representative and supported by at least five work groups each, studying business development, finance, quality, outreach, and operations. Legacy added six more teams in 1997 (for dialysis/ diabetes, imaging, nursing, ophthalmology/neurology, orthopedics, and trauma). Every major disease group is now represented by a program development team.

Second, Legacy moved to a new management structure in 1997, trading geographic focus for a functional one supporting the 13 PDTs. The Legacy hospitals no longer have CEOs. Specific sites have operational coordinators reporting to central executives.

An operations redesign task force to eliminate duplication concluded its work in June 1997, grouping all activities under six senior management leaders (Figure 3.1). The senior management team has a series of systemwide goals and performance indicators covering patient and employee satisfaction, market share, finance and cost, facilities and personnel planning, and improved community health status. It uses a broad range of committees and task forces to set and achieve goals across the various geographic sites and PDTs.

The depth and breadth of the senior managers' portfolios is noteworthy. The chief operating officer's responsibilities include physician integration, marketing and strategic planning. The senior vice president for finance manages material management and plant services, medical records and a clinical research unit. Clinical operations coordinates the 13 PDTs. The senior vice president for human resources and quality leadership has a strong educational focus, including graduate medical education and other professional education. The senior vice president for legal and information services, responsibilities include clinical information system, a data archive, a cost management system, and sophisticated case mix and case review systems.

Legacy Implements Its Strategic Pathways

Value to Stakeholders

Portland has been so successful at controlling healthcare cost that there are questions about whether its costs are too low, or as Don Sacco, president of Blue Cross Blue Shield of Oregon, says, "underfunded."

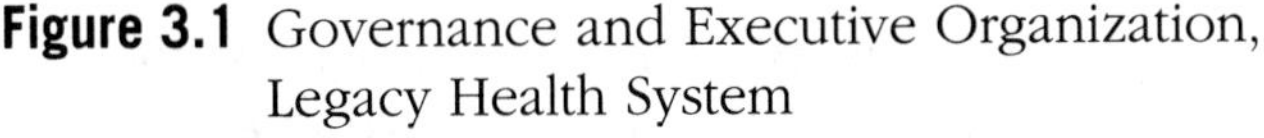

Figure 3.1 Governance and Executive Organization, Legacy Health System

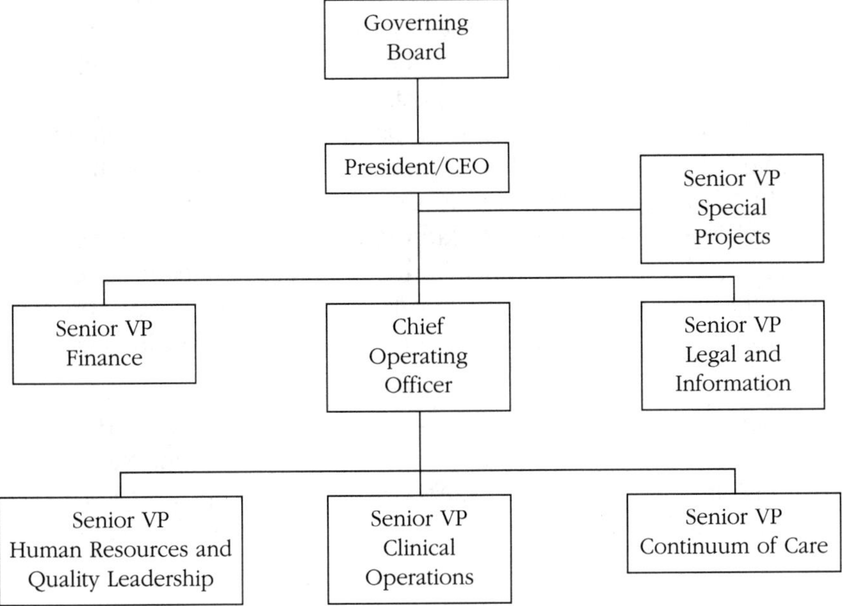

He goes on to explain some of the factors in cost reduction that contributed to the record and in the end became subjects of contention:

> "There's a lot of talk in this area of the country that healthcare is underfunded. I don't know whether there is truth to that or not. It's all in what you get used to. When you talk to employers, they sure don't think it's underfunded, and I think there is legitimate pressure for price improvement.
>
> "When you look outside the borders of the state, we look pretty good. When you look inside it still represents increases from year to year that have been modest. There's some real pressure being put on, and there are some real positive results. Kaiser has done some smart things, dumping their facilities and buying on the spot market for care. [Kaiser has begun decommissioning its hospitals.]
>
> "For whatever historical reasons, we are more conservative here in the Northwest in deploying the most expensive resources. At the same time, we are doing some things in preventive services and in protocols around chronic disease management. We have a lot of cooperative efforts, like the

> immunization project. The primary physicians really took hold of a tightly managed role. They really did start working with specialists and each other to reduce use. The doctors are on a fairly tight chain for what they can prescribe or order without calling the medical director. The old-style utilization review has helped reduce specialist costs.
>
> "On the other hand, claim-by-claim bullying can't be sustainable in a relationship between and among physicians. It led Blue Cross to be viewed in a very adversarial way back in the '80s. The medical groups claim that their doctors have been taking a hit in their incomes in the last couple of years. Several of the groups have complained bitterly, but they have grown substantially and they finance growth out of current income."

John King, Legacy president and CEO, describes the response of the provider organizations to the "old-style utilization review." By avoiding expansion as population grew and by slowly shrinking the hospital beds and inpatient staffs, Providence and Legacy kept their costs constant for many years:

> "The market went through a consolidation phase around Providence and Legacy that helped stabilize costs. There was one freestanding surgery center built in this town, and it went bankrupt. The doctors believed their patients were better off in hospital settings. There were a lot of conversions to outpatient business by the hospitals, to make ambulatory surgery cost effective and convenient. Those kinds of things kept us on a reasonable growth pattern. We had a huge excess of inpatient beds, but the doctors weren't going out and churning them. They just slowly shrunk away."

The forces that help Providence and Legacy hold costs down came more from the health insurance and healthcare provider competition than from the buyers directly. John says:

> "It's very much a small company town. The business community has no organized buyer group. Health is not high on the agenda of the big companies that are headquartered here—Nike, Fujitsu, Intel. They are not preoccupied with healthcare. Right now they are very interested in education. They need educated people, and the tax cuts could threaten that.
>
> "The healthcare marketplace has been led more by the insurers and the providers. Kaiser was a big factor in keeping prices competitive. They [Kaiser] had strong growth in the late

'80s and were one of the catalysts that got Portland moving in its current direction.

"The third factor was the doctors. Doctors here are very well trained. We have a highly skilled medical group, good people. This is the best-trained, most cooperative group of physicians I've ever seen. I don't know if the physicians here understand how good they are.

"Oregon has a lot of political liberalism, but conservative lifestyle. It was the first state to have a bottle return law; it started the Oregon Health Plan; it has a strict land use law and a solid metropolitan government. People are resistant to taxes on one hand, but they will spend on the other. They are trying to cut land taxes on the one hand, but they support an increased cigarette tax for healthcare at the same time."

The trustee role in value

Charles Heinrich, trustee and former board chair, tells how Portland companies got control of health insurance costs in the 1980s:

> "In the past, the companies around Portland were paternalistic about healthcare. My company, Portland General Electric, certainly was. The employees thought their healthcare came from Blue Cross, but the truth was we paid all the bills. As Portland became more high-tech, and also as competition increased, suddenly cost became very much an issue. Portland was one of the first places to have a business group on health, probably around 1980. The business group considered how to control their costs, whether they should contract directly or some other way. Our employees were aging. We did not want adverse selection, so we had to come up with a general plan. Kaiser looked like a good plan to be in when you were young, but then people would select a different plan with broader coverage.
>
> "The companies [that] were competing in metals or computers, or things that had overseas competition, were the most vigorous. The attitudes changed. I met all of Pacific Gas' largest customers for lunch, and sometimes I was lunch. Their concern was, 'I've got to cut my costs in all areas, and you are one area. How can we work together to get the quality and the price?' Hospitals have begun doing that now. 'How can we provide the healthcare you want at a cost you can afford?' It's not a fun thing."

Charles describes how the business group transferred some of the risk of healthcare cost to the employees. Under a menu plan, the employer selects several different kinds of health insurance, such as a rigorous HMO like Kaiser, a looser managed care structure or a PPO, and a traditional plan. The employer's share of the premium is often set at the level of the least expensive coverage. Employees are free to pay more for the other plans, on payroll deduction:

> "So the business group recommended a menu approach. Portland General Electric had five plans, including Kaiser and Blue Cross. We still had the old paternalistic plan, but it got priced out of the market, partly by adverse selection and partly by its benefit costs. The traditional plan now has a deductible of $2,000, I believe. Most people are now in HMOs."

Big companies, like Portland General Electric, can get what they want at a fair premium. Small companies have problems in two ways. They can't afford to pay somebody like Charles to become an expert in healthcare, and they can't get the premiums that come with large, stable groups. Charles explains how the Oregon business group helped:

> "One of the things the group did was to get the smaller companies involved. It was educational for them. The smaller companies can purchase in a pool through the Oregon Health Plan.
>
> "The business group was on the hospital boards, but for a long time they viewed it as an honorary job. Our board now is very much a working board, and people are very concerned about the wellness of the whole community. You have to know also that business concern has led Oregon to the Oregon Health Plan. OHP is quite unique, and it is a form of rationing."

And why, as John King goes on to say, Portland no longer has a business group:

> "The chamber of commerce took over the business group activities. Once it got inside the chamber, it started acting more like a place to have lunch than a place where you were working on a problem. I think it eventually kind of died. Two things happened. People who came to the business group were second-level people. Some of the people who understood it even left to go into healthcare. After we started changing our plans, cost became a less pressing matter."

James Perry, J.D., the current board chair, confirms some of Charles Heinrich's thoughts:

> "One of the reasons for Portland's success with healthcare costs is that in many respects, it is still a small town. Business leaders in Portland have almost to a person maintained a high profile in shaping and preserving the quality of life in Portland—education, health, all of that kind of thing. Affordable education and affordable health have been high priorities. We've had business leaders who had the ability, because they sit on the Blue Cross board and in other positions, to ratchet down the cost. It's the big business people who lead the United Way and sit on the hospital boards, and that kind of thing. It was to the advantage of smaller businesses. There has never been a we/they split between big business and smaller businesses here. The big businesses rely on the little businesses for their livelihood.
>
> "I think controlling healthcare costs was totally an economic thing. When costs began to go out of whack, the business leaders became very alarmed. I remember my own CEO [at a large bank] just raising hell with insurance companies. Others of the same ilk were instrumental in requiring the insurers to hold down premiums. The insurers in turn looked to the providers. Costs were out of control, and it's like a runaway train. The reason Portland is where it is today is because the brakes started being applied some time ago, and yet in a way that was not dramatic. The costs were not cut. They were kept level while everybody else's were rising. It wasn't a knee-jerk kind of thing but just a general recognition that costs needed to be controlled. We see the same kind of thing to a lesser extent with our education costs for higher education. Some pressures are being brought in the legislature to deal with that. Oregonians still feel this is a citizen-operated place, that we can get involved with and make a difference.
>
> "I started on the Good Samaritan board, nominated by the Episcopal Diocese of Oregon. I'd been interested in healthcare issues for a long time. My first act was to vote for the merger with HealthLink that formed Legacy. Cost control was not the dominant idea for the merger. Good Samaritan was in a good economic position, but we were a high-cost operation and our market share was deteriorating significantly. That could not continue; we needed help in turning it around.

HealthLink had been formed as an economic lifeline, but they were sinking financially."

Part of the reason the business group strategy succeeded is that Kaiser has always been dedicated to cost-effective care. So when the companies benchmarked their premium contribution, there was a reliable, low-cost solution for those who wanted it. Jim points out that although not everybody wanted it, competing with Kaiser was not as easy as it looked:

> "Kaiser has always been a player here, with at least a 25 percent market share. There's always been a feeling that they were a low-cost operation, but a low-quality operation as well. Some of us who didn't know any better had our eyes opened by those who were more knowledgeable, around 1989. It became clear that Legacy could not gain market share simply by being a center of excellence, because we are not that much more excellent than anybody else."

Measured performance and continuous improvement

Measured performance is a keystone of the continuous quality improvement concept, and Legacy has been pursuing CQI diligently since 1991. In 1996 it won the Oregon Quality Award, a prize awarded in a statewide competition to the organization with the best CQI record. The facts from the CQI program demonstrate its success. Legacy has stabilized its market share of hospital admissions. Given the growing Portland population, admissions have increased, from 38,884 in 1991 to 39,868 in 1996. At the same time, total expenses have been held to an increase of 8 percent over 1991 levels. (Inflation created an increase of 15 percent during that period.) Costs per admission have been held to an increase of just over 4 percent.

These savings permitted steady improvement in the operating margin, from 2.3 percent to 6.3 percent, and improved the balance sheet. An overall margin, including non-operating income of 8.5 percent, is well ahead of U.S. norms. Legacy has an A^{++} Standard and Poor's rating. Financial ratios reflect considerable improvement over 1991. The debt:equity ratio, which reached 1:1 in 1993, is now 0:53 (Table 3.3).

Employment at Legacy has diminished from 5,896 FTEs to 5,080, falling to 7.36 per 100 adjusted admissions. A deliberate effort has been made to retrain and assist downsized employees, with the result that about 70 percent have been retained and another 15 percent rehired as vacancies have occurred. Employee surveys show stable to

Table 3.3 Legacy Key Financial Indicators

	1993	1994	1995	1996
Income and Expense				
Net patient service revenues	$423,544	$420,528	$426,492	$470,261
Operating expenses	427,686	427,252	423,946	451,300
Income from operations	11,103	9,444	19,827	33,722
Total income	$24,076	$17,406	$19,779	$39,946
Balance Sheet				
Current assets	$158,194	$115,472	$128,556	$113,701
Limited and restricted assets	56,536	59,435	17,425	17,788
Other assets	332,492	390,121	437,917	472,140
Total assets	$547,222	$565,028	$583,898	$603,629
Current liabilities	$73,320	$74,169	$77,465	$83,355
Long-term debt	212,672	205,612	195,155	160,990
Other liabilities	19,755	20,911	24,105	21,299
Fund balances	$241,475	$264,336	$287,173	$337,985
Operating margin	2.6%	2.2%	4.6%	7.2%
Times interest earned	4.64	4.41	4.56	6.54
Debt/Asset	39%	36%	33%	27%

improving satisfaction. Legacy, which is the sixth-largest private sector employer in Portland, was named one of the ten best companies to work for based on an evaluation of pay and benefits, employee involvement, community involvement, opportunity for advancement, and workplace culture. As a result of Legacy Goal Share, the incentive payment program, Legacy was rated one of the top five companies in the state for pay and benefits in 1996 and 1997.

Measuring the quality of healthcare is a field in its infancy. Legacy uses one of the few national data collection efforts, nine quality indicators developed and administered by the Maryland Hospital Association (MHA). Legacy was better than the reported mean on all but one indicator, returns to the operating room after surgery (Table 3.4). The nation's MHA mean for this indicator was 1.13 percent; Legacy's was 1.39. Tom Hansen, M.D., vice president for medical affairs, reported, "We traced it to our heart program, where our heart surgeons have a deliberate policy of prompt return to surgery in the case of problems. The heart program overall has exceptional outcomes, and a national database."

All of this was accomplished without loss of patient or physician satisfaction. Legacy systematically surveys patient satisfaction using an

Table 3.4 Measures of Quality of Care

Indicator	1996	1997
Hospital-acquired infections/1,000 patient days	3.3	3.125
Wound infections as percentage of surgeries	0.72%	0.62%
Cesarean section rate as percentage of deliveries	16.32%	18.76%
Unplanned readmissions as percentage of discharges	3.20%	3.63%
Unplanned admissions after ambulatory surgery, as percentage of ambulatory surgeries	0.35%	0.32%
Unplanned returns to special care units as percentage of discharges	2.70%	1.34%

outside agency to ensure accuracy. Sample sizes are large enough for major units to check their performance quarterly. Satisfaction is checked against prior values. Physicians are also formally surveyed, but they also have formal and informal avenues to communicate within the organization.

Since it has been surveying patient satisfaction, the percentage of "secured patients" has stayed above 70 percent. A secured patient is one who was satisfied, would return, and would recommend to friends. The weakest of the Legacy units achieves 67 percent secured patients, and improving performance is a 1998 goal for all operating units. Similar values are reported for physician satisfaction (Table 3.5).

CQI has been central to these successes. John King talks about CQI:

> "I've had two opportunities at continuous quality improvement, and they both worked. At Evangelical Health Services, we were two years into it when I left, and I was afraid it might wither, but it sure did not. It also took root here, and has become a part of the organization. That sort of stuff takes tough CEO commitment."

Larry Choruby, trustee and chair, planning committee, adds:

> "This CQI has really been something. In many people's minds it was cost reduction. John never mentioned cost reduction; it was always quality improvement. That's what everybody was working on, and everybody was invigorated and having fun and accepting change. Along the way, the profits went up."

Barbara Zappas, senior vice president, human resources and quality leadership, describes some of the components of the CQI program:

Table 3.5 Measures of Patient and Physician Satisfaction

Percentage of "Secured Patients"* by Region and Type, 1997

All Legacy Patients	72%
Portland City	70
Meridian Park	76
Mount Hood	72
Visiting Nurse Activities	74
Outstate	69
All Hospital Patient Types	73
Emergency	63
Inpatient	77
Outpatient	77

Percentage of Medical Staff Members Rating Legacy Health System, January 1997

Attribute	Excellent	Acceptable	Needs Improvement	No Response
Patient Care				
Quality of care	59%	28%	5%	8%
Equipment	43	42	7	8
Facilities	48	40	5	7
Clinical services	46	43	3	7
Staffing levels	27	46	18	9
Collaboration				
Access to leadership	24	45	12	19
Quality of communication	21	47	13	18
Legacy responsiveness	17	44	18	20
Physician involvement in decision making	19	41	20	19

*"Secured Patients" are those who report that they were satisfied with service, would use service again if needed, and would recommend to others.

"As we eliminated the hospital CEOs, we centralized the quality leadership under one office. We've been working under a single approach, developing a single quality language using CQI, since 1992. That has been the defining structure that has made us an integrated delivery system. It has become the language, the culture, the way we do business. That capability has made us move forward and has started to break down the differences and the barriers between previously competitive hospitals. It has also allowed for a lot more appreciation and respect for the differences in our cultures. It defines our management style.

"The data revolve around the quality compass—financial, patient outcomes, clinical measures and indicators, and customer satisfaction. We are focusing on data across the system, across the business. Every department, every operation, every facility collects data on what's important for them to measure. Every clinical area has its measures. Those roll up into operating plans."

Barbara discusses how the CQI philosophy is presented within the organization:

"We don't want to overcomplicate how we approach quality. We've been very consistent in our language. How we approach it through the quality council is to be sure that we have consistent methodology and reliability and that the indicators are meaningful. We want people looking for stretch targets. When a measure gives us scores of 99 percent for three years—'Throw that out and push yourselves.' If the measures are not meaningful, or don't stretch, or are not reliable, then we'll find one that is.

"We've gone from introductory training, in 1992 and 1993, to where if the departments are comfortable with two years of trending of a quality indicator internally, we are asking them to do what we call 'little b benchmarking,' to look around the system for someone doing a better job. Look internally to model from each other so that all of Legacy can rise to that standard. Then we look outside, in our industry or outside our industry.

"At the close of every year, we take three days and look at every operating area using a consistent template to define our operating goals for the next year. We take all of the systemwide clinical programs, such as women's services and imaging, and all of the functional areas like quality, HR, legal. Everyone is required to follow the template in defining the high-level tactics for the upcoming year, the major implementation tasks, who is responsible, and what impact it will have on operations and capital."

Barbara notes that the CQI process is unending. Despite Legacy's success with it, there is still plenty more to do:

"We have a difficult time finding best practices within our industry that we haven't set or matched. In human resources, we went to INCO, Westinghouse, and Walt Disney World for

> benchmarks we are now using as part of our applicant tracking and employee turnover. Healthcare has not done a good job of managing work force development. If you go to airlines, car rental companies, large software companies, you will see how they do things from employee health management to moving an applicant through the system much more efficiently than hospitals.
>
> "The plan doesn't sit on the shelf. Every quarter we pull it out and look at it. It gets pretty dog-eared by year end. It goes to the board, the community boards, the medical staff committees, the quality council. The community boards have quality as one of their key areas. That's how we keep focused. If you get distracted, you have to come back and explain it. If you haven't achieved, then there's accountability. This is how we keep quality moving forward.
>
> "Our next step is strategic goals for quality. We have just been corralling what everyone's been doing. Now we want to be proactive. We have a double A rating in finance; where do we want to be in quality? Strategic quality goals would say to everyone that quality is going to lead this organization as much as finance.
>
> "We are proud of what we have done, and we think we can share what we've learned with others. So we applied for the Oregon Quality Award in 1996, and won. We were the largest applicant ever, and the most distributed in terms of sites. We are applying again this year, and trying for the Governor's Trophy."

The Legacy successes are interrelated, and are related to opportunities that arise in the local environment. Lowell Johnson, chief financial officer, explains how the Oregon Health Plan helps Legacy:

> "Legacy can succeed in its broader vision—healthy community, good citizen—goal only if it's got a bedrock performance that allows it. In '87 to '93, Legacy could think about good things for its employees, but it couldn't afford them. We had to build the financial performance base that generates a net income. I think Legacy is in its current financial position for three different reasons. The payment mechanisms from Medicaid are among the most generous anywhere—not from a rate perspective, but coverage. It's easier for Oregonians to help those less well-to-do, because they look just like the rest of us. They aren't 'The Others.' That generosity translates into

revenue for us, the ability to charge for patients that formerly, and in other states, we couldn't charge for. Oregon Health Plan expanded those who paid the bills and the people who came for service.

"OHP is a small percent of our revenue, maybe 5 or 6 percent, but much of this was not collectible at all before. It probably eliminated $10 million a year of bad debt and charity losses in the last three years. That's 20 percent of our bottom line. It's become a very accepted public program. The state passed a tax on cigarettes to pay for it in the last referendum. OHP has won in the court of public opinion in Oregon."

But Lowell goes on to describe the kinds of cost accounting and budgeting systems that are necessary to convert market opportunity into financial reality. First the cost accounting system, a technical marvel that allows the operator of a small activity, such as a nursing station, or a large service line, such as women's health, to know how much it actually costs to provide the services:

"First, we make it clear that we are going to do performance measurement. Finance staff is saying, 'Don't get all hung up about it, let's just do it. This is hard work, but not impossible work.'

"Our cost finding for service lines is business reliable, not accounting reliable. By that I mean a rational business person can make a rational decision from the information. We've invested about a million dollars and untold hours of hard work by financial and information systems people to take our general financial system and run it through a decision support system to program-specific and even physician-specific information. It's reasonably accurate. We know contribution margins [the difference between the direct costs and the revenue earned] by program. I like to stop there. I'm not enthralled with allocating depreciation, or plant costs, or front office costs. If my contribution margin is over 40 percent I'm getting by; if it's less, it's not satisfactory.

"Our accounting people have learned to explain to the operations people where the 40 percent goes and why it's important. The legitimate question from operations is, 'What are you going to do about the part I can't control?' It becomes a team approach. The number one thing that got this organization willing to go at the operating level was that, the first year I was here, I took $4 million out of the corporate office. When they saw the central office willing to go down by 12 percent in one year, they had a lot more willingness to do productivity. John King and I gave up assistants. I took the accounting staff from 300 people to 240. You gotta do it yourself before you can ask somebody else."

And rather than strive for general improvements in accuracy, Lowell's team goes to the areas where greater accuracy is important:

> "The cost accounting system is a painful bear to build on the front end. It took us untold effort. The cost analysts had to go one by one with the operating people to get the accounting right. It was a two-year building process to get where the operations people would say, 'I believe and I trust these data.' It is one of the hardest jobs a finance staff will do. You have to get into a level of minutiae you won't believe. If the user won't accept it, you can throw it out.
>
> "The labor cost is tracked on an electronic timekeeping system. Employees use telephones to track their actual work time and place. The management staff clocks in by function. You allocate your time like a professional service organization would. We all clock in, even John.
>
> "We have some needs. We are mostly using our own history. We do not do a good enough job of benchmarking the specific clinical services. The operating people are saying, 'Show us more specificity.'"

The CQI strategy is dependent on being able to move large quantities of information to people who need it in a form they can use. That calls for an information system and a deliberate information strategy. John King, CEO, notes:

> "We did not have a strong information system strategy when I arrived. We have one policy board of information users who really set priorities and policy. There is no question that there is a very centralized approach to information planning. That's another pitfall in a lot of organizations. Too many users are given too much latitude. We have one policy group that makes the decision. People don't always like it, but they know where we are going."

Mitch Olejko, senior vice president of legal and information services, describes a plan that some people would call excessively conservative:

> "Phase One calls for all of us to get on the same technology. By the end of this year, we will have a wide area network

> connecting all our sites, local networks within each site, a common phone system, e-mail, and a central financial system. We are starting a five-year, $23 million clinical information system project. It will automate each clinical activity so that the records and the data can be shared.
>
> "All doctors' offices will be able to tie into the system. What we don't have budgeted is what physicians need for their office practice and billing. We have talked about a medical services organization [a corporation providing management services to physicians] organized around that service. When you start looking at the dollars involved, it gets pretty threatening. The doctors have to agree on a common system, and many of them already have investments of their own. There is no screaming need for it. Physician offices are not aching for that kind of information.
>
> "We delayed installation because we wait for developed software. When a better system is ready, we'll be able to plug into it, and we'll have the money to do it. We won't have made another silicon forest millionaire in the meantime."

But Mitch wouldn't change to a more expensive, faster, and riskier plan, and he says the board is behind him:

> "Overspending your budget remains one of the biggest dangers of technology. When you sit where I sit, if somebody describes our plan as conservative, that's exactly what I was shooting for. Conservative—let's not get stars in our eyes—that's where our money should go. We don't see ourselves as an information technology company; it's not what we're about.
>
> "Since Matthew Calais, our current chief information officer, got here, we haven't had too many missteps. We've dropped systems in and they have worked. The board felt very comfortable about the decision and the rate at which we are implementing new technology. There were questions about whether we should have done it faster or earlier. Those came mostly from people from the Fortune 500 side of the street. The physicians were intrigued by the ease of use and information they could get. They saw it as a time-saving thing and something relatively robust."

Matthew Calais, chief information officer, amplifies Mitch's perspective:

> "Our operating budget costs between 2 and 3 percent of total operations. In '89, Legacy started with basically nothing as far

> as information systems are concerned. Cats and dogs, cousins and aunts. No leadership, no vision, and no software. From a capital standpoint, we are spending 20 to 25 percent of our available capital, roughly $10 million a year. That commitment is reviewed every year. There are specific milestones and checks and balances.
>
> "Healthcare's problem with information systems is much deeper than just a broad brush: 'Banking spends 7 or 8 percent and healthcare spends an abysmal 2 percent.' We could spend ten times as much on information systems and have the same delivery of information, because the practice of medicine is not ready yet, at least here in Portland. We feel pretty strongly about that.
>
> "Mitch Olejko characterizes our strategy as risk-averse. I call it common sense. We are going to use two different vendors. An integrated clinical, financial, and administrative system developed by one vendor on the floor, and another by a different vendor in what we call the factory, lab, pharmacy, and x-ray. Our 'floor' system is in over 100 sites and the 'factory' systems are in from 40 to several hundred, depending on the application."

The two-vendor strategy is unique. Each of the vendors could supply almost all that Legacy wanted, and each wanted the whole contract. Matthew explains how he thinks the strategy will pay off:

> "We are doing that because neither company had everything we wanted. It was not an easy journey. We spent a lot of money on due diligence, and we had an external consultant just for the due diligence review. In the end we said, 'Let's hedge our bets. If it's financially feasible and we can keep the vendors from being overly cozy, then if one does better or one has problems, we have a cushion. If one company excels, we haven't sunk all of our money into the loser.'"

Jane Cummins, senior vice president for clinical operations, describes how the strategy works in practice:

> "We started out about when John King got here. We established an information resources steering committee that agreed on some core principles to make information resources user friendly. We would not try to be experimental, not customize off-the-shelf products. We would always put the interests of the system ahead of the interests of any particular department.

> We would invest only in programs that would talk to one another. We built the philosophy that the system good is more important than any part's [good]. Under the principles, we were able to get the employees involved in the selection of the specific systems.
>
> "I was chair for the first two years. I didn't know anything about computers, but I knew something about hospital operations. Everybody in senior management is on the committee. Implementation teams for specific systems are made up of the people who need to know—who need the data. Team members are usually taken off their regular job for several months so they can talk to people around the system. They are there, coaching and troubleshooting, throughout the implementation period. You don't have external salespeople or information techno-nerds trying to teach an OR nurse how to use the equipment. It's her peer, Roxanne, whom she's worked with for five years, telling her how to do it and what the value is in it."

The Legacy strategy is to interface with existing systems in doctors' offices rather than to sell the doctors a common office information system. As a result, it will be dependent on insurance claims for critical clinical information about office-based care. Legacy will have difficulty collecting the clinical information it will need to improve office care. Mitch Olejko, senior vice president of legal and information services, discusses this unsolved problem for Legacy:

> "If we can get our inpatient and outpatient activities automated and pull our physicians along, this won't solve all our problems. The perfect system would be one information system as a public utility for all providers and insurers. We have talked about that, but I'm not sure how successful it would be. The perception is that information is a competitive advantage. The Oregon State Medical Society has its OMEN system. It's a way for the society to make some money, so why should it support a public utility? We talked to Blue Cross; they were concerned they would pay for automating some processes that weren't their problem. We will continue to talk with them, but we're not spending a lot of time thinking about it."

Training and incentives for value

Legacy deliberately motivates its employees through goal-setting, advertising and promotion, training, and incentives. It embeds the CQI philosophy in all aspects of its management. For example,

- Executives are responsible for initiating and overseeing the Quality Planning and Monitoring Process in each of their areas. Within this process, each group identifies its key services, primary customers, and customers' expectations.
- The senior management team formulates an annual quality dashboard with system-wide indicators that are monitored quarterly.
- The annual operations planning process incorporates quality and performance goals in addition to traditional financial ones.
- Quality councils review departmental performance on all goals quarterly, and reports are distribute bimonthly to community boards and the Legacy board.
- If customer satisfaction and operating performance goals are not met, action plans are developed to correct the shortfall.

—From the 1997 Oregon Quality Award Application

The weekly employee newsletter and the bimonthly *President's Report* are organized by the strategic pathways, to help employees connect day-to-day events and long-term goals. Legacy CQI principles (satisfying customers, empowering people, continually improving, and managing with data) and core values (teamwork, respect and caring, taking initiative, and using resources effectively) are publicized widely and frequently throughout the organization.

Substantial resources are devoted to training people. All new employees have a day-long orientation. After surveys showed that employees still did not grasp the values of CQI, a five-part set of courses on CQI principles, basics, and methods was taught to about 2,000 employees in 1996. Comprehension improved substantially. An additional 1,000 employees participated in more advance courses including group management skills, conflict resolution, using feedback, and training others. Total attendance at all classes was 6,800, an average of more than one session for each of the 5,000 Legacy employees.

Jane Cummins, senior vice president for clinical operations, explains how this works:

> "Motivation starts out with a firm foundation of understanding among the managers, vice presidents, and directors about the management imperatives of the market we operate in—managed care, contractual allowances, pricing contracts. We have a relentless barrage of meetings, conferences, readings, speakers, and dialogue with topics like write-offs in managed care and the ethical dilemmas around that—what does that mean?

How can we look at a continuum of care and really get our costs down?

"We've supported that knowledge base with a cost accounting system so that people can fully understand the costs. We've engaged the medical staff on a number of outcome studies and disease studies that have focused everybody on how we might mitigate the cost of poor quality.

"We have standards for productivity. We know where we've been, and we're very proud of seeing these measures come down. People know getting it down took a lot of work. There's a pride level in not letting it creep back up. What people pick up on is usually just graphs. People like to see trends—where are we going? Pictures they can grasp.

"We have gone much more into a systems approach. In the past, Jeff, who was vice president at Meridian Park, one of the smaller hospitals, had a lot of clinical departments reporting to him. Now he's in charge of lab and imaging at all sites. Steffani is now doing surgery at all the sites."

Lowell Johnson, CFO, describes how knowledge is translated to success:

"The biggest part of how we got where we are and what we have to do going forward: we were successful in getting every one of the 5,000 people who work at Legacy to understand that we must constantly improve our productivity. I think if you walk on the floor at Good Samaritan this evening at seven o'clock and ask any employee, 'What's Legacy doing financially in the coming year?' you would hear, 'We are going to get 2 to 4 percent more efficient at what we do, and we have to do that to survive in a competitive environment. We are going to improve our productivity through better clinical practice, better buying of supplies, and—grumble, grumble, grumble—tightening on labor.'

"The downtown operation constantly communicated to their labor force that we have got to get more productive at what we do. We gave them the tools to do it with. We have a very good labor productivity monitoring system that the managers use on a daily basis for staffing. Every two weeks we know where we are by department, right down to the employee level. We aggressively use it to hit our productivity targets. We adjust those targets on an annual basis. We have

> ownership at the manager-worker level. They say, 'I've developed these targets; they're mine, I can live with them.'
>
> "I would say 80 percent of improved productivity comes from the people who drive the organization. The remaining 15 or 20 percent is the development of a common goal, a common language, a common management team, and a oneness of system. There is something about what Legacy has become. Five years ago it was a holding company. Today it is an integrated organization with common objectives."

And Lowell goes on to describe a systemwide incentive program. He touches on one of the known problems with incentive programs. When the incentive is not earned, there is a strong negative reaction from the employees:

> "One of the big things that closed that loop was when we introduced the profit-sharing with the employees. The profit-sharing says that the organization needs a net of 3 percent to survive, and our long-term plan is based on 5 percent. We told our employees we would share any profits over 3 percent. Half of anything over 3 percent is yours. You have met customer satisfaction and quality goals. Last year three operating units failed on quality or satisfaction and did not get a check when the others did. Now all the sites are being judged together. If we don't make the 73 percent threshold overall, nobody will get a check.
>
> "The first full year, we paid almost $11 million in profit-sharing. The second year we raised the threshold to 4 percent, which was a mistake, and we paid about $6 million in profit-sharing. This year we took the threshold back down to 3 percent again. Four percent was a failure because there wasn't enough incentive left. The first year the employee got a check for almost $1,700. By going to 4 percent, the opportunity got down in the $700 to $800 range, and it was hard to keep them motivated. With no price increase this year and no market share gain, the 3 percent threshold will be hard to reach. In our mind, you have to deliver about a thousand dollars per employee to get their attention and support. Employees will get grouchy if the cash isn't there."

Marketing for value

Portland citizens have a choice of insurance and a choice of provider. The choice can be exercised at the annual re-enrollment period for health insurance, when a specific provider panel is selected, and in some cases at the time of service. The hospitals will absorb some of the patients' financial penalties for leaving the selected panel. Because the patients have this flexibility, Legacy must act constantly to protect its share of the market, and it has been successful at this. Marketing begins with well-designed systems delivering value and service. Jane Cummins, senior vice president for operations, talks about how Legacy positions its services to attract markets:

> "Lab, rehab, cancer, pediatrics, women's are considered to be the best of our centralized services. The lab is working hard to get primary care business. Dr. Millan, chief of pathology, has been very effective at sending out information on how to use the laboratory most effectively. We go to primary care doctors and say to them, 'Show us your lab data, and we'll show you how to reduce costs and improve your capitation.' That's been very successful with two of our largest primary groups.
>
> "We had two oncology groups, one at each downtown hospital. We now have one tumor board, one chief, Dr. Natalie Johnson, and one manager, Martha Wangenstein. All the cancer people are responsible to Martha. We have radiation oncology on all the sites, with a single group of managing physicians. People move around the system. If there is a backlog at one hospital, people move to take care of it.
>
> "Women's Services started out as a program at Emanuel and Good Samaritan only, around 1988. They were the only sites with OB. We determined that we were losing market share because the women in the suburban areas would not come downtown for care. A decision was made over great wailing and gnashing of teeth to start OB at both suburban sites. Meridian Park has been in operation for three years and it has already had an expansion. It was built at ten rooms and was completely undersized. It is now almost as large as Good Sam. It was a three-year fight until John King got here. He kind of blasted through the politics and made it happen.
>
> "We have four OB units, with one director, Terry Joyer. We talked about the fact that we have two OB units downtown, but right now neither one is big enough to take the whole load. Terry had to work through all the difficulties—anesthesia, standards, measures, nursing protocols, forms. She's also gotten involved in the pediatric politics to create a single standard of care in our newborn nursery. What we're striving for

> is a gold standard—a Legacy standard that a woman will get at any of the four sites. If we offer lactation services, we will have them at all sites. If we can't afford to do something to the Legacy standard, we are not going to do it at all."

Barbara Zappas, senior vice president, human resources and quality leadership, brings a quality perspective, marketing by "delighting the customer," meeting all needs in an excellent manner. She goes beyond that to patient-oriented marketing, which prevents illness and eliminates both the discomfort and the cost that go with it:

> "We do a quality matrix to understand what external users are interested in, like Blue Cross, its economic partners, community groups, HEDIS, and NCQA. We aligned all of these. The highest level of interest was in birthing and prenatal care. So we talk about women's services in terms of what the community wants: good prenatal care, good well-child care, good outcomes.
>
> "In women's services, the standard of care was not the same at the four hospitals. We said, 'If Legacy is going to have a standard of care, it has to be equivalent.' One of the things we determined was that we had to have standards for an infant in distress, or a mother in distress. At the downtown hospitals there were more people available to take care of both the mother and the baby. We realized we couldn't afford to have a nurse anesthetist standing by just in case, so we trained what we call the 'R Nurse,' a resuscitation-trained nurse, available on all the shifts at all the hospitals. The R Nurse manages respiratory distress until the specialist takes over. This year, women's services is looking at the rate of newborns who breastfeed within the first hour postpartum, compliance with home care plans, and Project Network. Project Network is for drug-addicted pregnant women who move into Project Network apartments for a process of detox. The goal is to deliver a healthy, full-term baby.
>
> "We have a collaborative program with Blue Cross to send out health risk assessments to our Medicare HMO patients. We are expanding the way we think about chronic disease. We are identifying risk factors and interventions for them, working with the clinics and the doctors. We want to manage selectively the patients who need the care. We do the education, trying to help the patients take control of their illness.
>
> "We don't have the vehicle to work in the doctors' offices. We have a couple of studies. The Robert Wood Johnson grant

is helping. We have members of each of the primary care groups, but we are working with them as individuals. We are up against the competitive nature of the three groups. We are not to the point where every doctor would say to his or her diabetic patient, 'There's a collaborative diabetic clinic every Friday. You go there and see a nutritionist, a health educator, and whichever referral specialists you need.' Kaiser does that. We are not there yet."

Sonja Steves, vice president of marketing and community relations, expands on the effort to get the right services in the right place:

"The program development teams [PDTs, clinical teams oriented around specific groups of diseases] are charged with staying on top of trends and analyzing the feasibility of new techniques, new equipment, and new services within each program. The local hospitals are charged with analyzing population trends, and recognizing unmet community needs. Our Legacy strategic planning will oversee the process. For example, we are developing a breast center. The idea is to improve all the steps involved from a patient's perspective—education about breast care, having a mammogram, communicating the results, and coordinating the follow-up. There are some problems now—too many delays in reporting and follow-up. The breast program is a cooperative of three PDTs—women's, imaging, and cancer. Each of the PDTs is now considering when they should decentralize their services throughout the area.

"We've also tried to establish a preference for Legacy services within each local market. So Meridian Park has done a lot in the marketing/communications arena to work with community groups, residents in the community, and physicians to establish themselves as the preferred provider in that whole southern part of the metro area. One thing they had to consider was expanding services for a growing population. They had to add a medical office building, OB, and other services. After we started OB, we had to expand it."

But marketing also includes promotion and affiliation with the right insurance vehicles. Sonja describes these efforts:

"Meridian Park started as kind of a sleepy hospital serving a senior population, and suddenly the whole market had grown with younger families. People weren't even aware the hospital was there. So [Meridian Park] had to start with basic information—advertising, community newsletters, health education, more community involvement, and [community] representation. It was two years before they began to see a significant result. The biggest expense was the advertising. We hired a firm to advise us on media and themes. We were able to buy localized television, as well as direct-mail, outdoor, and print advertising. Now, six years later, they have very high recognition and preference within their service area.

"The primary marketing strategy has been our affiliation with Blue Cross. It's brought us our target market share gains in the last few years. We've done some joint sponsorship with Blue Cross, but no advertising. Blue Cross works with other providers. We've assisted Blue Cross with prevention and health risk assessment and outcomes projects, particularly for the seniors in the First Choice 65 program.

"We have a lot of media coverage to promote Legacy. We keep statistics on the number of stories, evaluated as positive or negative, and stories that we originate. Our pediatric and trauma programs bring a lot of media inquiries. We suggest topics to the media. One of our TV stations did a round-the-clock story on our neonatal ICU. They ran it for several days, and some of the coverage was picked up by Seattle. We sponsor a number of programs with the cancer society and heart association. We use health education to promote Legacy. We send out a newsletter to 500,000 households. John King has been the most visible healthcare leader. He's been chair of United Way, involved in the Oregon Business Council, active with the legislature, instrumental in Oregon Health Systems in Collaboration. He's a good promoter of Legacy.

"Our current advertising budget is $565,000: $45,000 is for advertising specific health education programs; $120,000 is program specific. The rest is for branding. The community newsletter costs $120,000 a year. Our program to reach new arrivals to Portland costs $40,000 on direct mail introducing Legacy and telling them where their nearest facility is. We have an in-house creative team, and we try to do as much internally as we can. We have a contract with an agency for consultation and art direction.

"In the '80s there was a lot of advertising in the Portland area. I think the ad budgets were much larger. Then as managed care began to grow, advertising completely dropped

> off. We thought for a while that it did not pay to do brand advertising. Now we've returned to it."

Sonja also notes that marketing involves a constant, quantitative effort to understand the customers' needs:

> "We do an annual attitudes and perceptions household survey. We have a sample of 1,226 and we segregate it by service area so we can see the impact of the local programs. We survey our medical staff. We do consumer testing and focus groups all the time. All of our surveys show that people in Portland perceive quality as high and equal among providers. There is no differentiation between the systems. Before we go forward with any advertising message, no matter how small it is, we take it to a panel of people, even if it's just an announcement of a health education class. We did a series to get qualitative data for developing a branding strategy. We test everything."

Clinical Improvement

Legacy can document success with all three vehicles of clinical improvement: profiling, protocols, and case management.

Finding improvements

Tom Hansen M.D., Legacy vice president for medical affairs, summarizes the history of clinical improvement in Portland:

> "How has the philosophy of medicine changed? Clearly, there has been a decrease in length of stay. Oregon has one of the lowest lengths of stay around. Part of that is shifting to lower levels of care. We put skilled nursing facility units in both our downtown hospitals, and many procedures have shifted to outpatient. Physicians in this community have bought into the need for cost containment. They understand the need for it, and they understand it personally. When the competition heated up ten years ago, Legacy was second-highest cost in the region, behind the university. There was some loss of market share. The new leadership convinced everybody. We got our costs in line, and market share went back up.
>
> "In the primary care offices, they are very concerned about utilization. The groups review the need for high-cost procedures. They have productivity quotas for the doctors in terms of how many patients they see. They profile their doctors. The independent primary care doctors practice as usual, and

are just trying to do it smart. The medical groups with strong risk positions have a slightly lower stay and costs than the others.

"The insurance plans provide profiles on utilization performance, and the groups pursue it. We've been working on cost per case and LOS for ten years, although our first efforts weren't very sophisticated. We used a commercial program that compiled national profiles for a couple years, but it didn't seem to do much for us. We weren't seeing huge variation. We still have DRGs where our LOS and costs are high, but it is not because of the actions of a few doctors. Some of our medical admissions in diabetes, endocrinology, and nephrology are a little high, but we've approached them through our program development teams."

Legacy supports this effort with profiles, protocols, and case management. Tom describes the program:

"All of the Legacy programs are expected to have a quality planning and monitoring plan integrated with their operating plans. They choose the measures with their staff, and report quarterly. We've encouraged them to post and discuss their results. The medical staff quality council deals with both critical incidents on a peer review basis and trends in quality data. We've worked on waiting time in trauma and ED and gotten that down, and we've looked at trends in c-sections and are below national averages on that. We've used the Maryland quality indicators, and don't have any problem with those.

"We have admission and discharge criteria for intensive care. As acuity has gone up, the difference between intensive and intermediate has blurred, and so we have reduced the number of levels of care. A lot of effort has been put into the two biggest users of intensive care, open heart and trauma, and they have pretty restrictive protocols. The exception is trauma, which has so many head injuries and multiple fractures. The NICU, for the preemies, is participating in a nationwide study. They have been able to get their LOS down quite dramatically.

"Most of our protocols are nursing, not medicine. The doctors have input into them, of course. Our experience is that the protocols aren't particularly well followed, and it is hard to sort out how they really affect care. We've taken a little more of a case management approach. We try to predict the problem cases and deal specifically with them. We identify them by their charges, so it is hard to do early in the stay. Insurance companies could help us out on that.

"The large primary physician groups have their own case managers, so that in some situations we have two managers. Legacy managers try to make sure that the inpatient protocol is followed, and do the discharge plan, removing the roadblocks to discharge. We have programs in trauma, joints, congestive heart failure, bone marrow, and minimally invasive surgery."

And Tom goes on to some advanced efforts:

"Our congestive heart failure (CHF) program identifies patients either from the clinic or the hospital. We surveyed CHF patients to see their perspective on their disease. One of the most startling things that came out of that was that only 68 percent of the patients acknowledged that they had CHF. A lot of patients weren't meeting national guidelines for the use of beta blockers and advanced therapies. That's the start of it. There's a physician education piece, and a patient education piece, and follow-up surveys to measure improvement. This has been going about a year. The cardiologists have all agreed to participate, and some of the primary groups have agreed.

"We've spent a lot of time and energy on patient-focused care. We're working on service, not only clinical quality, because in this market patient satisfaction is clearly a determinant of where patients go for care. The public thinks the quality will be good anywhere they go, so the focus is on service."

Legacy's efforts have been going on for a long time. The list of program development teams covers almost all disease categories. The role of these PDTs is to analyze, integrate, and improve care for the diseases in their categories, cutting across the dozens of functional areas that are needed. In 1996, the Legacy PDTs reported the following:

- The heart program uses a special database involving hundreds of hospitals doing advanced cardiovascular work. Against that database, Legacy had better than average performance and a rising level of patient severity.
- Hip replacement patients report their own health in eight functional and perceptual areas before surgery and at six months, one year, and two years afterward. The results show improvements in most areas. They were used to extend the rehabilitation program in the only area not showing improvement.

- Outpatient surgery is monitored for unexpected returns. They have been below reported national averages consistently for the last five years.
- Patient flow processes, like admission and discharge, were reengineered to improve patient satisfaction. The number of specific admission activities was reduced from 184 to 16. The number of tasks for which employees must be trained was cut from 102 to 8. Cost per admission decreased 11 percent, and employee satisfaction also increased.
- Birth weights were raised in a program of medications for high-risk mothers before birth, and overall obstetric performance was monitored against 109 neonatal centers.
- The Legacy VNA monitored seven specific issues such as pain control, safety, and self-care, and achieved scores over 95 percent in all but one. In the lowest measure, 93 percent of mothers in high-risk pregnancies maintained fetal well-being and growth.

Ed Oakies, M.D., a cardiovascular surgeon, describes his practice. By "aggressive," he means willing to accept relatively high-risk patients. One way to improve surgical outcomes is to take only the easy patients; he's saying that Legacy does the opposite:

> "Practice in Portland is aggressive. I used to be in Houston, and we were very aggressive in open heart surgery. When I got to Portland, there was a low threshold for referral to surgery because the operations were successful.
>
> "A lot of specialists, when they saw managed care coming along, deliberately formed alliances that would keep them active in both Legacy and Providence. The Legacy staff as a whole is open, but we have the only cardiovascular surgeons on the staff in our group, the Oregon Heart Institute. The OHI has contracts with insurers that would be hard for an outside group to get. Some of our success is because we don't have different groups with different perspectives competing for patients. We have ten surgeons, and we are adding one in the summer.
>
> "We had three separate groups look at our quality: Travenol in the mid-'80s. Larry Verne and Associates did a survey and noted that OHI patients had the highest acuity and lowest mortality, around 1990. *Modern Healthcare* ranked Legacy number four in the country in cardiovascular surgery in 1995. One of the reasons this has happened is that we have been collaborating with our staff for a long time.

> "The traditional lines of medical separation no longer make any sense, but the people in control of those areas are having a hard time letting go. We have more in common with the cardiologists than with general surgeons. Our business is cardiopulmonary problems, and our department should consist of all the people who share that business. The one piece we don't have is nursing. Nursing has traditionally been a stand-alone deal. The program development team has all the people we need. The cardiopulmonary nurses are on the PDT, but the ability to change nurses' schedules and compensation is not under PDT control."

Darrell Lockwood, M.D., a diabetologist, discusses some other protocol efforts:

> "People are working on thrombophlebitis, asthma, and diabetes protocols. We use our consultants and try to get everybody to think through the issues—education more than force.
>
> "In diabetes, we have kept up with changes in testing and drugs. We are more likely to make a house call or a Saturday visit than we used to, if it will keep the patient out of the hospital. We're toying with using physician extenders but haven't so far—diabetes is usually managed by general internists or family practitioners. Primary care doctors are more capable of handling diabetes because of advances in diabetic teaching programs and improved monitoring. We have a belief now to monitor consistently and frequently. Keeping blood sugars under control has been settled; we are going to do that."

The agenda for the future

Legacy's plan for future clinical improvement is for better measures, more effective case management, and continued search for improved protocols.

Elaine Denning, a member of the corporate development staff, describes some of the measurement plans:

> "One of the places where Legacy will grow the most in the next year is in a more uniform approach to the dashboard. Like most systems we have been organized around hospitals. We are moving away from that to a programmatic base. Most of our dashboard indicators are around hospitals. Those indicators will shift more to a programmatic focus.
>
> "We don't have indicators that give us a global look at the market. We are looking at market share and trying to build a

more complete picture. I'm trying to build outpatient share data."

Ed Oakies, M.D., carries a pocket computer that contains a large database on cardiovascular surgery and that he uses not only to evaluate individual patient risks, but to explain those risks to the patient. The same database allows him to compare his practice to those of his colleagues around the country:

> "One of the reasons why our quality is as good as it is is because we have kept data on our patients. We have pooled it with data from other cardiovascular groups all over the world. One of our projects is risk assessment. We know the mortality rate and the stroke rate by age, sex, previous history, and laboratory values. The database is similar to the one used by the College of Thoracic Surgery, but we have more items. We now have 250 questions on each patient.
>
> "We have a very good relation with the cardiologists. They are contributing to the database. The current management of diabetes during heart surgery was developed here, with our diabetologists."

Ed sees his approach as the future. Not just surgical procedures but whole disease entities will be known in detail, and the management decisions can be based on sound statistical evidence:

> "More of these algorithms will be available to get people to the specialist before they become critical. The problem is financing the data collection. Nobody wants to pay for the follow-up data. We mail a survey to all our former patients every year, and pay for it out of our own pocket. We have done it because we think it is mandatory to know what the outcomes are."

Steve Johnson, senior vice president, describes two programs, one for Medicare patients and the other for young mothers, being evaluated with funding from the Robert Wood Johnson Foundation:

> "The project is called Community Resource Connections. We identify the patients and link them proactively with educational and community services to reduce their risks. In the Blue Cross First Choice 65 population, there are eight clinics. The clinics are learning to use more than the medical or clinical approach to problems. Patients complete a risk assessment form, which their doctor uses to assess their risk and the level of support they might need. Nurses then look for community

> resources. For example, an 80-year-old woman had to go downstairs for bathing. Our nurses found that for $500 we could help her bathe on the same floor. So even though it is not in the First Choice benefit, we did that. The research is funded by RWJ, but the cost of the staff and the interventions are paid by Blue Cross and Legacy.
>
> "Legacy is working with OHSU and Blue Cross on a smoking cessation program for women who have just given birth. We've helped get contact with the physicians and provide some of the educational programs. Legacy nurses track the home setting and monitor the smoking situation. Robert Wood Johnson [Foundation] has sponsored the evaluation of that, too."

Meanwhile, Legacy's strategic partner, Blue Cross and Blue Shield of Oregon, is responding. They are working through the Alliance to measure and improve seven important prevention areas. A major 1997 project has been a health appraisal for all Medicare HMO members. Eighty percent have complied. About one member in 20 has a manageable risk, and clinical, educational, and community resources are brought to bear for their problems. Don Sacco, BCBSO president, points out that there's more to be done:

> "We're beginning to understand the importance of data. Right now, a lot of the emphasis is on the individual claims data, as opposed to the aggregate. The aggregation may lead to things that alter behavior for the primary doctor and the specialist. Blue Cross hasn't done nearly as good a job as it should in getting and using the data. Our data have been messy and oriented too much to the financial side. We are starting to pay a lot of attention to that, orienting ourselves differently and developing some profiles. We've been criticized for not moving faster, and rightly so. The intent under the Alliance was to create an information interdependency, but we haven't gotten there. It's still a good, solid concept, but we never got to the point of a unified strategy.
>
> "From my perspective, the customer is the enrollee. From the doctors' perspective, it's the patients who show up. If we have 19 different medical groups, and each one looks a little different, Blue Cross has trouble making a uniform product for 500,000 enrollees. We're getting subscribers who ask why, if they change primary care providers, things are so different. That's the simple stuff, not the complicated problems. I've

been pushing the notion that what we need is protocols overarching the enrollment base, and the groups are pressing to do that individually. When we put those issues on the table, everybody agreed they had to be addressed, but no one knew how to get it done."

Physician Organization

How to organize medical practice is an unsolved question in Portland. Practically everybody has an opinion on it, and most of the opinions reflect dissatisfaction with the efforts to date. Portland has had the Kaiser approach for 50 years and a gatekeeper-oriented set of HMOs for a decade. The only thing they seem to agree on is that these two models are not what they want.

Developing the strength of primary care

The discussion centers on two relatively independent questions. The first is how to compensate and organizationally support primary care physicians. Compensation and practice organization are interrelated. The range of alternatives runs from salaried physicians organized by Legacy (similar to Kaiser-Permanente) to capitation models that leave the doctors free to organize themselves as they choose (similar to most of the rest of Portland's HMO contracts). In between are physician-hospital organizations (PHOs), collaborative models like the one being developed in Greensboro. These can accommodate several payment models at once, including the "withhold" model Greensboro favors.

The salaried model is not on the table. It usually involves buying existing practices and employing the physicians who formerly ran them to continue doing so. John King says:

"We didn't make the physician decisions in a vacuum; we sat with physician groups and other executives. Legacy had some hospital CEOs at the time who, frankly, given the opportunity, would have bought some practices. They [the CEOs] were floundering around. We usually found other places for them to land."

Mitch Olejko, J.D., chief legal officer, expands on the possibilities for Legacy:

"We have a board level policy that, except in exceptional situations, employed physicians and employed specialists are not where we are going. The policy is under active review. I don't

> think the polarity will change, but it may loosen a little. At the time we formulated this policy, we concluded that people who are buying practices are trying to buy something other than practices. They were trying to buy a relationship with their physicians that you can characterize in certain ways. What people want to buy is the relationship that the large groups, like Group Health and Virginia Mason (two long-established medical groups in Seattle), have—however you might describe that. That is, there is no distinction between the hospital and the physician; they are all providing something together: that we trust each other, that our agendas are all out on the table and open. I don't think you can buy that. If you try to buy that you will be disappointed. That's something that gets built, brick by brick, over a long period of time.
>
> "Hospitals tend not to be very good managers of physician practices. They refuse to do the things that permit physician groups to be successful. If you are going to use the acquisition of a physician group to turn back the hands of time, or to keep the tide from rising around you, that's probably not a good strategy."

In 1993, Legacy attempted in one bold step to solve its primary care organization problems and the arrangements with "aligned health plans." It formed a joint venture corporation, Northwest Physician Alliance, with Blue Cross and Blue Shield of Oregon and three medical groups, Cascade, Mullikan, and Metropolitan.

The alliance is governed by a board of nine, six of whom are physicians. There are no "super majorities" or special voting rights, but BCBSO sets the premiums and manages marketing and customer services. Medical care is delivered through the Northwest Group Practices Association, a subsidiary of the alliance formed by the medical groups and managed by them. Legacy has two seats on the association board and a dominant role on the hospital provider committee.

The alliance assumed the provider contracts for the BCBSO HMO and PPO business on January 1, 1996. Its goals are

1. To attain and sustain an enrollment of 400,000 lives
2. To develop a risk-capable primary care network of appropriate size and geographic distribution
3. To maintain a price-competitive market position for the Alliance health plans by effective clinical management, relying on full capitation to primary care groups.

The alliance anticipated that the association would grow through the expansion of the original groups and through contracts with other physician groups. It would be a joint venture to provide medical management and capitation management. Its goal was to have all payments to its physicians capitated by January 1998.

John King, Legacy CEO, describes how the alliance strategy arose:

"There was a tradition of solo and small doctor practices. Doctors were not entrepreneurial, and they were without cash. So we developed a policy in 1992 to give preference to larger primary care groups of a dozen or more, not to buy practices and not to assist recruitment to smaller groups. We communicated the idea that groups of two and three were going to have trouble managing risk. We made it clear that Legacy is not a source to bail them out of financial difficulty. We could do that because there is a sufficient supply of primary care doctors. The specialists were taken aback, but they began to realize the importance of the primary care base.

"The alliance strategy is to look to primary care doctors to select the referral specialists they want. The marketplace is at work here more than anything else. The primary care groups have clearly redirected some referral work. That's forced people to leave town, and some specialist groups to reduce recruiting. Legacy hasn't defined who we are going to work with and who we aren't. We've let the marketplace and the referral patterns handle that."

John goes on to tell how it worked out in practice:

"Blue Cross made an initial commitment to offer full capitation on the physician side, but it backed off when it understood the internal problems capitation created, and the market signals about it. The original commitment was for full capitation for OHP [Oregon Health Plan] in '97, Medicare in '98, and commercial in '99. They will continue to offer some of the business on that basis to the three groups, but they will not mandate it. They want to stay with a withhold model for at least some of their business. I think only two of the groups will accept the capitation, and the third will revert to a withhold approach. We have spent too much time focusing on reimbursement models, and not enough time on data and actually managing care.

"The three primary care groups have doubled in size, so that now 200 of our 400 primary doctors are in groups but no new primary groups have formed. Even though they have not collaborated as we had hoped, we have strong working relationships that are going to continue. We'll tweak this and find ways to get the specialists more involved, but on the whole, Blue Cross and Legacy have gained a fair amount. The question is how we can continue to move it.

"So we are back at the table, and where we think we'll go is to bring the specialists to the table and create a more balanced relationship between primary and specialty care."

Bob Pallari, chief operating officer of the alliance, gives the perspective of the primary care groups:

> "What happened is that OHP took off with a vengeance. It pulled down commercial premiums, which were already low. The three groups had been spending to expand. The increased risk and reduced revenue ate into the cash flow, and now they are in trouble. The major primary care groups had their worst years last year. The PCPs feel like the bubble burst. They didn't manage as well as they thought. The protocols weren't as good as they thought."

Like Greensboro, Legacy is moving to a complex risk-sharing arrangement. Bob Pallari continues:

> "We got everything we could out of the gatekeeper model. People who haven't gone where we've been think they've discovered an easy way to cut the costs. It's not that easy. The PCPs did call the cards on utilization. The three groups hired very strong medical directors who ride herd on the utilization. They established new prices for both specialists and hospitals. They caused free fall among certain specialists. What they haven't done very well is understand the specialty costs and the day-to-day management of the sick patient.
>
> "Doctors can form some kind of a physician association, or even a physician-hospital organization, if they want to, but the groups must be capitation capable. We started with withholds, and then moved to risk pools with a 100 percent stake for the primaries in their own pool, 50 percent stake in the specialist pool, and 25 percent stake in the hospital pool. The amount primary care physicians can make off their own pool will never offset what they can lose in the specialist and hospital pools. They have to manage the specialist and the hospital side."

Rebuilding the referral specialist capability

The other issue of physician organization is supporting and compensating specialists.

Darrell Lockwood, M.D., trustee and member of the Medical Affairs Committee, describes the problem:

> "Traditionally the medical staff has been pretty parochial. Doctors here are very independent, with a suspicion of hospitals and outside organizations. So progress has been very slow. The drive to organize has come largely from the specialists. We have sort of gone through the IPA phase. The specialists started that. We are seeing growth of larger specialty groups positioning themselves with the primary care groups to contract area wide. Orthopedics, ophthalmology, and cardiac surgery have done this."

Dick Zimmerman, M.D., an orthopedic surgeon, adds:

> "We have a group of 21 orthopedic surgeons. It's only been at 20 members for the last two years. There is one other group of 12, and the rest are solo or two-person partnerships. Our strategic plan called for being geographically diverse within the city, and specialty diverse within our group, so we could offer full-service coverage to any primary care referral source. We think the evolution will be partnerships between primary groups and referral groups. We have offices in every hospital in the city, including the Providence hospitals.
>
> "Our group is one of the largest and best organized. We're a little unique. Two of us went back to get master's degrees in business. We may be the only group that has a marketing strategy. I look at the dynamics of the local market, and the local market here is large primary care groups. I want those groups to be able to say, if a person comes in with a fracture on a weekend, 'Call the Portland Orthopedic Group.' The primary care doctor doesn't even have to think about an individual. He knows that no matter what hospital, he will get a person competent to assess the situation, and if that person can't handle it, there's a subspecialist in the wings to back him up.
>
> "We like the alliance. I see three big groups of primary care that I can extend my group's services to. We're working on electronic referrals with the alliance groups. We will have clinics without walls that are connected by the information system. I

want to get to the point where I can share the risk with them, rather than just do fee-for-service."

Dick goes on to explain why he thinks the specialists should have a share of the risk:

"All that's really happened is that we've cut the fees to the specialists, and taken away their independence. We have seven employees who do nothing but call primary doctors for permission to hospitalize. I get no reward for practicing cost-effective medicine. If I work with the hospital to develop critical paths, to move our patients along rapidly so that hospitalization days drop, it takes me time. I've given up income to do it. The hospital gets all the reward. If we standardize the prosthesis, I'm the one who has to learn new instrumentation and take the risk. I get zero reward for that. There's a natural tendency to be hesitant or passive-aggressive about doing this. We have to have strategic partnerships where we both share in the risks and the rewards.

"We have to stand up to the HMO as the patients' advocate. The other specialists are not as outspoken as I am, but they basically agree. The problem is that no one is addressing the underlying causes of cost increases. The problem we face is not what to do but when—do we do a bypass on an 85-year-old? Only the governor, a doctor, has said that we need to ration care, and we need to admit that we must ration care. I don't know how the problem is going to be solved, but I know it can't be imposed from the top down.

"The specialist concept is to narrow the field to an area you can master. That's still a good idea. The specialist has to decide when the procedure should be done. The primary care doctor does not have enough knowledge base to make that decision. The insurance companies can't make the decision. I can always tell one of those reviewers whatever they want to hear and not be lying. When Medicare first started asking us to call for permission to do an artificial hip, I got denied a couple times, so I told my clerical staff to keep a list of the questions they asked. Within three weeks, I knew the words they wanted. For instance, they didn't want me to use the words, 'x-ray showed degenerative arthritis.' They wanted me to say that the bones were touching. We never got denied again. Two months later, I got called. They said, 'You are obviously dictating from a form. Could we see it?' The point is that in the end, there isn't anybody to make the decision but me. The 'hidden hand' won't work in medicine—it's all thumbs. One of the biggest reasons is an information asymmetry. No patient, no primary care doctor, can have as much knowledge about orthopedics as I have."

Darrell Lockwood, M.D., echoes some of Dick Zimmerman's comments. "Subcapitation" means that the specialists would receive a regular monthly payment, in return for which they must meet all care needs of patients referred in their specialty. Under the traditional system, if Darrell can keep a diabetic out of the hospital, the savings return eventually to whomever pays the patient's insurance. Under total capitation, they revert to the patient's primary care doctor. Under a subcap, they would go to specialists. "Credentialling" is review of the doctor's qualifications, an essential protection for everybody:

> "Legacy has to turn its attention more to the specialists; I think that's proper. Some of the specialists are very upset. It's not just the fees, it's the constant limits on what you can do. We'd prefer that our specialists were subcapitated and managed their own risk. The old gatekeeper system is not going to last. Maybe we could subcap some patients for diabetes.
>
> "Credentialling is moving to the groups. We're considering whether the hospital needs to duplicate that effort. We're revising committee structures. I hope there will be a central credentialling service that is used by everybody. Right now, adding somebody to our group runs into all these obstacles."

Underlying the specialist organization question is the oversupply of many specialties. John King has already explained that Legacy wants to let the market settle that question. But specialists are produced through residency programs that Legacy and its specialists operate.

Tom Hansen, M.D., vice president for medical affairs, describes two positive steps Legacy has taken:

> "We have always had a primary care focus in our residency training programs. Three or four years ago, we switched from five preliminary areas to a coordinated primary care track. We don't take residents who are interested in specialty fellowships. We make a major effort to teach interactive skills, patient interactive skills, and send them into the community more to learn from community physicians. The new Pew grant will take six of our residents each year and train them in a managed care clinic.

> "We had a general surgery residency until 1996. We integrated that with OHSU."

But Dick Zimmerman, M.D., describes another dimension to the residency training issue:

> "They continue to train orthopedic surgeons. Most residents are used as lesser-paid employees to increase the productivity of the professor. The number of residents depends on how much help the professor needs, rather than what the system needs. Oregon Health Sciences University [OHSU] is totally responsible for the number of orthopedic residents in Portland, and it's based on the number they need to run their trauma system. The people at the medical school are not responsive to market forces because they are not affected by market forces.
>
> "We could do without residents. We would hire physician assistants to replace the work they do in the hospital."

And Ed Oakies, M.D., echoes his thoughts:

> "We are adding a clinical fellow in cardiovascular surgery, three-quarters in research and one-quarter in service. We don't have other residents. We tried to get a single program for Portland, but OHSU is a fickle partner. They will collaborate on what they want but not on anything they see as threatening.
>
> "We are running our program with a nurse practitioner and several physician assistants. Nurses are better than residents in a critical care unit. If you train them and they stay a long time, they get very good. Residents are very bright, but they rotate. You are much better off with a stable, non-physician team.
>
> "Why not train a group of physician assistants to take calls and support your program, and take only enough residents to meet community need?"

Diversification and Community Outreach

Diversification

Like Moses Cone, Legacy has an array of services beyond the usual office, outpatient, and acute inpatient. It has skilled nursing facilities, extensive rehab services, and a large home care program that includes infusion therapy and hospice care. The VNA subsidiary is a $25 million annual business. Legacy operates two day care centers for Alzheimer's patients. Its Care Mark Behavioral Program has been so successful that a national licensing arrangement has been considered.

Steve Johnson, senior vice president for continuum of care, discusses the diversification effort:

> "The hub of a system like this is not the hospital. It's the patient and the patient's family. If that's the case, we'd better figure out how to make them want to use Legacy Health System. I'm not suggesting we have to have a bunch of programs; we have to be very careful about what we offer; we have to learn how this all fits, what the value is to the system and the community. There's no magic here. We're looking at what we're going to be when we grow up in five or ten years. That's a good strategy for Portland now—you have to be cautious, but ready to move.
>
> "Our concept is to focus on families. We need to educate our boomers, 35- to 50-year-olds, on what Legacy offers for continuing care, what our programs are, how they coordinate with managed care for seniors. Often the patient we are reaching is their parent. Portland is moving up rapidly in percent of aged persons. Our challenge is to integrate services. We will fail miserably unless we can make the parts work together: make our hospice work with our clinics; make our rehab work better with our trauma center. This is our first step. Chronic care has to run through the whole organization. For example, cancer care now is 85 percent outpatient; we have to coordinate all those services in an outpatient setting."

As usual, there are plans for the future. Steve continues:

> "We have a task force, including Blue Cross and several of our physicians, working to develop a program development team for chronic disease management. Legacy is collaborating with Blue Cross on congestive heart failure and asthma, to develop comprehensive protocols for those diseases—how do we bring in all the resources, including the doctor's office and the community resources? The task force is working to define data needs and working with Blue Cross to get information. We had four comprehensive protocols, covering ambulatory and follow-up care, that did not work out as well as we wanted. Now we hope to do better. When we get comprehensive data on patients, then we can see what works. Blue Cross is pushing us to move forward.
>
> "We are working to get a broad spectrum of senior services into a single site, the Overton Center in northwest Portland.

We already have "The Front Door for Seniors," a converted warehouse with clinics, educational facilities, and counseling services at one site. We may be able to add congregate living. Providence is ahead of us: they have elder care and some other services that we don't. We are also considering expansion of our Alzheimer's facilities. We haven't made a big investment in congregate living [various forms of group housing for the active aged], although I think we might in the future. We will probably focus more on assisted living [supportive care for people with mental or physical restrictions].

"The traditional Visiting Nurse Association activity is shrinking under the impact of managed care. Our response to that has been to broaden out our services to the chronic sick, covering the whole spectrum of care. The VNA was 90 percent fee-for-service Medicare when I arrived in 1993. Now it is 60 percent. The growth has been in managed care. We now have 56 percent of the senior population in managed care, and we think it will be 80 percent in a few years. The VNA is adapting to that.

"I get great support from John [King] and the board. John is one of the few people in this country who recognizes the value of the continuum of care. John puts it on an equal par."

Sonja Steves, vice president for marketing and community relations, adds:

"We have resource centers in our hospitals for patients, with computers that access the internet, many books, and tons of brochures and literature. Our family support center has a lot of information on community resources and does a lot of referral. We have 56 support groups and quite a few health education projects. We had an 'Ask a Nurse' program, but we got out of it. It was too costly and not effective.

"There's a strong connection between our support groups, health education, and our resource centers, but there is not as much of a link yet with some of the higher-level concerns that we are addressing through OHSIC."

Community outreach

Legacy documents a total of $31 million a year, over 7 percent of operating expense, which it returns to the Portland community in what it calls its Social Accountability Program. Thirteen million dollars of the Social Accountability benefits have been targeted to the poor. About two-thirds of the total funds are for charity and uncompensated healthcare. The outreach programs targeted at prevention and change in health behavior cost $11 million in 1996. They reached 260,000 people through 154 different programs. The program has involved 3,500 volunteers who have contributed 400,000 hours of service. To put the numbers in perspective, the $31 million expenditure is slightly more than one-quarter of the total Multnomah County Health Department budget, and the programs have reached one of every six Portlanders (Table 3.6).

John King has been a strong supporter of Oregon Health Systems in Collaboration (OHSIC), an organization of Kaiser, Legacy, and Providence; Blue Cross Blue Shield; and the state and county health departments. Although the OHSIC effort hasn't gotten far yet, it represents a way to keep the local voluntary and government health organizations on track to meet basic Portland health needs, and potentially to keep the groups from destructive competition.

Inevitably, the local health department is involved in any significant outreach activity by a health system. Billi Odegaard, director, Multnomah County Health Department, describes how her department fills a unique role:

> "Multnomah County has supported an excellent program of public health services, with extensive direct services to the disadvantaged, for many years. The question is how or whether

Table 3.6 Community Benefit Expenses

Program Category	Individuals Reached	In-Kind Services	Cost/Contribution
Clinic Services	9,171	$1,173,043	$ 87,998
Prescriptions and Medical Equipment	6,815	300	230,898
Screening and Health Promotion	125,265	82,565	584,523
Social, Home, and Family Services	38,385	19,310	745,140
Employment Training	14,329	184,867	162,256
Other	9,367	1,179,507	626,356
Total Programmatic Benefits	203,332	$2,639,592	$ 2,437,171
Charity Care			$ 9,439,000
Total			$14,515,763

we can keep this program at its previous level of performance given the funding cutbacks we anticipate.

"You have to understand that the disadvantaged population has more than just illness problems. They have problems with housing, nutrition, transportation, and what you might call the mechanics of living that make things like a trip to the doctor a major undertaking even if the doctor doesn't charge. You have to do more than just offer care to our disadvantaged populations. You have to take care of them."

It isn't as easy as it looks, she says:

"Some years ago, we tried "Project Health," an effort to mainstream poor people into medical care. It went under. People who are destitute, who can't speak English, who are addicted or on the wrong side of the law—they don't mainstream. Kids and teens from broken homes don't mainstream. If you want them to get services that will keep them healthy and save everybody money—services like immunizations, management of diabetes and hypertension, containment of AIDS, tuberculosis, and sexually transmitted diseases, prevention of unwanted pregnancies—you have to seek them out.

"We computer map the incidence of these problems, so we know where to find them. If you want poor people to learn child safety, avoiding domestic violence, good nutrition, and the value of exercise, you have to go to them to teach them those things, and you have to look at other needs they have so they can practice what they learn.

"Multnomah County's been exceptional at doing this. We have six strategically placed health centers, nine high school programs, and two middle school programs. Most of them have been around for years. They are a serious part of Portland healthcare. Last year our programs provided 325,000 visits, the equivalent of 40 or 50 primary care providers. Half of these people spoke no English.

"Public Health is a patchwork of specific things for specific needs. We have a special AIDS program, and a field team in north Portland with a linkage program to help people with chemical dependencies. In southeast Portland, we have the MotherLove program for pregnant alcohol- and drug-addicted women. Our nursing program targets young families at risk, referred to us by anybody who identifies a problem situation.

"We follow the families, and work to get them what they need to be healthy, whatever it is. The STARS program

> [Students Today Aren't Ready for Sex] has expanded to 17 high schools. We've trained 78 high school leaders and have reached 7,000 sixth and seventh graders—all the sixth graders in the county. Our follow-up evaluations show more resistance to sexual involvement, and the students at greatest risk show the greatest improvement."

Billi notes that the financing is complex and that the county portion is at risk. She thinks OHSIC is a vehicle to continue specialized outreach activities:

> "Not all of this has to be supported by the county. The $27 million of county funds is matched by $58 million paid in fees, and $23 million of state, federal, and charitable grants. CareOregon, our Medicaid managed care program, is the third-largest OHP group in the state. Nearly 11,000 recipients were assigned to our clinic sites. We collaborate with nine nonprofit community health clinics.
>
> "The question is: Where do we go from here, given the cutbacks in state funding? [Oregon was voting on a referendum to make certain tax cutbacks at the time of this conversation.] Two of our clinics are on the block. Multnomah County can no longer support them. We need to expand the school-based program. If we give up on any one of these patients—AIDS, addicted, teens, stressed families, TB, whatever—it will cost big money in the end. Any one of these problems can generate a $100,000 hospital bill; some of them can cost a million. The two prongs of our effort should be Healthy Communities—the categorical programs that reach people at risk—and universal access.
>
> "We will have to have a partnership to succeed. OHSIC is a good start. I have a lot of respect for John King. The question is whether the others will follow and pick up a significant part of the problem. The immunization program is useful, but it's not the only problem. The problems are bigger than that. They have to be attacked systematically and aggressively. Immunization is taking longer than it should, and it still hasn't gotten to actually immunizing kids. It's a good start, but that's all."

Strategy

The strategies to run Legacy in a larger, more competitive environment are less clearly defined than those for Moses Cone. Legacy must keep focused on its own goals, maintain its financial strength, and continue to develop its alliances.

Keeping focus

Charles Heinrich, trustee and former board chair, discusses how Legacy emerged as a vehicle to get things done:

> "[Healthcare] is one of the most complicated businesses. I always remind myself it's hard to know who the customer is. I want to say always that the customer is the patient, but when you get down to it, there isn't a single service that we provide that isn't ordered by some doctor.
>
> "On the Mt. Hood hospital board [in the mid-'80s], just like the guy Deming [W. Edwards Deming, founder of the quality movement], we were looking at numbers. We could tell our doctors, 'Last month you had four appendectomies.' He could remember all their names, even. We'd say, 'Well, we had a total of 22, and the length of stay on the other 18 was three days, and your length of stay was seven. We don't know what it means, but maybe you could talk to your colleagues to see why they are letting them out sooner than you are.' It is a delicate thing, when you are in the doctor-patient relationship. Doctors are extremely smart. When you put the numbers before them, they are glad to make changes.
>
> "We got our monthly reports, and found we had lost money yet again. I kept hearing, 'This is an outlier.' This was the excuse for not doing what we are supposed to do. That's when we started asking for numbers, statistics so we would be able to look and say, 'This doesn't look right. We don't know what it means, but maybe you should look and see what the difference is.' We looked at FTEs per occupied bed, and cost per day, and length of stay. I went to Harvard Business School, and we had a case to study every day. Each case was a different business. I started out saying, 'This doesn't apply to my business.' Then I came to understand that every case applies to my business. So every time management said, 'This doesn't apply,' we'd say, 'Of course it does. You just have to find out how.' It's a job for management. Our job is to tell them what to look at.
>
> "If the industry hadn't changed, there wouldn't be any Legacy. We didn't form this because it was the best thing to do. We formed Legacy because it was the best way to respond

to the changes going on. I was on one of the hospital boards—HealthLink—and chairman of the VNA board, which was pretty independent. The VNA did a two-day session on strategic planning. At the end of the first day, we concluded that DRGs would decrease hospital demand for our services, and we would be out of business. So we merged with HealthLink to protect our business. HealthLink merged with Good Samaritan the same way."

Larry Choruby, trustee and chair of the Planning Committee, describes how Legacy is different now than it was before 1991:

> "I was introduced to one of the community hospitals, Meridian Park, by a fellow worker at Tektronics, in 1985. I saw at the time that healthcare was a problem for the company. We were the largest employer in Oregon, with 24,000 people. I thought it would be a good way to learn why healthcare was in turmoil. After a couple years, I was invited to the HealthLink board. After the merger I served on the Legacy board and the Good Samaritan board.
>
> "The planning agenda has changed a lot since Legacy started. It changed abruptly after John King arrived, and it has changed since. It got better through all those changes. At first the planning committee was the dumping ground for everything that didn't work. We had 47 strategic issues, and the number was increasing. When John got here that stopped. One of the things the planning committee does is supervise the process, and in planning, process is most of it—not all, because outcomes are important, too. We make sure people are doing what they should, talking things through with each other, and getting their strategies aligned with each other. That's most of the battle: really talk about the alternatives.
>
> "Planning is so integral to the success of an organization. In contrast to planning, if people are scrambling around trying to solve their problems without ever getting ahead of them—a one-damned-thing-after-another kind of thing—the place is doomed to fail. If the CEO doesn't manage the board, all hell will break loose somewhere."

It hasn't always been that way, Larry says:

> "John's predecessor as CEO of Legacy told me he thought he would be fired. He was old and tired. After he passed away, it seemed pretty natural to look outside. There was not a lot of

confidence that the direction we were going would work, and a lot of evidence to the contrary. It would have been irresponsible not to look outside.

"The merger gave rise to the need to revisit the mission. John's predecessor never started with that. He kind of accepted, 'Well, we all know why we are here.' We never did say, 'Hey, let's work on the mission.' The strategic pathways fly under the mission, but they define the mission. It's a mistake to ever say the mission is done. Why not pull it out every once in a while and rethink it. As new people look at it, it means different things. 'Has that been there all the time? Why isn't this there?'

"One of the strategic pathways is market share. I've always had trouble with market share. The first meeting I went to, the lights went down, and the charts came up on the wall, and they were saying, 'Revenue is up.' I thought, 'Is that good news or bad news?' That means people are sicker. But [it] was good news to that crowd. I remember thinking, 'You guys are all happy about that, and I'm not sure I am.' I thought, 'There are really three players here.' I never forgot that. We had to pull market share numbers out of management. They were reluctant to share them, and when they did they made excuses. Every time we got the numbers, they were down.

"John put market share in the strategic pathways, and I thought that was pretty gutsy. It set the stage for gaining market share despite where our facilities are and the other excuses."

John King, CEO, talks about the board:

"From the time I arrived here, this board has been very policy focused and has never meddled in operations. They understand and respect the distinction between board policymaking and management operations. I don't know that everybody is as fortunate as I am. This board has also been able to focus on the whole and not the parts. Even though some of the board members have long histories with the parts, they have been unselfish and able to let go of that. They have been interested in the integrated system. The physicians have also. They have been good, full-fledged board members. If there is a chance for the board to screw up, it is in those three areas—mucking in operations, dealing with the parts instead of the whole, and keeping the doctors less than full-fledged board members."

Mitchell Olejko, J.D., Legacy chief legal officer, further elaborates:

> "This board is nirvana. The board is the prime mover. It is willing to take risk and controversy. They were willing to close a hospital.
>
> "Many of the people on this board are pre-merger. Shortly after the 1989 HealthLink/Samaritan merger, the system lost money. The senior executive died, just after the heir apparent left town. There was a bit of turmoil, what can only be described as a couple of exciting years. They may have had a lifetime of excitement. They picked John, and one of the things he did was complete the merger. Since that time, we have had improvement in everything. The board has a certain amount of trust in senior management. That isn't to say they don't raise questions. I wouldn't say they are the driving force behind the organization: John sets the vision, or he reads it in the organization and sets it down. We bring the good news and the bad news to the board. They do ask questions. We have had some interesting stuff on one of our subsidiaries, a little trouble collecting accounts receivable. On three occasions in the last five months, we have had questions from board members. The first question was, 'What's this about?' The second question was, 'How is this going?' The third question was, 'How is this getting resolved? What's the plan? Are you sure you are on top of this?'
>
> "A lot of the board work goes on in committees, and the committees get into more detail. There is a lot of respect among the board members. I don't think people are perceived as having agendas or personal ego things. People respect the committee reports. There is a theory that if you don't know how the board will react to an item, it's not ready to go to the board. Maybe you need to do some education. Get the questions on the table and get them in order before you go to the board."

James Perry, J.D., the current board chair:

> "When I took on the chair, I had two goals. One was a strategic plan, and the other was a succession plan for the board. We need to be sure that we have the right people coming along to provide the kind of governance that will be required. We are paying a lot of attention to that. One thing that is very helpful is to avoid a self-perpetuating board. There are term

limits so you don't get the good old boy who goes on and on. We are less of a representative board, which I think is critical. I am to some extent a representative. There are four of us on the board, the two bishops and two of us elected by our churches.

"What's critical is to make sure that everybody on our board and our management team is thinking system, rather than representatively. We now have a group that almost universally has abandoned thinking about one facility; it is the growth of the whole that's important. The question is whether the constituencies get served, not who serves them. You are not trying to preserve a building, you are trying to provide quality healthcare for a community. You start thinking that way, then the bricks and mortar kind of disappear.

"The Nominating Committee is very important. The people we are looking for have CEO and senior executive experience. They are people where the buck stops, people who have had to deal with difficult things, who are able to look at the big picture. They will help us with our strategic plan because they think strategically. They may have had little connection with healthcare. That's okay. We have enough other folks who can take care of that. We need physicians who can think beyond their wallet, who have a grasp of where healthcare is going, not just in their own practice, but in respect to community needs. We identified a couple of folks last year. We actually changed our bylaws this year to add someone we thought was strong.

"Legacy has been the best organization that I have been involved with that has walked the talk when it comes to mission, vision, and strategic focus. That's right out there. The CEO talks about it constantly. It directs our board agendas. It's the focus of everything that comes out of senior management. He's made us a believer. Also with CQI. What he's been able to do there has been wonderful. He took it to the limit. That's why we have the luxury of this planning process. The fear that we will throw it all away for the bottom line is gone. We really are concerned about quality. We really are concerned about community need. There's a much higher level of trust, and that's a very important reason why we are where we are.

"The biggest threat on our horizon is some of our alliances. The alliance with Blue Cross had a positive impact on our bottom line and on Blue Cross. Maybe we need to look beyond Legacy, face up to what's being done in the rest of the community. We have to look at what's being done at OHSU and Sisters of Providence, and they have to look at us. I think we can get that dialogue going better—it just started. A lot of people will tell you it is going nowhere, but I don't think that is the case. OHSIC is a piece of it, but it's more than that. There is an understanding among them that there are some things they should collaborate on. We ought to collaborate in some of the really high-end things. We are collaborating in trauma and the transplant program. Some of them are not so easy to identify. It wasn't long ago that cardiovascular work was really high-end tertiary, but not anymore. That might help us see that we shouldn't invest too heavily in some of the new things. Maybe we should cut a deal with the Sisters and support their spending the money."

Setting financial policy

Legacy has to operate in one of the most financially demanding environments in the nation. Not surprisingly, it has developed a powerful system to do this, resulting in an objectively measured, multidimensional framework that generates goals and rewards for all employees. Lowell Johnson, CFO, describes how this works:

> "We project three years into the future. We project changes in costs and volumes, but not productivity improvements. We let the model run, and it shows that three years out you go to a $30 million operating loss. An then you come back and say, 'That shows you the change that has to happen if we are going to stay at an acceptable level.'
>
> "We have an operating plan, a quality plan, and a capital plan that roll together into the financial plan. The quality plan includes the quality indicators on a program-by-program basis.
>
> "If you are the manager of surgery, you have a plan for the next three years. Now suppose you feel you need to go from 16 to 18 ORs. You will develop a plan that analyzes utilization against national benchmarks. You show where the additional surgeries are coming from, the revenue and cost impacts. If you convince management it's a good idea, the capital budget is developed in detail and it goes into the queue. The tests are, Does it add to market share, can it be cost effective, what's the return on investment, and does it move the strategy?

"At the end of the annual budget process, we have about $60 million in requests, everything from 'Let's build a medical office building in the suburbs' to 'Let's replace one of the air conditioners.' What the system is willing to invest for the coming year is negotiated with the Finance and Planning Committees and the board four months before the end of the fiscal year. Typically, this will be about $40 million. We're in a pretty steady state of $35 million in replacement and $5 million in diversification opportunities, anything related to our core business. We try to distinguish maintenance capital and strategic capital. We do not have a dedicated stream for helping physicians, or for improving the information resources. Information has to justify its need along with everybody else.

"About four years ago, Legacy hit a high water mark of about $215 million in long-term debt. In 1993, we started a discussion of the affordability of that level of debt. Out of that came a board directive, which I emphatically supported, to repurchase up to $100 million of long-term debt, and to finance all of its ongoing investments out of its own generated cash. A number of the board members are financial executives who felt we had excess debt. We have pushed the debt down to $135, and I'd like to go to $100. We now have a AA^{+} rating from Standard and Poor's. The level of debt is not a factor now in looking at opportunities for the future. It was a factor, major league, a couple of years ago.

"We had a whole lot of help generating that cash. Jim May, who ran the downtown hospitals; Pam Vukovich and Jeff Cushing, the regional finance officers; Jane Cummins . . . . There was no role from governance other than 'Atta boys.' A lot of support, but no involvement in the daily business. They approved the overall direction, they approved the overall guidance to reduce staff, get more productive, and hold the line on prices. They did not specify what to do. They are a contented, watchful board."

Alliances with other institutions

The Legacy alliances strategy has three major parts. First, Legacy will continue to build the capability of its primary physicians and specialist physicians, attacking the problems that have come to light through the alliance. Second, Legacy will continue its Social Accountability program with the Healthy Communities effort, supporting programs that address the Healthy Communities goals through financial and in-kind contributions. As part of this, Legacy will cooperate with and support the operations of the Multnomah County Health Department. Third, Legacy will develop OHSIC, a collaboration with its three major competitors, Providence Health System, Kaiser-Permanente, and Oregon Health Sciences University, and its strategic partner, Blue Cross Blue Shield of Oregon, to address high-risk and high-cost health problems that none of the five can effectively attack alone.

Don Sacco, president of Blue Cross Blue Shield of Oregon, discusses the problems the alliance encountered from a community perspective:

> "I had a set of critical questions about the alliance when I came here, and many of them were not answered to my satisfaction. We had been in a period of five or six years of premium growth, but in Portland the competition was getting tougher from PacifiCare and others. Plus, in 1995 and 1996 the investment income [from the reserves Blue Cross must carry as an insurance company] was buoyed. I think Blue Cross had more of a sense of security than we should have had, and that distracted us from careful analysis of our underwriting results. In 1994, the bottom fell out of utilization and the underwriting gain was enormous. That misled people too. It made it look like there was a lot of money in insurance gains. In 1996 we had to respond to price aggressiveness.
>
> "We took on a big burden in the Oregon Health Plan. Blue Cross had 38 percent of the Medicaid business. The first year of Medicaid business was a little deceiving. We started out paying commercial rates. For a while that looked okay. It turned out it wasn't okay. The alliance risk model negotiated the capitation split between the hospitals and the primary care groups; the groups would manage the entire non-hospital portion. The risk for the groups was substantial. [When the full force of the OHP utilization hit, the doctors found themselves unable to manage the risk.] The doctors' perspective was that Medicaid would pay the full commercial rate, but, as it turned out, we couldn't afford that. So the rate and the utilization had to be reduced simultaneously. It led to a different outcome than people anticipated."

Primary care has been in the spotlight of managed care for some years. Don suggests that the Portland experience shows some unexpected limits to the primary care contribution to healthcare value:

> "I think that the belief when we formed the alliance was that we were all going to win riding primary care as the vehicle,

even more than the gatekeeper; that they were going to organize themselves and then the rest of the system, especially specialists, in a way that led to efficiency. We were going to force everybody to join up with one of the groups, or emulate the group performance.

"We missed the point that what's pushing medical care costs is 'sick care,' the management of serious illness and injury, outside primary care. The issue of sick care was played out in the alliance and led to less agreement rather than more. I don't know that anybody anticipated the way in which primary care would try to get even with the specialists. They didn't really build good relationships. Medical management became the PCPs and individual relationships, instead of developing perspective on relationships—when it's best to refer, when to let go, when to keep control. The 'get even' tactics just interfere with the handoffs. The organizations that figure out the handoffs will be the winners."

He notes that the alliance has not succeeded as he and others had hoped, but that it will form the basis for the next steps:

"The alliance is not a failure, but it's not what we anticipated. The lesson is to avoid putting too many entities together that might end up competing with one another. There are integrated systems being put together with the notion of buying and controlling primary care practices. I don't know that that approach is working well. It's very expensive. The alliance was on the other end of that, to create a virtual system with no commingling of assets. Possibly because of the competing interests, possibly because there wasn't enough tying of the asset base, they first attacked Legacy, and then they attacked Blue Cross. The coalescing force among the physician groups was, 'Legacy is taking too much money; they had their best year ever'; and 'Blue Cross isn't going to give us capitation the way we want it.' Some place in that spectrum is something better.

"We are going to dissolve the alliance. We'll maintain our relationship with Legacy. We are going to restructure our efforts with physicians, and Blue Cross will take a much more active role in managing and creating the network. We'll probably contract directly with each of the physician groups. Then we will create a basis for those who are unaffiliated to work together with us.

"I would still like to have an organization with strong physician input that is devoted more to best practices and medical management tools. My idea is taking a strong core group of primary care physicians, not forcing them to integrate, but using the core group to do some medical management, and to share infrastructure development that cuts across the smaller practices. A lot of doctors in the smaller practices know they have to do things differently, they just don't have the resources to invest in it. If they feel they are not being forced to go under somebody else's control, they will be more willing to participate voluntarily. We can wed that base to a group of specialists, with an incentive that commingles the payment for primary and specialty care. We can play on the forces in today's marketplace for freer access to specialty care. Maybe we can end up giving the consumer choices of insurance plans within the HMO."

Mitch Olejko, J.D., chief legal officer, develops the idea of managing "sick care" further:

"We talked about developing a care management organization with our specialists. That's a way to organize the hospital and the physician around the care of patients, rather than what some physician-hospital organizations do, which is focus on getting managed care contracts or providing services to physicians. We are still a sick care hospital company. We have sort of neglected our relationships with our specialists over the last few years, and it's time to focus on them, not take them for granted.

"The idea of a care management organization with global capitation would allow us to share risk with our specialists. If Legacy had a global cap, or episode-of-care payment, or just a deal for sharing cost reduction with the insurance company, we could share gains with our physicians. The care management organization is an idea that risk and reward should be the same for the doctor and the hospital. Any money that falls to the bottom line can be shared. With the payment system we now have, that's not possible. We've identified a couple areas where at least 40 percent of our business could be on a global cap or episode cap. We could grow it from there by showing success in the marketplace. Whatever legal format doesn't matter. We need shared decision making and a risk contract with the insurer. The care management organization would be

> a kind of tool box, with whatever services it needs to make the care management work."

Meanwhile, Legacy's commitment to diversified health services and outreach continues. Judith Anderson, trustee and chair of the mission affairs committee, is a nurse who also chairs the Northwest Parish Nurse Group, supporting parish nurses in four states. She describes the committee as working to identify a strategy:

> "The committee is in transition, trying to find its role. Each Legacy operating unit has its own mission effectiveness committee, charged with monitoring the unit's performance. Historically, mission affairs has been a place where they could report their activities, emphasis, focus, and direction. I think we're seeing that we can have a much more effective role if we can integrate those reports with the new strategic plan.
>
> "One of my biggest concerns is how to balance a solid fiscal picture with providing services—how we can balance prevention which doesn't pay except in the very long term (but in the long run has got to help) with our more immediate needs? If I had my druthers, I'd drag up every penny I could to support primary care and health education. That's exactly what we are doing in parish nursing—health counseling, referrals, family support.
>
> "Over the past several months mission affairs has discussed the potpourri of experiences, and how to not just jump on the next bandwagon and do somebody's pet program. We've asked each mission effectiveness committee to look at what it feels could be a more effective strategy to coordinate our efforts. They are to report at our next meeting. Then we'll get all of the Mission Effectiveness representatives and look at a more intentional program, aligning with other major groups like Healthy Communities and the OHSIC group. We should look not just at every good project, but at what will be our thrust based on need, how we assess the need, and how we evaluate its effectiveness."

It's clear, she says, that the strategy will emphasize collaboration:

> "The community is where a lot of health system activity will be. A couple of main issues are, 'Where do we interface the community and the healthcare system?' and 'What portion do supplemental activities take on?' Are we an added frill, or can we plug in to the main vision? We are also looking at whether

> it will be more effective if we have participation from foundations. We've pretty much decided that someone from the foundation world should sit on mission affairs, to see the direction we're going and why we are asking for funding in a particular area. We are turning to alliances with some of the major groups, such as Healthy Communities, and seeing that we aren't duplicating activities being done elsewhere.
>
> "Healthy Communities is a national agenda supported by the W. K. Kellogg Foundation. In 1995 they convened all the agencies in Portland—police departments, schools, health departments, hospitals, organizing projects, the Urban League of Portland—every major organization coming together to talk about 'If you were to look at how Portland could be a healthier community, what would the community look like?' We identified common themes from the groups and asked for volunteers to work on an ongoing project. They are selecting a common agenda. They targeted some of the same areas as OHSIC: teen pregnancy and domestic violence.
>
> "I'm an optimist by nature. I think we can work toward collaboration. Without it, we wouldn't have either the humanitarian effort nor would we get the best from life. The Sisters of Providence and Legacy both have a strong commitment to the poor and community service. If we can draw on our religious background, it can help us. Ecumenical Ministries of Oregon is a unique contributor. The Interfaith Volunteer Caregivers will help. The Atlanta project has taken a lot of diverse community organizations to work together, with a pretty good track record. In the L.A. area there is a pretty significant movement.
>
> "I think it's wonderful that John King has gotten us into this. Anything that gets past the competitiveness is a step in the right direction. It's fairly threatening, not knowing the other person's reaction. I think the dialogue will not happen instantly, but I think the trust level can certainly be built. John King is a key person to do that. If people can see the advantages to collaboration, it will work. I think we are in the fetal stages of it right now."

Finally, Legacy is committed to collaborating with its competitors, and has moved to implement Oregon Health Systems in Collaboration. Jim Sanger, Vice President for administration, describes OHSIC:

> "OHSIC has been around three or four years. There's a steering committee of CEOs that meets quarterly, and a management

group meets monthly. We have picked four topics—teen pregnancy, domestic violence, immunizations, and access to care. The topics were picked by the Portland Progress Board. They benchmark various problems, and these four were high on their priority list.

"The teen pregnancy thing is the simplest. STARS is a statewide program, focused on specific schools and supported by a number of groups. We put up some of the money and do the evaluation scheme, and others actually do the work.

"We started a survey of what was being done in domestic violence—leadership activities, patient activities, workplace activities, community activities—for all the participating organizations. We were looking for dedicated response teams, screening policies, weapons policies, nondiscrimination policies, employee assistance programs. We were hoping to find out whether it made any difference. We got into a big debate about how much to spend. The survey will cost $175,000, and it seems like a lot of money. We have a lot of anecdotal evidence that we have a lot of violence right in our own workforce."

Jim explains how difficult OHSIC's first major project turned out to be:

"Immunization started the earliest and everybody thought it was going to be a no-brainer. It turned into an administrative nightmare. We had an initial estimate that only 50 percent of the kids in this state were fully immunized. Then it turned out that nobody really knows. We will have spent in the neighborhood of $1 million to get a methodology to collect and report immunization status. The State Department of Health and the private groups who want to do these things don't get along very well. We had to take the system away from the state and give the job to a private contractor. We persevered through all that, and we do have a working system. The contractor and the state are at loggerheads, and the contractor will have to be replaced.

"The problem is that the families go to a whole variety of places. They change plans, visit different doctors, and go to ERs. To get an accurate picture you have to go to all of them. You have to have capability of getting data from several sites and then coordinate the records, usually in the face of slightly different identifiers. We have a tested system for collecting immunization data, using bar codes, postcards, and scanners. It will notify providers and parents when the kid is short of immunizations."

Jim looks to the future with guarded optimism:

> "Access to care is a problem because of all the tax concerns. The fact is the county clinics will go away, and the providers need a plan to replace them. If we didn't have OHSIC, I'm not sure there would have been any way at all to work on the access problem with the clinics closing. I don't know that OHSIC will come up with an answer, but without it we wouldn't have a place to start. My concern about OHSIC is that it holds out a promise that there will be an effective working relationship that will produce something. That promise has now been recognized by the governor's office, backed by the Multnomah County Commissioners, which is trying to issue challenge grants for public-private partnerships. Now OHSIC has to step up to the challenge.
>
> "There's a lot of promise here, and a lot of expectations. You can see where this could be the beginning of some kind of a civic decision-making process that could be expanded to take on more important issues and bring others in to participate in the solution."

John King, CEO, reflects a similar perspective:

> "OHSIC is still feeling its way. Competition here is not an emotional issue, but it is severe enough to hamper collaboration, especially when the CEOs are not present. We'd like to get OHSIC to think more on a community-at-large basis. Kaiser has helped support that, and the W. K. Kellogg Foundation [with a grant for a Healthy Communities Forum and some developmental assistance]. The governor's wife has been very supportive of the STARS program. The topics we have picked are useful, but there's not a lot of strategy yet. We have begun to leverage our efforts, tying the business community to health initiatives, but we have no outside trustees."

CHAPTER

4

HENRY FORD HEALTH SYSTEM, DETROIT, MICHIGAN

The Metropolitan Area

The city of Detroit, with one million people, is the center of a metropolitan area including seven counties and a population of four-and-one-half million, half the state of Michigan. Wayne County includes Detroit and several smaller cities. Three suburban population centers, Ann Arbor to the west, Pontiac north, and Warren east, are about 45 minutes from the city center by freeway. Windsor, Ontario, Canada lies to the south, across the Detroit River.

Manufacturing, principally automotive products, is by far the largest source of employment, followed by retailing, health services, and education. The area is notorious for cyclical income and employment. While work has been diversified and job security has improved, it remains true that "when the nation catches cold, Detroit has pneumonia." But the '90s have been prosperous. Employment, income, and tax revenues have been high; crime and welfare have been declining. Family income for the metropolitan area is high and poverty low compared to other metropolitan areas. Crime, education, and homelessness are somewhat worse than metropolitan medians.

Detroit proper is a rust-belt city, still in many ways recovering from the problems of the '70s and '80s. The racial divide remains; the city is over two-thirds nonwhite. The crime, low-income, and homeless rates are among the highest, and the number of educated families is well below the median. The city has made some recovery from the 1967 riots, which devastated large areas near the main campus of Henry Ford Health System (HFHS), but the problems are obvious and entrenched. The contrast between the city and the suburban population centers is striking.

Table 4.1 Detroit Metropolitan Area and Wayne County

	Detroit Metro.	Wayne County	Detroit City
Population	4,266,654	2,111,687	1,027,974
Median Age	33.0 yrs.	32.4 yrs.	31.5 yrs.
White Population	75%	57%	33%
Median Household Income	$34,389	$28,208	$21,454
Income Below $15,000	8.3%	11%	40%
Total Crime Index	146	197	192
Educated Families Index	117	63	76
Homeless Index	130	194	195

Source: 1990 U.S. Census. Crime, Education, and Homeless Indexes by Easy Analytic Software, Inc., U.S. mean = 100.

Health and Healthcare

The Detroit area, like many rust-belt cities, has supported broad-benefit traditional health insurance for most of its employed population and has been relatively slow to move to managed care. Despite the high costs that have resulted, unions have protected the insurance benefit. Even so, HMO coverage has grown steadily in the last decade and now approaches 25 percent of the population. Health Alliance Plan (HAP), owned by Henry Ford Health System, is the largest in the metropolitan area, followed by Blue Care Network, owned by Blue Cross and Blue Shield of Michigan, and Care Choices, owned by Mercy Health Services, a Catholic health system principally serving Michigan and Iowa. Several smaller HMOs compete in the area. Three locally owned PPOs have a combined subscription of about 250,000 lives. They have not been a major factor in Detroit. The state of Michigan has moved almost all Medicaid coverage to managed care. Intensive marketing of Medicare HMO coverage is just beginning but is expected to develop slowly because many retirees enjoy generous supplementary protection for traditional Medicare. The balance of the insured population has traditional insurance, largely Blue Cross and Blue Shield.

Health insurance premiums are high in Detroit. Traditional Blue Cross coverage can run near $200 per member per month. The HMOs are offered at about $130 per member per month, with competition driving the price down slowly. The Medicare cost per member per month was $628 in Wayne County in 1996, among the highest in the nation. The three surrounding counties were all over $500, as compared to a median of $400 for similar areas.

Public Health and Indigent Care

Wayne County suffers from serious health problems. It ranks among the ten highest metropolitan counties nationwide in age-adjusted mortality from all causes, and also for heart disease, cancer, and stroke individually. It is among the worst ten in low-birthweight babies, has a poor record on child immunization, and is 15th in homicides.

Almost 20 percent of Wayne County is on Medicaid, and a larger number are estimated to be uninsured. Much of the indigent care is provided by three healthcare systems operating in the city. The Detroit Medical Center leads in obstetrical and pediatric care, but HFHS and Mercy Health Services also bear a substantial load. Henry Ford operated the most comprehensive trauma center. All operate clinics for indigent patients at their larger installations and selected community sites (Table 4.2). The Detroit Health Department also operates clinics.

Healthcare Provider Organizations

Care in most of the metropolitan area still follows the traditional pattern of independent medical practitioners and competing hospitals. Henry Ford Health System is the largest of six systems at various stages of integration.

Table 4.2 Wayne County Scores on Available Measures of Health and Healthcare Quality

	Wayne County	Nation
Health		
Age-adjusted mortality (per 100,000 pop.)	352.7	281
Cardiovascular	66.0	56.4
Cerebrovascular	228.3	204
Cancer	40.9	29.4
Accidents	1,007.9	871.57
All Causes	−108.2	−71.18
Change, 1985–1992	2.39%	1.49%
Low birth weight*	16%	13.39%
Health Insurance		
Household reporting		
HMO coverage	22%	22%
PPO coverage	15%	11%
Fee-for-service coverage	53%	39%
Uninsured	10%	15%

*Births less than 1,500 grams.

Source: National Center for Health Statistics for mortality data; Robert Wood Johnson Foundation for national health insurance; and local surveys for Wayne County health insurance.

The Detroit Medical Center operates principally in Detroit and the northern suburbs. Mercy Health Services has facilities in the city, the northern and western suburbs, and a joint venture with HFHS in the east. St. John's Health System and William Beaumont Hospital Corporation serve markets in the northern and eastern suburbs, and Oakwood Health Services serves western suburbs. All six of these systems have physician affiliates in conventionally organized solo and small group practice; only Henry Ford has a large multispecialty group. The University of Michigan Medical Center, located in Ann Arbor, competes with Ford, the Detroit Medical Center, and William Beaumont for the highest levels of tertiary care. It has a large salaried faculty. Fifteen smaller hospitals and hospital systems also operate in the metropolitan area, with 4,045 beds, a quarter of the seven-county total. Several of these are affiliated with systems operating outside of Detroit.

Use of hospital services, as indicated by admissions, has been declining in recent years. A small decline in the population has increased the effect of declining rates of use per person. As a result, occupancies of hospitals have fallen, and beds have been taken off line. Several mergers have occurred in recognition of this trend, strengthening all of the large systems.

Henry Ford Health System

Henry Ford Health System began as Henry Ford Hospital, a unique concept modeled in part on the Mayo Clinic and developed by the auto manufacturing pioneer himself as a deliberate alternative to the prevailing medical organization in 1913. Ford sought an employed medical staff and emphasized a more integrated, less fragmented approach to medical care. Despite strenuous opposition from the local medical community, the organization thrived and achieved national recognition. By 1990, the major elements of the current system were in place. Those include a comprehensive panoply of healthcare available at multiple sites, an emphasis on outpatient and office service, a commitment to prevention and health promotion, and a health insurance vehicle designed to minimize costs. They also include a substantial commitment to medical and other professional education and to clinical and public health research. Over the years, the name has been changed from "Hospital" to "Health Care" to "Health System," reflecting the broadened interests.

The mission of HFHS is "to provide exceptional quality, cost-effective care, strengthened by excellence in education and research.

We work together to improve health and quality of life in the communities of southeastern Michigan and neighboring regions." The vision emphasizes

- needs of patients and communities;
- integrated, complete, lifelong healthcare . . . [that] our customers find easy to use
- innovative partnerships, managed care, and health education; and
- measured patient satisfaction and community health.

The values, which put patients first and the people who work at HFHS second, specify "continuous improvement," "community health," "diversity," "compassion," and "social conscience." Among the innovations HFHS cites as implementing its vision are a primary care delivery system that coordinates a team of providers under a personal physician, measured quality of care, patient-focused care that brings service to the patient instead of moving the patient, a computerized medical record, and research and training programs in proactive and preventive care.

In the past decade, Ford has grown substantially by merger, as well as by "same store" improvement. It has solidified its merger with two independent hospitals and has developed a joint venture with another. It merged with Horizon Health System, a system of smaller hospitals emphasizing osteopathic medicine. It also expanded its collaboration with Mercy Health Services, providing contract management for an inner-city hospital, operating two hospitals jointly, and developing strategic affiliation with Mercy's large hospital in Pontiac and its medical staff.

By 1996, HFHS was a $1.8 billion corporation with 17,000 employees serving almost 20 percent of the metropolitan population. It had affiliations with three medical schools and programs supporting 850 physicians in training. It had 1,500 research projects with $40 million in grant funding. It was the sixth-largest employer in Michigan and one of the largest health organizations in the country, and it was nationally recognized for its contributions in managed care, clinical research, community health research, and medical education. HFHS has nationally recognized programs in transplantation, neurosciences, and athletic medicine.

Governance

The governance of this organization relies on a uniquely complex network of community input. The board of trustees has 44 members, and

Figure 4.1 Henry Ford Health System Trustees' Report

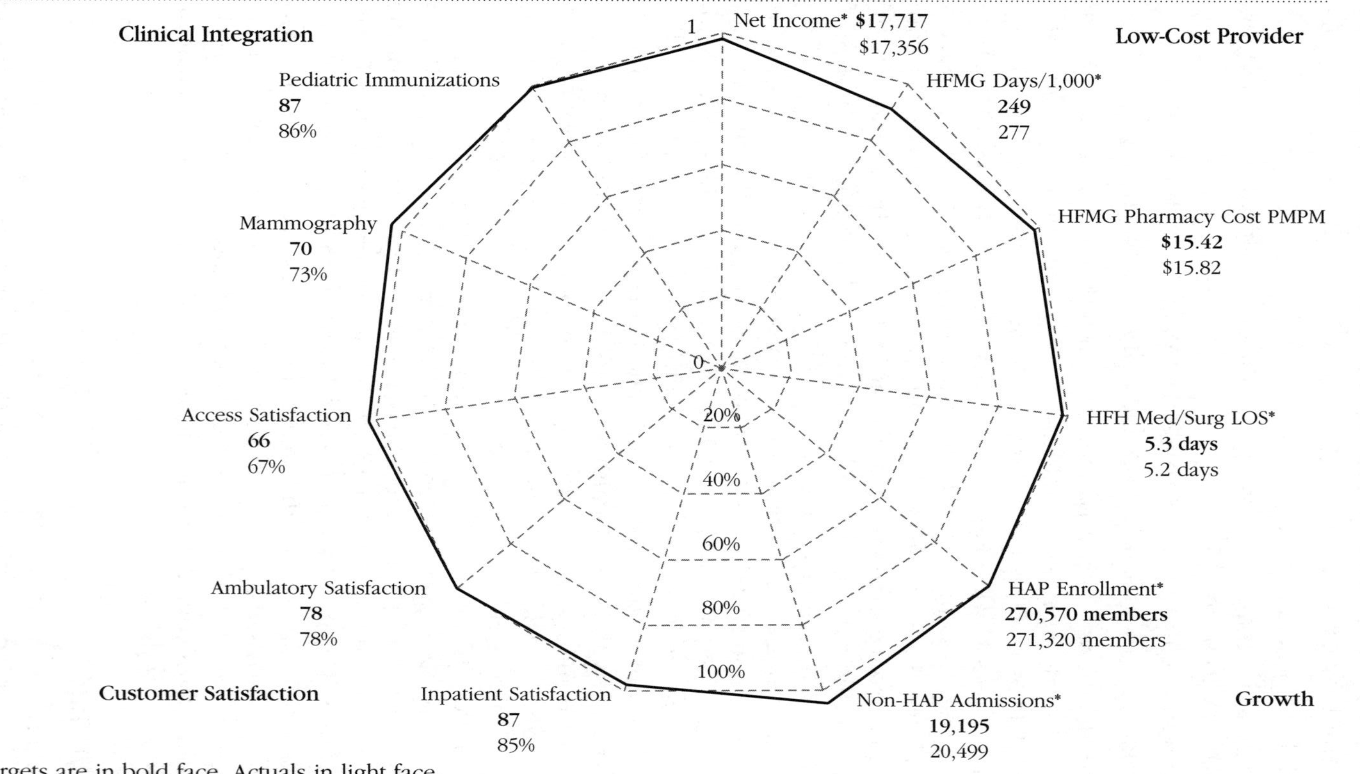

Targets are in bold face. Actuals in light face.

Each measure is expressed as a ratio of target to actual, expressed to show shortfalls as less than 100 percent.

*Asterisked items for current month, year-to-date. All others lagged two months.

their efforts are supplemented by 180 volunteer leaders who participate in advisory and affiliate boards for 14 subsidiaries that include six regional organizations, two insurance plans, Horizon Health System (the osteopathic affiliate), a hospice, continuing care, behavioral services, a heart and vascular institute, and a health sciences center. Subsidiary boards focus on assessing and guiding the direction of their units, and are represented on the board of trustees by their officers. The structure, which many would call ungainly, is made to work by sophisticated use of measurement and a powerful office of the president.

Quantitative performance measures and continuous improvement principals drive the Ford organization. Four strategic objectives, Customer Satisfaction, Growth, Low-Cost Provider, and Clinical Integration, were established in 1991, and efforts were begun to measure them. The board notes great success with spider diagrams (Figure 4.1), summarizing current operational targets with several measures representing each of the strategic objectives in a "quality compass." (Quality of care measures dominate the Clinical Integration dimension.) The focus on numbers allows HFHS to run many diverse organizations; assure quality, patient satisfaction, and financial performance; and support continuous improvement. Goals are proposed by operating personnel, compared to past performance and available benchmarks, and are approved by the boards with the central board in overall control. Performance is assessed versus established goals.

One perspective of Henry Ford is as a conglomerate of enterprises operating under shared rules. The focus on outcomes measurement allows individual units substantial autonomy, a characteristic particularly noticeable in the ongoing competition between the original Henry Ford Medical Group and the "affiliated physicians," independent practitioners who also provide care to Health Alliance Plan members. The lines of accountability focus all activities under seven senior and corporate vice presidents who, with the president, comprise the office of the president.

A Diversified Services Group operates pharmacies, medical equipment and home health services, and kidney dialysis companies. These are the only care activities reaching beyond the Detroit region. (Health Alliance Plan operates in Flint, Michigan to the north and has a subsidiary in Toledo, Ohio to the south.) A sometimes confusing proliferation of "centers," directly funded units independent of the operating lines, are supported to develop innovations and pursue special projects. The Center for Clinical Effectiveness, the Center for Health System Studies, the Center for Health Promotion, the Center for Urban Health, and the Center for Medical Treatment Effectiveness Programs all carry out a range of research and demonstration projects on different models of care and on organizational and clinical performance. The centers pursue grant-funded research and provide expert resources for operational questions. All of these operations, and the Diversified Services Group, have an entrepreneurial character that keeps the organization flexible and innovative despite its size (Figure 4.2).

Figure 4.2 Major Operating Units of Henry Ford Health System

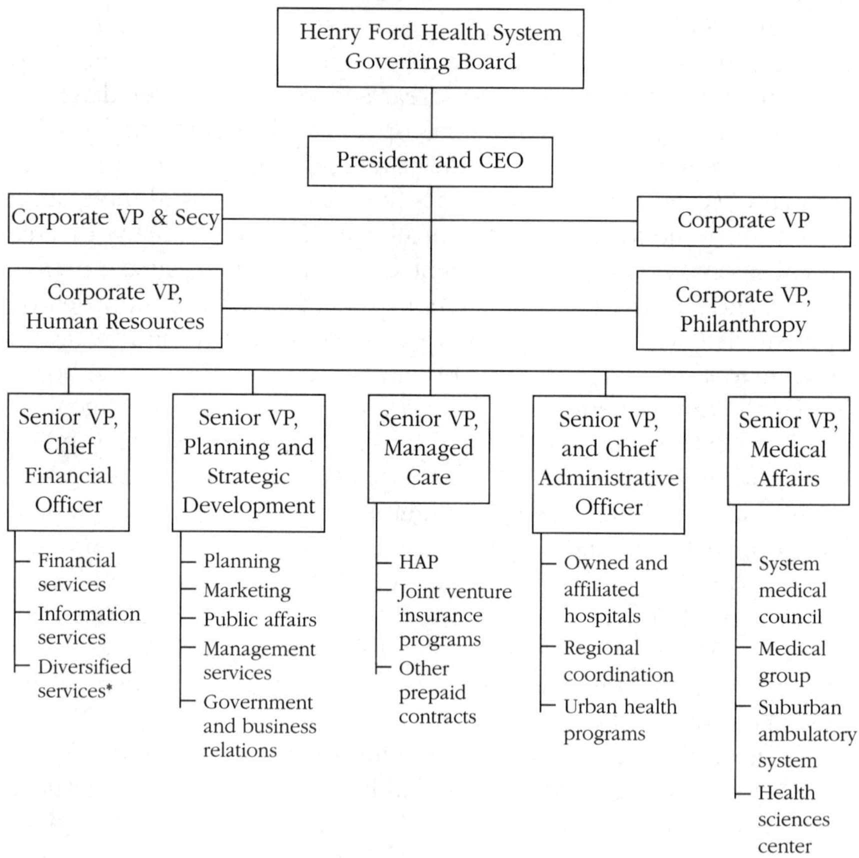

*The Diversified Services Group includes pharmacies, dialysis, medical equipment, and home health services.

Note: Several centers for research and innovation are not shown. There are extensive formal and informal cross-cutting or matrix relationships that are not shown. Most of the owned hospitals and several units have their own advisory and other operational or affiliate boards.

Henry Ford Medical Group

The Medical Group is a 1,000-member multispecialty group practice that has migrated relatively successfully toward a managed care configuration. Historically, the practice was a tertiary care, specialty-oriented activity supported by referrals from a broad area. Many members and most leaders came from academic medicine, and the group was noted as a clinically oriented alternative to the bench research emphasized by leading medical schools. The model began to crumble with the Detroit riots, which led many suburbanites to avoid the center city.

Over three decades, the Medical Group has decentralized to large ambulatory facilities in the north, west, and northeast, and to over 30 smaller primary care sites. The group has slowly changed its membership, compensation, leadership, and outlook to accommodate the changes introduced by managed care. Two mergers, one with the Metro Medical Group, a primary care–oriented group practice supporting a predecessor to the present Health Alliance Plan, and the second with Horizon Health Services, which was much stronger in primary care, helped redress the specialist–primary care balance. The need for change continues. Recent HAP marketing activities have increased the number of referral specialists among the affiliated physicians. While the group retains tertiary capability at the downtown site, it has conceded to patient demand for local care even in areas as complex as cardiac surgery.

Affiliated Physicians

The first obvious crack in the hegemony of the Medical Group came in the 1980s, when Ford acquired Wyandotte Hospital, a 349-bed general hospital serving a suburban community in the near southwest of Detroit. Wyandotte had a typical medical staff for its time and place, primary and specialist physicians in solo and small group practice. Such a group of affiliated physicians could easily have viewed the Medical Group as a threatening competitor. What happened was that the affiliates grew faster than the group, through subsequent mergers and contract service arrangements, until it is now more accurate to say that the affiliates threaten the group.

The driving engine is the patients' need for convenient care. Most large Detroit area employers now offer a menu of HMO and traditional health insurance benefit alternatives. Subscribers are unwilling to travel long distances for care. HAP must seek local care sources in order to be competitive. Although the medical group strategy of the

1980s greatly increased its geographic dispersion, further expansion of the group would be expensive. As a result, HAP has contracted with doctors and hospitals in all of the four large counties of the metropolitan area.

The form of contracts with affiliates varies, but most are fee-for-service, at rates substantially below traditional Blue Cross and Medicare. Much of the cost and quality control has been by centralized case management under the HAP medical director. It has been successful in keeping affiliate performance equivalent to, and sometimes better than, that of the group. Only a few of the affiliates are organized to manage capitation. Whether more organized structures will develop in the regions probably depends on their effectiveness. HAP has transferred risk to physician organizations in those groups that have indicated their willingness to accept it.

Operations

Henry Ford Health System has used quality improvement as a core competency. It began extensive investment in total quality management (TQM, conceptually similar to Legacy's CQI) in the late 1980s and has continued to emphasize empowerment, customer focus, objective measurement of performance, and process improvement as its basic control mechanism. TQM is supported by extensive education, vigorous leadership from the CEO, the performance measurement system, and an incentive program for the office of the president and about 200 managers. The TQM concept is enthusiastically supported by the board. TQM has been popular in automotive management, and it is well accepted in Detroit at large. The result has moved Henry Ford Health System to the front of the Detroit market.

Improvement goals are established through an ongoing dialogue that includes the operating units, the office of the president, and the extended board structure. Maintenance of financial stability, and of the AA bond rating, has been a critical part of the strategy. Most units expect to make a contribution to profit. The quality committee of the board reviews progress quarterly, and subsidiary boards are deeply involved in setting and improving goals for regions and specific services. Recent concern has been with patient satisfaction. Systematic surveys made clear that patients of affiliated physicians were generally more satisfied than those of the medical group, and that some low scores threatened further growth. These data generated a response that has reached from the board through the office of the president to the smallest caregiving units and their support services. A plan of "dyads," coordination between the appropriate medical officer and administrative officer, has been developed and rolled out to the regional units. Dyads now address the satisfaction issue in each hospital and clinic, working on amenities, scheduling, support services, and clinical issues. Various task forces and teams are at work, crossing regional lines and bringing in resources from planning and strategic development, human resources, and the centers.

The financial performance of Henry Ford Health System is shown in Table 4.3. Much of the growth shown is from acquisitions, and it is difficult to track "same store" performance. However, cost growth has been limited for several years. The HAP premium was once $10 higher than its largest competitor. By 1996, the gap had shrunk substantially; by 1997, HAP had become a price leader. The summary of

Table 4.3 Trends in Key Financial Indicators

	12/31/94	12/31/95	12/31/96
Net patient revenues	$ 626,543	$ 673,311	$ 852,108
Health insurance premiums	756,948	790,692	787,029
Other revenues	115,097	134,387	135,936
Total Revenue	$1,498,588	$1,598,390	$1,775,073
Operating Expenses	$1,448,543	$1,559,948	$1,731,206
Income from operations	$50,045	$38,442	$43,867
Non-operating income*	6,369	17,203	16,235
Total Income	$56,414	$55,645	$60,102
Current assets	$354,541	$409,481	$498,041
Investments	387,697	381,435	450,428
Limited and restricted assets	687,394	723,700	942,787
Total Assets	$1,429,632	$1,514,616	$1,891,256
Current liabilities	$360,652	$399,442	$ 468,934
Other liabilities	170,675	172,371	211,701
Long-term liabilities	263,215	248,886	422,630
Total Liabilities	$794,542	$820,699	$1,103,265
Fund balance	$635,090	$693,917	$787,991
Operating margin	3.6%	2.6%	2.7%
Total margin	3.8%	3.5%	3.4%
Times interest earned	4.5	5.2	4.9
Long-term debt to equity	41.4%	35.9%	53.6%

*Includes fund for Henry Ford Hospital.

financial operations is that the system assimilated growth, overcame market threats, revised patient care, stimulated extensive investment in information systems, supported community outreach, and still maintained a small surplus.

Continuing Care Services

Ford has a comprehensive array of services, including long-term care, rehabilitation, behavioral and substance services, hospice, home health, dialysis, and pharmacy. It operates two nursing homes and a center for the frail elderly. It has an occupational medicine program that it operates as a joint venture with Occu Systems, a for-profit national company. While these are generally excellent services, they are much smaller than the needs of the whole Ford market share. They serve more as benchmarks and competitive opportunities. Ford patients are referred to many similar services in the metropolitan area. At the moment, expansion of Ford-owned services is not a high priority, and whether it will become so as HAP enrolls larger numbers of Medicare patients remains to be seen. The answer probably depends on whether other providers in the community can meet needs at a standard of quality and cost that Ford finds acceptable.

Community Services

Henry Ford bears a substantial share of the indigent healthcare in Detroit through its clinics, emergency rooms, and senior centers. It has won local and national recognition for its efforts in community health. Its activities are deliberately tailored to the needs of its regions, with particular attention to the inner city. In central Detroit, HFHS operates three activity centers for seniors, with personnel specially trained in the health and welfare needs of the elderly. It operates two clinics for people unable to pay and staffs several Detroit Public Health Department clinics under contract. It supports a debt forgiveness program for patients who contribute volunteer hours. It has constructed a housing subdivision near the hospital, and assists the neighborhood association. In the suburbs, it has run depression screening, started a charter school for students interested in the health professions, and stimulated breast cancer screening. In addition to these formally sponsored activities, many HFHS employees participate in volunteer activities.

Several inner-city programs are oriented around children. Henry Ford began a unique school health program that had great success in its pilot middle school, and has since been expanded to 13 schools with support from other healthcare systems and the W. K. Kellogg

Foundation. Each school is provided with a team of medical and social work personnel who work with the school and families on prevention, counseling, and health education. A pilot violence prevention program identifies children at "moderate" risk in middle school and works with them to improve health status through conflict resolution, substance abuse prevention, and fostering self-esteem. A New Beginnings program provides on-the-job and college training for healthcare positions. Ford supports ten high school students a year in summer apprenticeships in science.

The impact of Ford's community outreach programs is shown in Table 4.4. While the program is substantial, it amounts to only about 1.5 percent of the system's total operations. This is partly because of the success the organization has had in raising outside grant support. Many of its programs, such as the school health program, are funded by grants from other agencies. Still, the total for Ford is much smaller than that of either Moses Cone or Legacy, which are close to 7 percent of operations. Several centers are exploring community needs and evaluating programs for them. The Center for Medical Treatment Effectiveness Programs studies differences in the health needs of the African American population from those of other populations. It has identified treatment response differences and has developed protocols to accommodate these. The Center has studied the epidemiology of asthma, has developed education for asthmatic teenagers, and is funded to develop smoking cessation for adults around asthmatic children as well as church-based outreach programs and inpatient education modules.

Research and Education

The Henry Ford Medical Group conducts a program of clinical research similar to that of leading academic medical centers, funded by the National Insitutes of Health and private foundations. The

Table 4.4 Measures of Community Contribution

Contribution	1995	1996
Uncompensated care	$42,846	$47,900
Health promotion, education, and prevention	*	1,995
Donations to community charities		1,714
Community health education/outreach		3,607
Total	$42,987	$55,216

*Detail is not available for 1995.

program is large enough to make it one of the top 10 percent of that group in the country. The system also includes a number of projects that are more population-based in nature, as well as several ventures, supported by one or more of the expert centers, which are on the borderline between conducting research and changing clinical behavior.

The Henry Ford Medical Group has a historical commitment to medical education. It has over 800 residents, 350 in primary care, 50 to 60 in research, and about 400 in specialty training. Glenn Davis, M.D., vice president for academic affairs, explains how this contributes to the overall goals:

> "First, we think that education helps provide a better quality of care and an environment of learning that makes people want to come here. The Henry Ford Medical Group identified the practice of medicine in groups as a core competency. Doing that well means scholarship and professionalism, and creation of a common culture. Second, we can hire out of that pool. Third, we think certain kinds of benefits will be linked to medical schools, and we don't want to forego them. Medicare graduate medical education is net money to the system, and residents are cheap labor. At least on the inpatient side, even if you increase the quality of education and reduce the workload, they earn more than they cost. In the ambulatory setting, it seems to us that we are at worst breaking even.
>
> "Part of the problem is replacing the residents. You have to produce alternative care. Most of the specialist education programs are small and tight. We couldn't reduce them further; we'd have to close them. If you start without residents, it's one thing, but making the transition from a resident-driven inpatient service in a highly tertiary inpatient setting with intensive need for physician involvement and restructuring that for clinical nurses, PAs, and house physicians is extremely expensive and culturally challenging."

Henry Ford Implements Its Strategic Objectives

Henry Ford Health System is eight times the size of Moses Cone in Greensboro, and four times bigger than Legacy in Portland. It is the only one of the three that operates its own health insurance company. It wrestles daily with all of the problems of large eastern U.S. cities. It deals explicitly with a problem neither Moses Cone nor Legacy faces, the fact that the metropolitan area population expects to be treated in its own home region rather than being referred to the city.

HFHS expanded its strategy in three major steps. Vin Sahney, senior vice president for planning and strategic development, explains that evolution:

> "The strategy in the 1980s was to expand in the suburbs. That would diversify our revenue base and balance the inner city population with a paying one. It would also expand ambulatory care. Around 1990, when Gail Warden came on board, we decided that we wanted to have a close tie with a medical school and to be in teaching and research. We discussed getting out of the 'cutting edge' and just becoming a second-tier tertiary care hospital, not into getting NIH funds and independent research. The board said no; they wanted us to be in research. It was a very conscious decision.
>
> "Out of it came three things. One, that we had to raise funds to support teaching and research. That was the origin of the Fund for Henry Ford Hospital. We said to the board, 'If you think this is important, you must help us, because in the long run it will not be viable financed from patient care.' The second was that we needed a better partnership with a medical school. Our relation with Case Western Reserve is going well. It generates 20 students per year, and has been supported by the Robert Wood Johnson Foundation. Then we developed a multischool strategy, so now we have three or four relationships, including one with an osteopathic school.
>
> "We also decided to expand our insurance program. Until about 1988, we offered only an HMO with employed physicians. We decided to offer a broader physician panel, a PPO, and point-of-service products. In the '80s we were looking at HAP as a means of filling hospital beds. Now we look at it as a business in its own right. So we have opened up to independent physician networks in all the suburban counties. The reason is quite simple. If we don't open it up, someone else will use those networks.
>
> "The third part of the 1990 strategy was that we should be big enough to have about a 30 percent market share. We really wanted to protect ourselves from for-profits coming into the market, either provider companies or insurance companies. We needed to be of sufficient size and distribution that would be hard to ignore. That's about one-and-one-half million people. Also, size is important to support our tertiary business. We need a base of a million people to do a good program in heart surgery or brain tumors. So acquisitions and partners have

been an important part of our strategy. We looked globally and by regions in the metropolitan area. We also are working on Detroit. It has a million in population and a lack of primary care. So we are going to expand primary care in the city. We have a plan for centers throughout the city, which we have started to implement."

Value to Stakeholders

The trustee role in value

Allan Gilmour, chair of the board of trustees, describes how the Henry Ford board functions:

"I've been on the board since 1987. I was on the first futures committee, in 1989. When they learned I was going to retire from the Ford Motor Company, they asked me if I'd be chair. I said no, I wasn't interested at all, but they came back and asked me if they divide the job in two, chair of the board and chair of the executive committee, and I agreed.

"The board's job is to support some of the priorities, quantify some of the objectives. It's different from a corporate for-profit board, because on those I can exchange Ford Motor experience, readings from other companies, whatever. Some outside observers believe that business people aren't forceful enough on nonprofit boards. That's true; we're not. We're scared we'll come across as the mercenaries, or mean people. It is harder for the layman to make a contribution in healthcare than it is at XYZ company.

"The first futures committee was several years ago. (We had another one last year.) It looked at strategic positioning. From my experience in business, the first objective of any organization is survival, and the second is success. We used those thoughts as we figured out what we should be doing."

Allan identifies four broad issues in the Henry Ford strategy: "retailing healthcare," value, survival, and continuing its wholly owned health insurance company. Then he adds a fifth, which commits Henry Ford to pioneering changes:

"First, we have a pretty broad-spread system of clinics and hospitals. That's an important part of our strategy. What our customers want is convenience. I said to some of the management and doctors last month that we are in the retailing business, retailing healthcare. Some of the doctors thought that was a low-class way of describing what we do, but there are many parallels. It is convenience, access, the right kind of facility, the right kind of professional to do the job.

"The second thing the board has spent a lot of time on is quality. It includes customer satisfaction, patient satisfaction, physician satisfaction, and employee satisfaction, but the ones who really count are the patients, both the ones we've got and the ones we wish we had. It includes access and convenience, but also a certain warmth and character that big institutions find difficult to carry off. It clearly includes professional care. It is closely related to price. In a relatively short number of years, there has been a shift from cost-plus to price forced on us by government or by employers.

"The New Century Program here will cut $20 million to $30 million a year out of expenses. We have already looked at next year. It's a heck of a job, but there isn't any alternative. First, we have to be competitive in our own market; second, to learn from what other people have done. What we are seeing is improvements in everything from capacity utilization to labor productivity to pharmaceutical costs.

"The car dealers are interesting. How do they find their futures—best practices, whatever? It's certain the manufacturers don't know. The so-called "20 groups' get together two or three times a year—twenty dealers, same brand, not in competition—to talk about it. That's an interesting way for smaller enterprises to work on their problems. Ford management participates in the Six Clinics Group and the 50-member Group Practice Improvement Network.

"The third thing is the rapid change in this industry. How do we ensure that we are one of the successful survivors? There is no law that says we have to be, but we think we've done enough—enough traditions and enough value—that we should be. So when we see mergers and acquisitions, the growth of for-profits and the growth of HMOs, we try to see how we can participate in that. That was the principle of the futures committee. It's facilities and people, goals, competency, and the financial wherewithal, and trying to put together a reputation for excellence in a very big place where excellence takes on different meanings. If I come for a physical exam, it's a very different problem than if I'm here with a serious cancer problem. Trying to figure out that range of customer wants. We will see more well people than we have in the past, I hope."

Allan's fourth point, owning a health insurance company, is different from most American healthcare organizations, including Moses Cone and Legacy:

> "The fourth issue is the right positioning for Health Alliance Plan. I'm not sure the record of healthcare organizations owning insurance companies is terribly good. As a member of the board of Prudential Insurance, I'm not sure the record is terribly great for insurance companies owning HMOs, either. It's something we are all trying to figure out. We have to run an efficient, responsive, and growing business.
>
> "I'm not sorry we own HAP, but we board members haven't paid nearly enough attention to it. We need to find a new CEO. The ideal combination is someone who can run the place and also lead it to new heights no one has ever thought of. We think we are good enough on the operations side that we can go for a visionary in marketing and product design. One reason I hesitate is that what makes an insurance company successful is not what makes a healthcare company successful.
>
> "Ideally, HAP has the potential to teach the organization how to manage risk. It's a source of patients. It's more profitable than the rest of the place. It's an opportunity for growth. There's plenty of pressure on HAP to cut costs, but at this point it's been 'What do we have to do?' 'What's the competition?' and so forth, as opposed to our own internal, 'Hey, just go do it.'"

And Allan Gilmour's fifth "broad issue," changing philosophies about medicine and healthcare, is even more radical:

> "The last issue is putting all the pieces together, figuring out—this is shorthand—how to move from some of the concepts of medical schools to more of the concepts of public health schools, population-based medicine, a much better statistical analysis of results. It is surprising to me how little evidence-based medicine there is.
>
> "I don't want to minimize what medical schools are doing, but I do want the whole place to understand that living is much more about evidence-based medicine, much more about customer satisfaction, much more about population-based medicine, where we are responsible for a number of lives in the broadest sense. We are not Henry Ford Illness System or Sickness System, or Tertiary System. We are a total health system, and it is immunizations of little kids, and hospice, and

working in the public schools, all of those things. When I see the Senior Plus program at HAP assigning patients to a panel and then having them come in for a history and some checks right away, it is almost the principle of insurance.

"We haven't pushed this at the board, but we are increasingly talking about it. One of the disconnects in our merger talks with other systems is that the other trustees don't talk this language at all. They talk good old academic departments. If you are good in urology, and ophthalmology, and podiatry, and everything in between, you'll be all right. We are on a different wavelength almost. There's some feeling like that here. A substantial number of our doctors would love to be called professor. I don't disagree with that, but I want to segment the market more. When I have my appendix out, I'm not interested in statistics. But later on, I'd like more involvement in downstream and upstream, and some outcome measures."

Allan goes on to suggest three pieces of advice for Henry Ford and others interested in the same path—stay local, keep the board out of operations, and focus on the insurance premium:

"We should stay home, continue our focus on Detroit. Healthcare organizations underestimate the management problems of size and geographic spread. It isn't the same task, just four times bigger. The complexities are more than that. I think we should be able to drive to anyplace we operate in an hour. Things are obviously going more nationwide; perhaps healthcare will too. The auto companies run much more easily on an international basis than healthcare, in part because we delegate the retailing to a whole bunch of independent people. Wal-Mart is a national retailing company, but they don't manufacture or engineer their product. This is a personal service business with a professional content. Who knows if I'm right, but I wish to be conservative on this. The consequences of taking too much risk are very severe.

"We have a board that is not meddlesome. That doesn't mean we don't have things to say, but we are not trying to micromanage. It's not even setting the broad direction, it's agreeing to it and commenting on it: did it get changed a little from the futures committee? Boards don't run things, in the for-profit world or the not-for-profit world. If they do, we are in real trouble. Boards listen. They bring experience and judgment, but they don't say, 'Go this way instead of the other,' because they don't know enough about it. If we see companies that are off track, the board's only real remedy, other than selling out, is to change the players. We don't say, 'I'll give you a strategic plan. We board members will have it written down a week from Thursday.' No, we won't.

"Employers in general should focus on the insurance premium, rather than the pieces of the costs, because they don't know enough about the pieces. All of us have enough to do running our own businesses not to try running someone else's. However, they will want to be knowledgeable about the trade-offs—the quality trade-off, the education trade-off, and so forth. Most of the hospitals won't be bashful moaning and groaning about those things. We pushed on the organizations like this one, and we got results, but as outsiders we could never tell what the cost structure was and what was possible. And we are all skittish on the tradeoff between cost and quality. In the car business, of course, they go together. Indirectly, that's being worked on here, through clinical pathways and similar methods. All these things need to be considered."

Mariam Nolan, trustee and chair of the quality committee:

"I think Henry Ford is a leader in healthcare. We ought to let people know what we are doing more aggressively, because I think there is a lot they can learn from us. I think we are a very important research institution. I don't think we get enough visibility for the quality of research we are doing. It's important for this region and the world. To some extent, we underplay our leadership role. We don't tell enough people what we are doing. I bet we are better known for quality outside this region than inside.

"My opinion is that there is a place for driving down costs. It's an issue the board addresses, and Gail [Warden, CEO] and other management focus on. Some feel maybe too much so. Part of my role is to balance making sure we find the highest quality at the lowest cost, but not driving costs down so far that you sacrifice quality. When push comes to shove, we need to make sure the quality is where it needs to be. Maybe they are not mutually exclusive, but you can't talk just about driving down costs. So we look at all the indicators, not just one of them. The final question at today's meeting of the quality committee was, 'Are we hurting ourselves if our efforts to cut cost reduce the quality of employees we want to hire?' A regional board member raised the question. It's always a balancing act. There is a very high priority on being the low-cost provider in this region, but not at the sacrifice of what we also think is important.

"One of the things Henry Ford is good at is educating us as lay trustees and getting us smart enough to understand the conversation, through large day-long sessions to committee meetings that are learning and trying to figure it out. This is as opposed to decision making—how to understand enough of the complexities that we don't make dumb decisions. Secondly, I think as trustees we continue to ask the questions that may not necessarily come from management, bring a different perspective, and continue to push for looking beyond the system. We make sure the targets set for next year's improvement are aggressive enough, and there's accountability for whether they are met. It's a steady, informed pressure. There was a question at the last meeting about clinical pathways. We had a 15-minute discussion that made it clear none of us understood what they are doing. We spent half an hour this morning trying to understand what they are, why they are important. Now we can deal with those issues."

She describes the role of the quality committee, which monitors all performance measures for the board:

"We are not a bashful committee. We may be wrong, but we don't back off. At the same time, we have a very deep respect for the quality of our management. We know they know a whole lot more about each one of these numbers than we do.

"We have to be smart enough and nimble enough to move with what is incredibly rapid change. The volunteer trustees need to understand that they are here to help the system move. I know charities where the trustees are being served by making them feel good. You can't afford that in healthcare today. Yes, you want them to feel good, but I'll be darned if they shouldn't also want to really talk business. One thing that Gail does is give us stuff to read. I can't take a course, but if I can read three articles every other week, I can get a little smarter.

"We try to do our business in a way that is acceptable to the system but that pushes. We organize how we do our work. We are getting better at rolling stuff up so we can look at the system rather than the individual units. We are looking at five or six cross-cutting themes. We try not to do what the other boards and committees do, but to ask the broad questions and keep our eye on the ball as to the key places where we can intervene to make major differences. If there is a central theme it is customer satisfaction. We go through a fairly elaborate agenda-setting process, which we negotiate with management. Sometimes what we ask for is new information that they haven't assembled before.

"We have certain responsibilities, like medical staff credentialling, but what do we really do? We raise questions. Provide support. Push hard if we have to. Help people think about things a little differently. The whole spider [that is, all of Figure 4.1] is our domain. Today they were showing us patient days per thousand in the various regions, 247 per thousand versus 139 benchmark. We need to understand why it is this way, what to do about it. We'll decide in September whether we should change our focus, or stick with it a while longer.

"I think it's important for volunteers to feel that the time they are giving to a healthcare system is worth it. That relates to having enough skill to make a contribution. To help volunteers know the areas they are good at. I'm incredibly glad I joined the Ford board. It's helped me in my own job, and it has helped me help the community, and it's fun! I chair the Michigan Foundation board, but I have no experience with a large business like this one. When I joined the quality committee, I said, 'I don't have a clue what's going on here.' They said, 'You can learn.' I'll be better next year, better yet the year after."

Gail Warden, president and CEO:

"We try to build an approach to managing that enables every level of management, medical staff, and board to understand the direction that the organization is going. The organization is a learning environment that exposes the physicians and managers to the principles of quality management. Although there were a lot of different cultures in each of the business units, quality management became a common way of approaching issues that makes us a collegial kind of organization, kinder and friendlier when you are trying to deal with problems, rather than one that fosters turf battles and a lot of silos. The other thing is that, starting with the board and then moving down, we really tried to get a sense about our environment, our future environment, and the strategies we will have to employ in order to be successful.

"The futures committee made a real effort to educate us all on the environment. From the very beginning, I tried to make everybody feel that there were no second-class citizens, and that everybody had an important perspective that had to be incorporated in any strategic plan.

"Third, we tried to dictate a process that encouraged people to develop the strategic plan in their business unit from the bottom up. The only thing we dictated was process—things you had to include in your plan. But we let them 'flow their plan up' instead of planning from the top, once we got agreement on the environment. The operating divisions and the staff divisions developed their own strategic plan."

Gail gives an example of how Henry Ford uses its planning process to identify and resolve potentially troublesome issues:

"One of the most successful things we did, we had them identify the issues they thought senior management and medical leadership had to deal with if they were going to do a good job. Each plan has a system issues section. We tried to deal with the systems issues, to remove the obstacles the units perceived. For example, the Health Alliance Plan CEO was the enemy across the street, even though Henry Ford owned HAP. The Medical Group says, 'You have to stop creating all these damned networks that compete with us.' HAP says, 'We have some criteria on it. How will networks be selected?' We resolved a lot of it by giving HAP a seat at the table in the management team, and letting them participate in the discussions.

"We reconciled the conflicting positions. We worked through the issues in retreats. We worked through some in one-on-one discussions. We used the HAP board, the system board, and the advisory boards in the regions. I had caucuses of the board members so everybody knew what we were up to. I created quarterly policy issues lists that all the boards discussed. When it came clear we were going to compete for the Medicaid managed care contract, the same person led a discussion at every one of the boards about the implications. It was a revenue stream we couldn't afford not to have, and we could not afford a reputation that we would not take care of that population, even though we did not covet it. We talked about the need to create a better delivery system and move it out into the neighborhoods. When we finished the discussion, everybody had been exposed to it; they felt like they had some input into it; and they bought in to what we were doing."

Measured performance and continuous improvement

Quantitative and comparative self-evaluation is a way of life at Henry Ford. Gail Warden talks about some of the issues that have stimulated the development of measures:

> "We have done pretty well in bringing down utilization and costs among the under-65 patients. We were $145 PMPM a few years ago. Now we are below $130. If the drug costs didn't kill us, we'd be even better. Our reading is that even though there is a lot of rhetoric, the employers are pretty happy with where we are. They are unhappy with the drug costs, and so are we, but neither they nor we can do much about it. We are doing a pretty good job with drug utilization, but prices are rising 9 or 10 percent a year.
>
> "In 1994, we thought we would take a bath on Medicare, and we were getting a lot of heat from the auto companies on reducing price. In a way, we let the autos create a crisis that let us consolidate, cut costs, and reduce utilization. It really was a campaign. We had videotapes, speeches, flyers. In the end we only laid off about 300 people, but we eliminated a lot of jobs.
>
> "A lot of the overall satisfaction numbers are driven by Henry Ford Hospital, which is an old facility. When we get the new wing open and the patient-focused units, and the systems reengineered and parking made easier, those numbers are going up. When Mary Hitchcock [a medical center in New Hampshire] opened its new facility, it went from 65 percent satisfaction to 85/90 like that! Wyandotte's new wing is getting much better satisfaction scores.
>
> "Seventy-seven percent of our employees say they know what our mission statement is. That's normally about 30 percent.
>
> "Henry Ford is for innovation; that is what attracts a lot of our people here. We make the resources available for people to innovate. We don't use resources just for some guy who thinks he has a research project, we do it to support the organization. That's why we have the Center for Clinical Effectiveness, the Center for Health Systems Studies, and the Center

for Health Promotion and Disease Prevention. All of these centers more than pay for themselves between the contribution they make to the organization and the grants that they attract."

Vin Sahney, senior vice president for planning and strategic development:

"Four years ago we decided we wanted to focus on four key system initiatives, with measures for each. One was growth. One was customer focus, satisfying the customer. The third was cost and financial performance. We looked at cost per member per month. We decreased our premium in '96 and '97, and held the increase this year to one percent. We agreed that the market will set the price and we must come below it. We made $40 million last year and $50 million this. That meant we not only had to meet inflation, but generate another $10 million on the bottom line. It comes in cost per discharge and days of hospital care per 1,000 members.

"A lot of the efficiency gains come from system integration. We have consolidated in the administrative areas—purchasing, laundry, finance, and planning. Now we work in the clinical areas. Pharmacy was consolidated to a product line last year. Optometry was moved to a joint venture with an outside company. Laboratory is under study now.

"It's not the kind of pressure like Minneapolis, with the Buyers Action Group coming together and saying to cut costs; it's not there yet. Our trustees might ask, if slightly differently, 'How does your cost compare to your competitors', and how will you bring your costs down?' This happened when Blue Cross priced its HMO $10 a month below ours. It's more of a competitive-based discussion than a community-based discussion. If all our competitors' costs were two dollars higher than ours, I don't think our trustees would have asked us to lower our costs.

"Don't underestimate Gail's role. A lot of the way the institution goes is his doing. He's kind of quiet. He's the most quietly effective person I've ever met. He created the Center for Clinical Effectiveness when the doctors really did not want one. He just set a little money aside and started it going. The Center for Health Promotion, the doctors didn't want that either. He just got it going. The community program, government relations, business relations, he just created them. He has a much better view of what needs to be done."

Peter Butler, senior vice president and chief administrative officer (shortly after this interview, Peter resigned to become CEO of Methodist Health System, Houston, Texas):

> "The spider diagrams (Figure 4.1) are a major innovation. If you ask our trustees, they were tired of looking at net income as the only measure of performance. They said, 'If we are going to meet our objectives, we need a balanced scorecard.' You set this in motion and people come up with a million things. We can't keep track of all that. We began to narrow it down to the key indicators. What is exciting is that we have quantifiable objectives for all our strategic goals, all our regions, and down to the care team level. You've got a consistent way of looking at how you are doing from the board level to the individual provider. Days per 1,000 members, pharmacy costs, med/surg length of stay across, customer satisfaction, and clinical integration are available all the way from the system level to the individual.
>
> "I present to the quality committee of the board every quarter and say, 'Here's how we are doing.' The diagram is a clever way of showing achievement versus goal. If you get the red line [marked with small triangles] outside the blue line, you are doing well. It identifies things that will make a difference.
>
> "The regions get similar reports, usually with additional measures. They see how they are doing relative to the others. Suddenly we get internal benchmarking. We also have best in the country for every one of the measures. You learn about your population, too. When you look at central Detroit, sitting up there with 393 days per 1,000, while the northeast region is at 188, you really start drilling down into your individual communities and getting into some of the variance. The northeast region is spending $17 per member per month on pharmacy, by far the leaders. Then you find that they have two AIDS specialists. The cost per discharge breaks out into the hospitals in the region. Workforce representation is a diversity measure, and we add employee and physician satisfaction at the regional level. Many of the measures will be revised or changed as strategic issues change. We are missing some clinical outcomes, and so forth. We'll develop those."

Peter describes the issues behind the spider diagram. Accuracy, credibility, incentives, and a way to reach consensus on improvements are all involved:

"We've been at this for three years. This took a long time, because you need to have a source of truth, some group designated to make the measurement and report it, and a regular schedule for reporting. Some measures are not here because we haven't been able to get them accurately. This is the year we really solidified it, and attached incentive compensation. We have three-year rolling plans and commitment for what each region is going to do in the next year. The Medical Group and the hospitals in a region come forward together, somewhere between two and four people, to describe how they are going to provide services and be number one or two in that community. We are getting more collaboration leaving it that way than trying to create a formal regional budget."

The quality initiative has passed a test under fire, Peter says:

"Four years ago, Blue Care Network gained a $10 premium advantage on Henry Ford. HFHS responded with three major initiatives, thinking through regionalization issues, measurement and incentives issues, and patient care delivery issues. Those were the responses that had some payoff.

"The real response was that we sucked it in and said, 'We're going to lower our price over three years to match the competition.' We were able to do that because the hospitals did so well reducing length of stay. The Medical Group laid the groundwork, but when all is said and done, Henry Ford Hospital [the downtown flagship] went from zero bottom line to $54 million profit last year. It and Wyandotte Hospital's dramatic turnaround paid for the decline in premium and for losses in the Medical Group that resulted from the same changes. We have overcome inflation, and customer satisfaction had to be improved. That's why the group incurred a loss."

Tom McNulty, senior vice president, chief financial officer, and treasurer, describes the evolution of the financial operation:

"In 1983, Henry Ford Hospital was successful in terms of reputation, but not as a business. The reason they weren't successful as a business is that they did not perceive themselves as a business. They did things like failing to convert their revenue to cash, and like accepting their way or process as the best without seeking outside competitors or benchmarks. As a result, no one was in charge of the business. They found themselves without cash. When I was recruited here, we actually had no cash in the bank. We had borrowed money against our fleet of cars.

"We began to use the assets of the corporation more actively in the business, getting joint ventures [with real estate investors] to support clinic expansions, for example. We also put in a budgeting system. The operating units did not want to be accountable for the budget, so we had to push it down and get them to understand they owned it. Once it got played back to us, I set a target for net income. I just said, 'We gotta earn 2 percent.' Once we broke out of the shell, then Henry Ford started to grow. All of those strategies are still in place. Not only are they still in place, they are not challenged. Most people understand why they are there and that they are necessary."

Tom says that the Henry Ford board finance committees have set the tone:

"We are more conservative than aggressive. We are conservative on reserves, and on filings for cost reports. We run a little under 3 percent operating profits. We could ratchet costs down and do better, but that seems to be the comfort zone between earnings and expenses. The net income is targeted to meet our capital budget over five years.

"The finance committee has had some pretty smart chairs. The chair I started with was the chief financial officer of Ford Motor Company. He introduced the concept of unit costs. We still look at that. His successor was a vice president of finance. They asked very good questions, and there weren't too many places to hide. They wanted to know why and where about costs. Now the chair is CFO at Chrysler Corporation. They have for years created the discipline that says, 'I need to understand what's going on here, and I'm not just going to accept what you are telling me. If you are going to try to give me a snow job, I've got my overcoat on.'

"We've created enough credibility in our financial division that we have the opportunity to do good reporting without any criticism from other officers. Before we get into a financial presentation where I think we have some differences, we sit down with all the officers and discuss how we want to present. We can't not tell the board, but we can tell them now how we are going to change. It's been a culture that we created.

"The credit for the turnaround in the hospitals goes to the operating folks, who did a good job of managing their costs.

Revenue increased as well. Even though the number of patients did not change much, payment per unit increased dramatically. A lot of the reduction was clinical decisions. The doctors just did not admit as many less severe patients and found more of the sickest ones."

Tom goes on to describe what's coming next from financial operations:

"The financial officers of the subsidiaries do not report directly to me. I felt that the CFOs should be part of their local operating teams. Indirectly, they are all part of a financial officers group that I chair. We create policy and direction, and they work with operations. Last year I was really concerned about the changing nature of the financial officer role. The group decided to develop a list of questions over about ten dimensions of what a financial officer would want to know. So we sat down and reduced it to 40 questions. Then we picked six organizations with good reputations and good financial records—for-profit and not-for-profit, outside healthcare, and in healthcare. We had representatives of our group visit them with our outside auditor.

"They came back with comparisons of how each one does things—everything from financial reporting to staff development to internal audit. Then we looked at what we called 'successful practices.' We asked each team to describe how they would perform these activities if they could start with a clean slate. I did not participate. The members of the group did it on their own. That became the basis for our strategic analysis division.

"The strategic analysis division will spend a lot of time working with the operating people to understand what is happening. The division will do four things. One is the budgeting. The second is forecasting, which will be driving our costs in the future. The reason is that the board officers now say, 'I don't want to know what happened; tell me what's going to happen.' They want to know next-quarter earnings. That means that you really have to understand your business. Not only do we have to prepare a forecast for the second quarter, we have to explain what we know now that we did not know in the first quarter.

"The third function of strategic analysis is product costing. We truly should cost our product like industry does. We have to have activity-based costing, which will tell us what the relationships are and the residuals are and how it affects the distribution. Fourth, we have to provide performance analysis. There has to be a group of people saying, 'Hey, here's how the rest of the world is performing. And, by the way, that doesn't mean they are right. It means that's how they are performing.' One of the things wrong with this industry is that we measure ourselves against bad benchmarks. We just assume that they are right.

"The strategic analysis division will try to create this kind of intelligence for the operating units. We are going to force down as much data as possible on the operating divisions, with . . . analysis of the data. We are creating a source of truth that makes sure we've got the right data and everybody's using them. The accounting and financial reporting division will concentrate on the internal accounting, to make sure it is consistent with standards. The internal audits division will check on compliance. The accounting offices in the business units can concentrate on generating reports and information for their CEO and not worry about these functions."

Information services is an area where Henry Ford has invested heavily. Tom describes some of the progress:

"We are following the same approach in information services as we did with strategic analysis. We've identified six sites with dimensions we are interested in. So far, we are ahead. Our managed care product is one of the most advanced around. Our operations people are spoiled. They keep saying we are way behind the curve, because we don't have fancy things like laptop computers and these gadgets you can walk in and out of rooms with using radio communication. We have almost 80 percent of the lab information in our system automated. We are not trying to tout it as an automated record, although that is what we are moving toward. We are doing fiber optic wiring at 150 settings. People can sign in at any time, and access all our systems.

"I've been saying, 'I'm not going to spend $30 million on improving information services, because I don't know what the value added is. Show me what value you add to the clinical or management process. If you bring great value, we'll add your equipment. If not, we will keep going with the tried and true.'

"We are going to build the infrastructure. Creating knowledge for the physician is absolutely important. Computer literacy is going to drive the use of information systems. If we could create interactive virtual databases that allow people to get in and out, I would feel comfortable. The real issue is twofold: to create the system that captures the information, and to create the corporate data store. As our needs change in the future, it's a matter of knowing how to access the stuff. Not only retrieval and analysis, but also maintenance, how long you keep the data and in what form."

But if the glass looks half full to Tom, it looks half empty to some of the physicians. Rick Ward, M.D., director of the Center for Clinical Effectiveness, looks at the progress of information systems and points out its limitations:

"Information systems are the only feasible method for implementing practice improvements that will stay implemented and that can be scaled [that is, distributed effectively to all the caregivers in the system]. There's a finite number of things you can bombard a clinician with. It really doesn't work unless you can get to the system the physician uses, every encounter, every day. If you are not working on that, you are not working on anything permanent. What we have now is not that. Our systems so far are largely about looking up data, access to what would normally be on the chart. They don't actually do much yet. They don't accept an order, they aren't the basis of communication between physicians, they are not reminders or alerts, there's no automated work flow. Nevertheless, we are closer to the launch pad than others are. There's nobody that's really head and shoulders ahead of us. There are now a lot of organizations working on the problem, and a dozen recognized leaders. It's been poorly supported by vendors. Some people think that the vendors are too invested in the existing systems.

"We have our corporate data store, which is an archive of administrative data, and a clinical data repository. We are well prepared for the work station, but we are quite a way from it. It's been very frustrating to me. We have had very good consensus in the medical community about what we need, even to the architecture we need to do it, but it has been a tremendous battle within the organization to push that agenda forward. It gets funded, but not at the level we need.

"The technical issues are not that difficult anymore. We've had connectivity at every location for a long time. The last two years we have been upgrading that, making it more flexible. The pathways database only cost about $50,000 to add to that. I think it's one of the applications of a future work station, where the clinician is directly recording information. There will be a default to the pathway, and a way to review the documentation for the default, and a way to override it, so the clinicians are not being victimized by a computer system. It's definitely necessary to get practice improvements that stick and that are scalable."

Training and incentives for value

Henry Ford Health System aggressively enhances the skills of all its workers. Learning something new is so deeply buried in the culture that it is taken for granted. If you are an hourly worker, there are courses offered by human resources and tuition assistance for outside training. As you rise in the management and professional ranks, more resources are available. The managers have advanced training in total quality management and in supervisory skills. Doctors and nurses have a Managed Care College to learn what Ford is doing to improve patient care.

You can call on consultative assistance from the various centers and several of the units operating under Vin Sahney. Most of this support is without charge, either to you or to your operating budget. Management services has help available for eliminating costs and for process improvements, supporting doctors and care teams, and developing annual budgets and three-year financial plans. For larger undertakings, planning and marketing offers service comparable to outside consultants at substantially lower costs.

The people providing this support expect to respond as part of their job. You will have a chance to influence their annual performance evaluation. On top of this, as part of the Ford System you will probably be invited to join one of the endless parade of task forces, work groups, and committees set up to address specific problems. These activities are purposeful, effective, multidisciplined groups with extensive staff support. If you contribute, the reward is more assignments and promotion. If you don't learn from them, you probably aren't cut out for Henry Ford.

The principle incentive is achieving the goals of the spider diagram. You set your own objectives, with a full understanding of their importance to the organization and the approaches you would use to meet them. Almost all of the time, you will succeed. The goals are set so that you can improve: you're not being set up to fail. If by some misfortune you do fail, you will know you let the team down. The close attention you get from your colleagues and your supervisor will help you succeed on the second try. In a very small number of cases, they may convince you that your career lies elsewhere.

Dennis Dowdell, corporate vice president for human resources, describes the basic training programs:

> "Human resources is very much into performance management processes. That's our largest strategic issue. In the next month or two we will be changing the performance measurement tools to include competency for each position, business literacy, customer service, interpersonal skills, teamwork—not necessarily tasks, but the competencies you want someone to have to do a specific job. The competencies are rated by peer evaluation, by '360 degree' evaluations, and by customer satisfaction.
>
> "We are spending about $5.2 million to create a state-of-the-art human resources information system. The return on that is about two years, one of the best returns in the organization. It's been benchmarked across the country as the best model. Along with it, we've created a succession plan. As the organization grows, we can create development plans not only for the organization but for physician leadership. We can identify gaps down to the director level. We can also look at the promotion of minorities and women. The program is beginning to give us the database we need.
>
> "Quality classes, Managed Care College classes, labor relations, diversity training, and management skills are offered on a continuing basis. We've had about 27,000 enrollees in courses, for 17,000 full-time equivalent personnel. We pay for external learning options for physicians and for management. The physicians have agreed that they will take three of these a year. Most managers take at least two.
>
> "People don't fail because they don't know how to do the tasks of their jobs. They really fail because they are not customer service–minded, they can't work in teams, and things like that. A tremendous number of people take our change management courses. We select 45 to 50 people from throughout the system for our leadership class. They go through an intensive exposure to all parts of the Henry Ford Health System. That's an attempt to create health system executives, rather than hospital leaders or outpatient leaders. We also have about 40 people in our mentoring program, managers who are teamed with a

formally designated mentor other than their boss. Many of the senior management team participate as mentors. Mentees are diverse, including supervisors in hospital and business services. They attend board meetings and high-level meetings.

"We want to be able to demonstrate the relationship of initiatives in human resources to improving actual patient care. We know that we have improved our customer service ratings by 4 percent. I think it's a combination of our training, behavioral and competency interviewing, and the decentralization of the human resources function. Whatever the cumulative effects, the results are getting better.

"Our diversity program has won seven national and local awards. We have been selected by the Hay Group as an example of the best reengineering in the industry. We did it ourselves, and we are very proud of it."

Additional financial reward is a minor incentive. Dennis describes the limited incentive pay program:

"We have very little in the way of incentives for the hourly group, but for the past three years we have awarded an annual all-employee bonus. This year it was about $167 per employee. Part-time employees get a fraction. There are no gainsharing plans. The best incentive plans are ones where the worker can see what has to be done to receive the incentive. In a large healthcare system like Henry Ford, it is very difficult to see what creates success; there are a lot of factors outside the employee's control or understanding. It will be a disincentive if we introduce a plan where the employees feel we stacked the deck with measures over which they have no influence.

"The top four levels of leadership have an incentive plan. It covers 150 people. It works reasonably well. It ranges from 2 percent of base to 25 percent. We have no plans to expand it; the next level of managers would bring in 2,000 people. When you consider the next level, you have to recognize that our overall combined time-off benefits program is the most generous in the area. We are achieving our goals without an incentive plan like that, and 85 or 90 percent of our people think this a quality place to work. We are continuously stressing innovation to achieve higher levels."

John Wisniewski, M.D., director of the Managed Care College:

"The Managed Care College is a small program designed for healthcare professionals and historically has attracted almost all its enrollment from the Medical Group. The concept is to combine professional development with clinical improvement, to use hands-on improvement projects as one of the learning vehicles. We have a voluntary enrollment. About 325 out of 1,000 doctors in the Medical Group, and three to four times that many nurses, administrators, and others have gone through the program.

"We try to bring a multidisciplinary team to the classroom. It's all centered on what it means to manage healthcare here at the Henry Ford Health System. What can we do as front-line providers to improve the value of healthcare, to work more effectively together, to analyze where we are weak and make it strong, to analyze where we are strong and make it better? How can we tap into the resources of HFHS? What does all that mean to our patients, and the front line of care? How much of this system is set up to serve the interests of its management and succeed as a business, and how much is really oriented toward improving care where it counts?

"We pose the questions just like that. It's not a propaganda program. It's a place where it is safe to come and talk about the experience of working here, and about the organization, to share opinions and ideas, but also to acquaint yourself with what's going on in other parts of the system and the country. Most importantly, the program really seeks to help people feel more comfortable about working here, to help them discover new ways to tap in. We bring people from different sides of town who have never met one another to sit and discuss common cause issues, and learn together the gap between the system's aspirations and its actual performance. We hope they discover what it means to them, and where they can contribute.

"We also try to get people involved in some small clinical improvement projects for their local population. They identify a group of patients, usually peple with the same chronic disease, and over the ten months they look at what they can do to improve the care and actually make some or all of the improvements they come up with."

Patricia Stolz, director of healthcare quality improvement education and research:

"My department is the owner of the 'Quality 101' teaching programs: how to flowchart a process, how to think about your work as a series of steps, how to collect data about your process. It's a three-day program. We reach about 500 people a year with that. We are now reaching front-line supervisors. We also teach 'Advanced Statistical Thinking and Tools,' 'Facilitating Change,' and a monthly seminar, 'Foundations of Continuing Improvement' taught by Paul Batalden [a nationally known physician and leader of clinical quality improvement, who holds a part time professorship at Ford].

"We want to work as lean as we can on the front line, and we don't want to take people off line for education activity. Putting people through courses is a useful index of how your teaching resources are utilized, but I'm less certain that it puts skills in place. I've talked to a number of people six months after the early classes, and they hadn't done anything yet. As the concept of work as process and a focus on the customer become ways we regularly think about work, the local units will train their own people. So I am redesigning our curriculum as a toolbox for first-line supervisors and team members. We will supply the toolbox through a loose network of facilitators. The facilitators are leaders of formal local networks. The course will be for supervisors and managers.

"We use a self-assessment workbook to help our leadership team to identify improvement targets. This year, as a first step in developing their plan, the leadership team in each one of the business units talked about their short list of key measures in each one of the results areas and used that list as a way to focus their thinking."

Taken as a whole, the Ford educational opportunities rival any in the country. Vin Sahney, senior vice president for planning and strategic development, is a key voice shaping them. Surprisingly, Vin is not satisfied:

"The programs we have now are not well related to our needs. You can select a topic, hire a good teacher, advertise classes, and a lot of people will go to them, but the line people can still have a different need. Right now, the line doesn't buy in to all of the educational programs, so they look at it as an infringement, taking away from their time.

"People confuse good class evaluations with meeting needs. It has been just a bland mix of things without focus. The Managed Care College is an exception. It is really able to change doctors' cultural focus in a nonthreatening environment, enabling them to understand how to practice under managed care. The line managers want more people to go through it. We put 80 people through; they wanted 200. That's what happened with the quality program, but it's missing in much of our other training."

Marketing for value

Modern marketing is far more than advertising. Henry Ford has chosen a marketing strategy that emphasizes being competitive on price and service, and devotes relatively little to promotion of either its insurance product or its care network. Still, it's essential that your customers think well of you, and know where to find you. Bill Schramm, vice president for planning and marketing, discusses the Ford branding strategy:

> "I want to do enough promotion that the individuals who haven't touched us, when their physician wants to refer them to Henry Ford, they say okay. Brands evolve over time. You can't go out and create a brand with promotion. The image is more than the advertising. We subscribe to a national corporation that does household surveys of brand recognition, and we do some of our own surveying, around specific projects. The issue around the Henry Ford brand is whether we are going to build the brand itself, like Kellogg, or around our products, like Proctor and Gamble. A fair number of people who recognize the Crest toothpaste brand won't know that it is a Proctor and Gamble product. For example, one of our diversified services relies on referrals from a direct competitor. If we had labelled that service 'Henry Ford' we would not have built that business. Now the Henry Ford brand is developing an image that's okay. The negative impressions caused by the downtown location are going to be difficult to change.
>
> "We also need to think about people who are not ill, making sure that those are the patients who don't walk away from the organization simply because there has been no contact. We are identifying those individuals, putting literature in front of them, putting them in contact with a care provider. Those are the individuals we make money off of, but they are the ones most likely to change because they don't have a tie to Henry Ford."

Carol Bradford, vice president for public affairs, adds:

> "Now that we've diversified, with joint ventures and contracts, an HMO, home health, hospice, other services, even our own

> people find it difficult to explain who we are. While the term 'integrated health system' is understood and holds value among benefit administrators and employers, patients find words like 'integrated' and 'system' less appealing. They feel it suggests massiveness and something less than personalized care. Our goal in public relations is to convey the benefits patients receive from a system.
>
> "Issues management is the number one thing I do. We do presentations for the major media, briefings on healthcare. In an organization this size, a lot of things that can bubble up do. If issues or crises aren't handled well, that's what people remember. Exxon had a terrific public relations plan, but the Alaskan wreck was badly handled. It sticks in people's brain. Tylenol had two crises. They handled them well, and their market share went up.
>
> "We notice our competitors have really become aggressive in advertising. We hear numbers like $2 million for one competitor, over a million for another. Some of this is targeted to subregions. The system covers a broader geographic area than many competitors and is far more complex to explain. Our advertising programs have to work harder and more creatively to be remembered. Fortunately, because we have so many locations, our blue facility signs have reinforced the message that we are conveniently located throughout southeast Michigan."

Don Hirt, associate vice president for research and planning, Health Alliance Plan, discusses the promotional issues for HAP:

> "Our advertising budget is about $1.6 million, and it has been cut over the last three years. It is much less than our competitors'. We have multiple marketing audiences—employers and the general population. General marketing is the highest-cost, and it focuses on the fall season when most of the plan selection occurs. You are creating an image trying to differentiate yourself, but it's not a true call to action. The advertising may create a framework, but what happens at the employer site has a great deal of influence.
>
> "A plan like ours needs to move into a much more aggressive public relations campaign, one that tells people—particularly the employer customer—the positive side of what we do rather than reacting to criticism. I think the employer needs a sense of the strength of HMOs and the things they bring to their members. There are things we can explain to the

employers that we may never be able to make clear in the general market.

"One of the key drivers is the relationship to the personal physician. That fit between the provider and the patient is one of the key drivers to keeping people in our plan. If it's strong, they are much less likely to leave. Cost does drive people out of the plan, but you can overcome costs at a certain level with a strong provider relationship. Supporting that physician with customized information for preventive services and risk management is important—and the patient as well, reaching her with information that addresses her problems. Some plans are aligning their service representatives to physician panels, so that there is a point of accountability on customer service.

"HAP leaves a lot of things up to the individual provider. We don't ask for 'driveby' deliveries. Gag rules don't exist here. We do a tremendous amount of prevention. We are continuously working to meet preventive goals in HEDIS. We do a lot of piloting to see what works. Getting women to come for mammographies is a big challenge, for example. We've tried targeted mailings and we've found it doesn't work. So we've moved to a strategy working through the primary physician. We are evaluating that right now. I don't think we highlight that enough to our employers."

Don goes on to talk about the general marketing strategy for HAP. For the "commercial market," workers and their families, Don envisions a family of healthcare financing products with different benefits and insurance structures from the HMO, which is limited by law. They ride the coattails of the HMO in the sense that the doctors providing care will probably transfer much of the HMO care management to other patients, so that the premiums for these patients will be lower than they would be in a purely traditional situation. The lower the premium is, the more people will be able to afford it, so that this strategy has the potential to reduce the number of uninsured patients.

"We have about 35 or 40 percent of the Detroit HMO market. Blue Care Network is our biggest competitor. When you look at all products, including PPOs, Blue Care and HAP are pretty much equal. That's why we've recognized the need for a multiple array of products. Specific products will drive additional growth. It's hard to say how fast that will occur.

"There are no big opportunities for under-65 employed subscribers. The major employers are looking at slowly influencing movement through the monthly premium, but there's a general resistance in this market to forcing all employees into one option. I don't see us moving away from multiple options, which means higher premiums.

"We can offer a limited traditional insurance plan with some managed care features through our Alliance products for the small employer market. Some of those people pay very high premiums, and some don't buy any insurance at all. It's a deliberate strategy, a market we recognize as one we have not pursued over the years, where we could compete. We can offer a personalized product with managed care attributes that some of the other plans might not be able to provide. We are hoping to win on both price and service.

"[From an employer's perspective] your employees may not have had access to all the provider groups who are part of the Health Alliance Plan. And, we can customize the insurance to meet your needs—the level of coverage you want. We are not locked into the HMO standard. The rate will depend on your own population base, and we will give you the record keeping you want. It will be an uphill battle, because there's a sense of security with the Blues [traditional Blue Cross and Blue Shield, which still has the largest overall market share]. So our marketing strategy will link it directly to HAP. 'Backed by HAP and Henry Ford Health System' is another selling point. We've been very competitive on price."

And Don notes that HAP has committed to sell both Medicare and Medicaid managed care:

"We've been aggressively marketing our Medicare senior risk product for a year and a half. It has 17,000 members now. We've added over 10,000 members in the last year. Now our competitors are in that market as well. I don't expect it to grow fast but to continue at about the same pace. We have had some discussions of more creative ways to manage the care of the non-union motors retirees—maybe having special plans for seniors with high-risk profiles or chronic conditions, and other plans for young retirees who have limited needs—something the HAP network could deliver but that wouldn't be an HMO and not subject to Medicare HMO regulations.

"Medicaid will have an impact. We already have 25,000 members and we expect to at least double over a couple years. The largest market share, 125,000 members, is held by a company that is predominantly Medicaid. The total market is near 500,000. The challenge is to balance membership growth and service capability. If we grew too rapidly, we would sacrifice employed-subscriber growth. If we grew by merger with another plan, they would probably have to bring some service capability that meets our quality and service checks. Some of the Medicaid requirements are unique. We have to have patient literature written at a fourth grade reading level. The word 'referring,' as in referring physician, does not meet that test. We have to have the literature available in several languages. We have to have all-night member telephone services."

One serious marketing problem is the public backlash against managed care. David Nerenz, Ph.D., director of the Center for Health Systems Studies, discusses this problem. Dave's center is a leader in developing reliable measures of quality of care. In the absence of these measures, a lot of the backlash discussion has been based on unique incidents that may have been preventable problems, but that also may not have been preventable, or that may not be as harmful as they sounded:

"The current backlash against managed care is a witch hunt. It's based on an anecdotal reality, fed by a bias in favor of the traditional approach. We don't read articles about people being harmed by unnecessary surgery in a fee-for-service environment with the same frequency we read about the harm of withheld care in a managed care environment. There's a filtering effect. There were several articles published last year that compared fee-for-service with managed care that showed no difference or an advantage for managed care. What article got the big publicity? A *Journal of the American Medical Association* article using ten-year-old data on a sample of three or four hundred people showing a deficit in the functional health status of elderly patients enrolled in managed care plans. It was on the front page of every major newspaper in this country.

"Not only do we have to be better, but we have to gather the information that shows we are better. We have to make sure that all of our care processes, from the earliest prevention and screening to primary care access to the highest level of intervention, offer the highest possible quality measured against costs. At the moment there are bits of information that can demonstrate our superiority or our areas for improvement.

Some of that has to do with our satisfaction surveys, some with clinical outcomes. The data are not as well established or as pervasive as they ought to be. We can't go into our database, pull up information on diabetes care, and say our care is better than that of our competitors. It's a challenge. On the other hand, traditional insurance plans and fee-for-service organizations don't have as much data as we do.

"We can meet the test in some areas like transplants, and we have some ideas about how we can expand that capability. On outpatient mastectomies, our surgery department designed ways to measure patient satisfaction and outcomes. Once enough patients have been treated with the new approach, we can compare satisfaction and outcomes information on the new approach with the traditional one. We have data on short-stay obstetrics that suggest that it's a good thing. We've designed a program around expanded prenatal care, short stay, and follow-up care in the home. We have had to scuttle promotion, though. We can't talk about how good the program is, because the public is predisposed to view such managed care programs as bad."

Clinical Improvement

Behind backlash lies the question of whether managed care is truly superior. Backlash is an expression of the fear that, when all is said and done, the traditional way was better. Henry Ford has a cadre of physicians who are completely convinced that properly managed care is and will be better. It will yield a healthier population, make the patient happier, and cost less. Under the general direction of Tom Royer, senior vice president for medical affairs and chair, medical group board of governors, the cadre's efforts split into two major directions. One is to make the medical group the leader in designing and implementing the best care. The other is to bring the practice of the affiliated physicians up to higher and more uniform standards.

The best will never be perfect. John Wisniewski, M.D., one of the physicians committed to the managed care concept, explains:

"We need to understand that everything we do for our patients involves some sort of trade-off. We need to anticipate in advance what those [trade-offs] are, and plan around them. There are systematic ways to analyze the care that you provide, to make it better, and to measure the effect. Teamwork is better than non-teamwork. Sports teams go to the locker room and look at tapes. They talk about positions and how the play worked and so forth. They have a playbook. What would a playbook for clinical care look like here at Henry Ford? If you looked at our playbook, how would it differ from the one of a guy sitting out in his private office or somebody sitting in the competitor's office down the road? What makes a winning play in healthcare, and how many of those do we actually run here?

"Patients take the technical competence for granted; they expect that. They also expect and deserve a lot more—humanity, consideration, and integrity in our dealings with them. How do you deliver the goods on that? What do you actually do on the front line?

"Medical care is not the center of the universe. I think that's a problem that afflicts a lot of people in medical care. We become so imbued with what we do that we view the whole rest of the world as unimportant. What are we trying to do with medical care? We are trying to extend some comfort and succor to those people who ask it of us and to grant them some piece of mind, some ability to enjoy the free exercise of their will. We're damned lucky if we can deliver even part of the goods on that."

Finding improvements

Tom Royer, M.D., senior vice president for medical affairs and chair, medical group board of governors, notes that you must have accountability for clinical improvement, and patience:

"My office is responsible for the quality of care throughout the entire system. At times that has been an issue because all clinical parts of the system do not have a direct reporting relationship. But we now have people in medical leadership roles who understand collegial and collaborative relations, and they are developing uniform processes through the IPA networks and among private practice physicians who work in HFHS hospitals. We have a hospital council organized where the private practice physicians have representatives.

"My major concern is that changes in medicine do not occur incrementally. They have long, painful lead times, and all of a sudden you get a crescendo. I think people forget that it takes that much effort. I think we have paid that price. We put a lot of effort into utilization, our bottom line, and quality of care. Our HEDIS quality indicators are up 8 percent, our market access went up 10 percent, physician satisfaction moved almost 2 percent in 1997. Almost unbelievable for the size of this ship. It's because we concentrated on operations 90 percent of the time, and growth and innovation 10 percent, whereas through the 1980s decade, growth was the driver."

. . . and motivation:

"I think you have to motivate medical practices on what they need to be doing to be successful in their costs and in managing that capitation. You'll always have your vision that you'll share risk for those things you can't control and take total risk for those things you can. Unless you can get everyone sharing the risk, you enhance the polarity between primary and specialty. The primary will keep the patient too long; the specialist will encourage too early referrals. They won't want to do handoffs to home nursing, pharmacies, and so forth. They have to be organized enough that the leadership comes together.

"The changes have to be led by physicians. The leadership has to be visible and accessible. These lessons are only learned by physicians when other physicians are teaching them and saying, 'It's all right. I've been through it. It's not destroying my clinical practice. I still have some autonomy.' That's the fear; you go into managed care, you lose control. To me, the experience in the exam room is identical to what it was 30 years ago. I get paid a little differently for it, I may have to follow a protocol, but the protocols are really helping me give better care. The decrease in length of stay which have been forced upon us by payment mechanisms and by a managed care mentality created better care today than it was in the past. We don't have pulmonary emboli or strokes; we get cataracts done in six hours."

. . . and education:

"The educational component is more important than the financial incentive. If you don't understand protocols, how to apply them to get length of stays down; if you can't access nursing homes and sub-acute units; if you don't understand how to use a generic drug; if you are not interested in bringing a group of people in to teach them diabetic skills; if you can't look at your panel and identify your hypertensives and

> check their therapy; if you don't have the skills to identify the high-risk patients in your practice so you work harder with them than with the walking wounded or the worried well—you are going to lose. We expect the market to drive the physician. But the physician can manage resources by withholding or by allocating. There's a very big difference in quality."

The medical group has begun to exploit its core competency through its regional medical directors and through a unit called Clinical Resource Improvement Service (CRIS). It has chosen pathways as the key. Reginald Baugh, M.D., medical director of CRIS, explains what has happened:

> "Care pathways work at Henry Ford. Since 1993, we have made significant savings. We have reduced charges 20 to 30 percent across the board. The hospital length of stay has dropped from seven days to five. Some cases have 60 or 70 percent reductions in length of stay. We can get contracts with other insurance companies because we can demonstrate both quality and cost.
>
> "Our strategy is process improvement. We use total quality management to change clinical processes. We select targets that may be high-cost, but our process improvement focuses solely on quality. We've approached them not necessarily as inpatient but as a continuum for the patient. So there is an inpatient pathway, but also a change in ambulatory care.
>
> "Pathways have been around since 1991. In 1993, we decided to reduce the number of doctors treating patients in the hospital, so we have to reach a much smaller number of doctors with each pathway. Each doctor who uses the pathway is familiar with it because he or she treats a lot of patients with this condition. We can involve them in the pathway development and build in residency training and so forth. We involve the chief resident in the development.
>
> "We try to identify the diseases where it makes a difference in the population. We know that in Michigan versus the United States, and Detroit versus Michigan, there is a higher incidence of smoking, a more sedentary lifestyle, more overweight, higher incidence of diabetes and hypertension. Other major initiatives are childbirth complications and low birth weight. It will make a difference in the short term and the long term. For us to do well, we have to address these problems."

Reggie notes that Henry Ford can now develop pathways quickly, but their contribution is measured and evaluated:

> "We can develop a pathway in six to eight weeks. We develop the measures and the implementation. That's another six weeks. We make a trial. We use severity-adjusted information, and we examine what went well and what did not go well by severity. We look at cases where the physician leaves the pathway to see if we should incorporate that. We get a clear understanding of what parts of the process contribute to success. The natural work group for the disease is involved in all that. We involve the nurses and other staff.
>
> "The pathways increase the demand for measures. There's a whole piece related to functional outcomes [measures of the patient's ability to perform basic tasks or functions] that's difficult. Medicine in general does not measure functional outcomes. It's a tough challenge to follow these patients over time and collect information about how they did and how they liked it. Having an infrastructure that will support that measurement and the need for information is not a small undertaking. We have many people devoted to cranking information, mining data sets, and collecting information from primary sources. Not everybody has the infrastructure to do that."

As Reggie describes several important diseases now covered by pathways, he reveals the complexity of modern care. Getting the optimum outcome involves the contribution of many skills in the right order, the right quantity, and at the right time. Spending more for the wrong resources does not improve the result:

> "Intestinal bleeding, for example, begins with the patient's initial presentation in the emergency department and extends to ambulatory care after discharge. It involved changing how we staffed the ambulatory care, how and where we did consultations, interactions with the emergency staff, changing the physical layout of the emergency room. One of the problems was the consistency of emergency department decisions. We established ED protocols that ensured complete information and quality care. It's very much an integrated approach—coordination of care. The key leverage point was understanding how long the patient needs to stay in the hospital after the bleeding has stopped—understanding by age, by condition—to be sure they are not going to bleed again. And making sure when they are discharged from the hospital that the handoff is

> secure, that somebody's going to follow up. Against prominent commercial pathways, we equal the rigorously managed length of stay, even for an unselected urban population coming to our emergency room. We are able to achieve that through coordination, careful attention to details, and analyzing information to understand what works. With each round of information collection, you define a new reality."

The answers come from unexpected directions, Reggie says:

> "In the ambulatory arena, we have done a similar thing looking at asthma. The whole world is looking at asthma. We don't have anything special, but in a system with 41 practice centers and over 1,000 practitioners, having everyone say the same thing, having everyone teach patients how to manage their asthma, represents a significant improvement in the quality of care. Now, when patients come into the emergency room, the ED queries them, 'Have you received education?' The answer is increasingly, 'Yes.' Then, 'Tell me where they left off. Tell me what your level of understanding is.' So with a few questions we understand where the patient is. The educational material is modular, so that we can start there. No matter where you go, you get the same thing. We can ask, 'What is your peak flow? What is your range? How long has it been there?' So very quickly we can ascertain what needs to be done. People are using the same sort of model, the same sort of phrases. The family is not hearing different things, different philosophies. It's reinforced. They hear the same thing wherever they go.
>
> "We are working on stroke now. It will involve 1,500 patients a year. We wanted to incorporate the anti-coagulation treatment and the rehabilitation arm, so the pathway is much longer than anything we've done so far. We will have to affiliate with rehab facilities, and we expect the patients to go there on the fifth day. That's a lot sicker than a lot of nursing homes are used to seeing. You have to partner with the nonacute providers to help them train their staff.
>
> "We've tried very hard to bring our physicians along. Most of these initiatives are driven by physicians themselves. We did a statistically valid survey of our medical group to identify their beliefs about patients and diseases. We tried to learn more about the population and how people feel about their diseases. We have a mixture of ethnic populations in southeast Michigan. How does a provider adjust to that?"

And the answers include the patient:

> "We found that diabetic education was traditionally sort of a one-time thing, a relatively short period of time. The vast majority of the diabetics said they needed more information. We began to think, 'Gee, maybe that one intense period is not enough. We need to build in a more consistent, continuous educational process.' We identified 10 percent of our diabetics, with proven laboratory evidence, who were denying they were diabetic. That's kind of illuminating. That's a big deal. So we are seeking a better understanding of why they deny their disease.
>
> "The support departments, such as home care and therapies, are involved in the pathway implementation. Our orthopedic pathways created a problem in physical therapy staffing. We had to do a very detailed analysis to solve it. We try to do that in the implementation, before the pathway gets installed. We identify everything we can up front, and we modify the pathway or the organization to make things go smoothly. We understand that it's more than just the pathway design. The design can be excellent, but the organization needs to support it. We found that if a pathway isn't used in over 50 percent of the cases, it tends to die.
>
> "Our pathways are paper processes now. The information system priorities have not yet gotten to computerizing the pathways. We found that the pathways are transportable to other hospitals but you have to understand how to install them. A pathway developed in the medical group generates substantial profit for the group, so the distribution of pathway information to a competitor is not taken lightly. Some pathways have not been shared. The pathways shift care from inpatient to outpatient. The pathways have routines to make sure the patient makes the follow-up visits. That's easier for the medical group than it is for private doctors."

Tom Simmer, M.D., acting medical director, Health Alliance Plan, describes the other part of the Ford clinical improvement strategy, how HAP attacked the problems of clinical improvement with its affiliates when it expanded beyond the medical group:

> "I sort of look at it as a Star Wars analogy, where the Empire is the medical group and the rebel force is the affiliated physicians. The rebels are something of a rag-tag group. They don't have any infrastructure at all. Their office is often their wife or

their daughter; they don't even have a nurse, let alone a healthcare team. Some of them, of course, are further along, but the vast majority are very primitive. It is a rarity to have a large group that provides them with an infrastructure and supports a more strategic approach to managing individual patients. To the affiliates, the model is the doctor and patient in a room. Beyond that, it's basically sending people out for a particular event and pulling them back for a follow-up. Because the team approach is lacking, the role of the HMO becomes considerably greater. A lot of what we do is developing networks of offices into an organization that can compete in a monitored, measured environment.

"As it turns out, the rebel force has some advantages. First, there's no bureaucracy. They tend to answer their phones on the first ring, and say, 'If you are sick, come on in.' The simplicity, the personal nature, and the high service quality makes them a preferred source of care. Patients look for those things as their number one satisfiers. When we actually measure quality in terms of things that are important, such as the percentage of patients with congestive heart failure on an ACE inhibitor, the percentage of two-year-olds with all their immunizations, the percentage of diabetics who've gotten what they need, there is no comparison. The medical group does a far better job. So HAP's job is to improve the affiliates' clinical performance, while maintaining that service and personal attention.

"Right now, the membership of the affiliates is rising, while the group membership is static. HAP finds itself advocating for competitors of the medical group. My predecessor had real difficulty in managing that conflict. The medical group viewed the affiliates in almost a colonial relationship, physicians we signed up so they would refer patients to them. I think that's natural, but HAP has a different vision. We enthusiastically try to improve our affiliates' ability. When the HAP members don't want to go downtown, we try to meet their needs where they want. That improves member satisfaction, and gives the customer what they want."

The challenge for Tom is to change clinical practice without a bureacracy. HAP has successfully begun doing that:

"We have gotten the cost of care in the affiliate group lower than in the medical group. It's not entirely a fair number, because we haven't exactly matched patients. For example, the affiliates have much fewer obstetric complications, which tend to be referred to the group.

"The costs have been brought under control through a series of strategies developed over time. Initially, the strategy was inspection and interference. The HAP medical director's office got involved in all the decisions. This turned out to be very useful. HAP's clinical review physicians were sound, and contacts were viewed favorably because the affiliates needed somebody to discuss their cases with. The HAP doctors have read more, have broader experience, and are respected as clinical leaders. In the beginning, we had some people near retirement who were particularly outstanding."

The HAP strategy began with credentialling, the selection of properly trained and motivated physicians in the first place. Tom says:

"Our credentialling process has been a significant strategy in keeping out physicians who don't have the skill sets that are needed. In the medical group, the doctors who are too far off the track cannot hide behind anything. The records are uniform and everything is very visible. A salaried structure tends to discourage the ambitious, even while it screens out the unqualified. The affiliates tend to have a much bigger range.

"Our selection process in the early 1990s was not very rigorous. We raised our criteria to board certification and two postgraduate years of study. I'm not aware of any other HMO in Michigan that is that rigorous. The vast majority of candidates who are not accepted into our network are denied because of problems we see on site visits to their office. We rejected about 20 physicians from one area because they did not do the record keeping and office practices we want. They really hate that, and they say our competitors accept them."

The protocols were used in a different way. Instead of developing them, which was impractical for the affiliates, HAP bought them and used specially trained nurses to encourage the doctors to apply them to hospital patients:

"The next thing was that more and more 'cookbook' models became available—protocols that could be purchased from national suppliers. HAP superimposed these, using nurses to identify patients who were not following the usual path. We have nurses in 15 area hospitals. The patients they identified were referred to our physicians. That also educated doctors whose practice had fallen into a path that wasn't really great—such as doing hysterectomies before starting hormonal treatment, colonoscopies more frequently than needed, or for the wrong indications. It basically moved the care over to a more appropriate but somewhat leaner approach.

"It looks as though we can mature out of the protocols completely, but we are not positive of that. From one set of 25, we are now down to about 5 that we still use. The other 20 are procedures done by specialists who follow the protocols automatically.

"The protocols divide patients into usual and complex. Complex patients are excluded from the protocols, so the protocols cover only about two-thirds of hospital cases. The protocols have 'loosely managed,' 'moderately managed,' and 'well managed' standards. Our plan is close to moderately managed. We try not to be heavy-handed. The protocols are only guidelines, and we think it would be wrong to use them in a heavy handed manner. We don't think you need to, to get reasonable costs."

After the success of the commercial protocols, Tom says that HAP is moving on to outpatient and emergency care, and to simplifying the review of care for doctors who have a reliable record:

"We are going to start applying the protocols in the emergency room. If the protocol suggests admission is not necessary, we can avoid it. But the affiliates don't have the resources to manage complex outpatient care as well as the group. So we have to develop those resources.

"Now we are using a practice profiling approach. We will eliminate the review process for physicians who routinely follow the protocols. The review will be for those physicians who are new to the plan, or only have a few patients under the HMO. The reviews are very burdensome to the physicians, and if we can avoid them we should. We had trouble profiling physicians before, but software to do that is now available nationally.

"For the future, we will improve our profiling on inpatient, outpatient, and quality, and we will probably nudge up our incentive plan as a percentage of total earnings. We will improve our case management of complex cases and provide better methods for chronic patients like diabetics. The doctor groups will develop a more sophisticated model within their offices. We have a program in our Managed Care College to educate doctors' nurses on managing patients. We need to develop the infrastructure that allows patient education and case management within offices that now don't even have the beginnings. As we develop that infrastructure we expect to improve our performance."

The agenda for the future

With the successes of Reggie's Clinical Resource Improvement Service and Tom's efforts with the affiliated physicians, it might appear that the issues of clinical improvement are solved or, at least, that the battle is in its final stages. Henry Ford people would not agree. The attitude at Henry Ford is one of beginning, not ending. This is a journey just under way, with a clear vision of the future and sense of shortfall. John Wisniewski, M.D., the Managed Care College director:

"Over time, Henry Ford has acquired a wonderful reputation. We are quite successful. We are growing; we are competitive. We are enabling a lot of improvement activity, exploring and investigating and improving, that you wouldn't find in other organizations. But internally we are not what we could be. We are not well organized. We have at least half a dozen different departments that are there with the express purpose of improving quality, and they don't work well together. One of our regional medical directors characterized this as 'a drunken stagger toward quality.'

"In terms of utilization we are still far from national benchmarks. On the quality side, some HEDIS rates are okay, but others are weak. Our vaccination rates, for example, are still lagging. We are in the high end of the national range, but not as good as we could be. We are not tracking our populations well enough yet to have a good understanding of their needs and how those needs are changing. We don't have the push-button type of response that one would hope for in this type of system, that when we see an opportunity for improvement we go after it and four months from now it's widespread in the system.

"The most successful efforts become invisible. That's probably why we should continue to support competing units. We make our gains in small, sometimes tortured steps, not quantum leaps. But our patient-focused care effort could be a quantum leap. Patient-focused care has been a sinkhole for cost in some organizations. Here, so far, thanks to the efforts of people in Henry Ford Hospital, it seems to be working well. It's been well received by the patients, but it hasn't been big enough to tell whether it really pays off. Notice that effort did not arise out of any of the units that are there to promote quality and effectiveness. It came out of hospital management looking for a better way. I think TQM made that possible, but you'll never find people giving it the credit."

And Richard E. Ward, M.D., director of the Center for Clinical Effectiveness, describes how his center provides guidance for situations where the answer is not simple:

"The Center for Clinical Effectiveness is about 50 percent research and 50 percent internal process improvement support. The Managed Care College started out as a CCE project and is now independent. Our role is to provide system-level support for practice improvement. We have carved out a couple niches since 1989.

"One is to be the most methodologically rigorous, trying to be thorough enough that we can write the projects up and publish them, and hopefully get grant funding. Part of our role is to contribute to the reputation of the system. That gives us a lot of clinical capability that comes from being very science based and evidence based. We do literature review, analytic modeling. Some of the other units either outsource protocol development or use consensus methods. The results tend not to be very scalable. They achieve improvement in one local setting, but you don't see it catching on in other sites. A year later it's back to normal, even at the original site. In other situations there is a lot of controversy.

"We come in when the answer isn't obvious and consensus isn't emerging. An example is the requirements for credentialling practitioners to do conscious sedation—who should be allowed to do what. I'm working with the anesthesiologists in their battle with the certified registered nurse anesthetists. I'm trying to walk them through an organized process of resolving differences. There really isn't any evidence one way or the other. The argument was about what drugs would be defined as conscious sedation, who could do it, whether there had to be a nurse present, were there specific certification and documentation requirements, did we need a resuscitation setup in

> the room. These standards become very controversial because one group of people is thinking of it as a matter of safety, with no data, and other people are thinking about it as a matter of revenue and patient convenience. They can't do their procedure at a certain site because it doesn't have the right equipment or personnel. People take it very seriously.
>
> "We do things like the framework for how protocols are going to be developed, and the standards and references for protocols. We do 'explicit method' protocols, in David Eddy's term. That's a method where a group of people can't agree, so you explicitly outline the alternatives, estimate the various health and economic outcomes, and then step back and discuss values. We use the explicit methodology for some of our most controversial issues, for example, the role of mammography in the 40 to 49 age group, or genetic screening for breast cancer, or PSA testing for prostatic cancer, genetic screening for cystic fibrosis. These are painful issues, but they must be answered."

Given the importance of accurate data in both care and profiling, it is reasonable to have a group like the Center for Clinical Effectiveness work on the information system design. Rick describes what the center has done:

> "We also have taken on medical informatics. Ford doesn't have either an academic informatics function or an operational one, to take clinical information technology and develop it in such a way that they support practice improvement, utilization management, and clinical integration. Partly from my own interests, we've gotten more and more involved. I drafted the medical group's strategic information plan two years ago.
>
> "I lead the medical group information planning committee, which has a grant from the National Library of Medicine to do information planning on a corporate level. That activity has been productive in developing a lot of core technology. For example, we developed a pretty extensive system to support outcomes measurement and the national standards for outcomes data coding and transmission."

Expanding managed care to Medicare patients is a major step, because senior citizens need about three times the care of younger populations. Like most places in the country, Henry Ford is just beginning. Tom Simmer, M.D., the acting HAP medical director, talks about some of the learning that is occurring:

> "Medicare has strengthened us at HAP because the sick Medicare patients forced us to learn how to manage complex illness much better than before. We put a lot of resources into that. Our Medicare risk product costs have come down quite a bit over the last six months as our model has kicked in. That ability to manage complex cases is a core business strategy. That's why we are training nurses in doctors' offices. We will allow the physicians to bill for the nurses' services if we train and certify them. We think they will be able to handle cases that only the group can handle now. These will be registered nurses, not nurse practitioners. We have a variety of means to identify the complex cases. For a complex patient, like multiple sclerosis, we have the protocol for each visit. The nurses follow a recipe that is embedded in an encounter form. She or he has a process that comes with all the material for each kind of patient."

And the lessons learned from Medicare help with younger patients:

> "The part the nurse is performing is not all aspects of care; it is the routine aspects the physician is not all that good at. Let's say you have a patient with multiple sclerosis, and their main issue is urinary tract infections that become complicated. They have to follow a better method to prevent these and to respond as soon as the first symptoms appear. That may be all that nurse is doing. There is usually one issue that tips the patient over, and that issue is usually not a complicated one; it is a breakdown in good routine care for chronic illness. Even though they are simple, they lead to large costs. We take each patient, one at a time, and meet their needs. It's a different thing, and it may not work as well as we hope, but that's what we've learned from Medicare.
>
> "Most doctors don't have enough complex cases to keep the nurses busy full time, so a lot of our training has to do with well-patient visits. We have an excellent set of protocols for well-patient visits, segregated by age and based on the U.S. Preventive Services Task Force. Every recommended education, counseling, and screening event that is supposed to occur for that age group is in the protocol and is handled by the nurse. These are things our affiliated physicians never had the time to do. We think we'll get both better proactive prevention and better complex case management this way."

Physician Organization

So far, what we have learned about medical organization is that we don't know very much and that many of our preconceptions were wrong. There are two basic ideas—an independent practice model, like the Ford-affiliated physicians and Greensboro's Eagle Physician Associates, and an employment model, like the Henry Ford Medical Group or the Permanente Groups in Kaiser—and countless variations. The former may work better for primary care; the latter for specialty care. But no one is bragging about their results.

Developing the strength of primary care

Tom Simmer, M.D., acting medical director of Health Alliance Plan, talks about the incentives and organization of the affiliates, the group he calls the Star Wars rebel force. Like most revolutions, the picture is confusing. At least for now, the payment method and direct case management by HAP are the central activities, although some affiliates are beginning to organize themselves:

> "HAP's basic payment is fee-for-service. It averages about 80 percent of the Medicare fee, but it is about 75 percent for specialists and 85 percent for primary care. We are not a generous reimburser. We don't have any trouble getting physicians at that price. We have very low turnover in our network.
>
> "We are also linking the profiles with incentives for primary care physicians. That incentive is not large—a 5 percent bonus—but it is a significant factor in their behavior. There are some extra incentives, about $1,200, that they can get for complying with specific measures of quality of care and overall costs. The primary care physicians have to approve extra tests ordered by the specialist. Because of the incentive, they are asking for data on the costs incurred by the specialists. They want to send patients to the specialists who will spend the money wisely and who will do what they consider to be the best job from a managed care perspective. We are with them on that.
>
> "We have not invested in doctor's office organization, because we don't have a capitated payment system. A lot of competing HMOs have capitation, and some of the affiliates develop an infrastructure so they can market themselves to other HMOs. If the doctors form a group that has some data on performance, they can evaluate capitation offers. They exert a pressure on their own members that is greater than

> what HAP is bringing to bear. Philosophically, they can accept that pressure better from their own members.
>
> "One well-known consulting company has developed a payment strategy that doesn't include capitation. Their view is that capitation itself is not usually practical, because the number of the patients in any one practice is small and the variation in the needs of the patients is great. They also feel that capitation leads to doctors disliking and avoiding their sick, resource-intensive patients. It puts the physician more in conflict with the patient. The doctor can't take an advocacy role. We have bought into this philosophy, trying to incentivize in a balanced quality and utilization way that isn't so austere as to raise this conflict. We may find in the end that our model is too costly, because the motivation under capitation is very, very strong. One wonders if that isn't one reason that managed care is so negatively viewed."

Tom points out some of the complexities involved in lowering the premium and in reaching benchmark performance:

> "The question is, Should we be at a premium of $100 a month, or $120, or our current $130? Some argue that the West Coast has gone further than they should. In order to be a Portland, we will need more time because the fixed costs have to be eliminated. That is a wrenching thing. This market hasn't driven us to make those types of decisions, because that involves closing hospitals, laying people off. In this market, the medical infrastructure costs are too high to achieve $100. Our incentive compensation model may be strong enough to get us there; it may not. I hope it will, because it appeals to me as statistically more reasonable, and ethically it puts us into fewer dilemmas. One could make the transition to a capitated model if it becomes a necessity.
>
> "I think the auto companies want to see a fairly static premium. They consider their role to be one where they provide continuous pressure for us to improve. They haven't really given us ultimatums, such as, 'Next year if your premium isn't as low as [a large competitor], we're pulling 50,000 members and you're dead.' They have that kind of market power, but they haven't used it.
>
> "I think General Motors believes that there are no benchmark plans in this area. They are correct. No plan can get too far out of its market. The plan that had such austere utilization

that it could come in for much less would also be less friendly to the public in comparison to its competition. The fact that our market has not had 50 years of Kaiser-Permanente puts the benchmarks farther ahead. I don't think they are following a sequence any different from ours, but they started first. We were glad that although we weren't rated a benchmark plan, we were 'above average.' We picked up significant membership as a result of that position."

Rebuilding the referral specialist capability

Meantime, the Henry Ford Medical Group and the Henry Ford Hospital have been losing market share and profits. Yet the group sees its future as being the leader, gaining a stronger, more complete understanding of disease management that will attract patients and provide exportable protocols for the affiliates. Peter Butler, senior vice president and chief administrative officer, and his counterpart, Tom Royer, M.D., senior vice president for medical affairs, are cooperating to design a new organization. It turns out to be a job that's more complicated than anybody anticipated:

"About 18 months ago, we came up with a chief medical officer/chief administrator officer team for each region. They would coordinate product lines. The implications include pulling apart the Ford Medical Group, aligning it with hospitals and the rest of the continuum within the regions to become more customer-focused. We piloted this in the eastern region. We took Cottage Hospital, wiped it out as a corporation, wiped out its board, created an advisory board for the region, created a chief medical officer and chief administrative officer for the region, and incorporated both the medical group and the hospital staff in the continuum of care.

"We learned in 18 months that this wasn't perfect. Not the least of the reasons that led us to abandon the model was that we spent all our time trying to organize these boxes, our structures in the corporate office. No matter how we did these things, we began to recognize that the communities we were serving and the individual people could care less. It wasn't necessarily improving what we were doing. Are we cheaper? Are our customer satisfaction results better? Can we explain what it means to be under the HFHS blue sign? The answer was, No, not really. We were busy designing our car, but we were still putting defective parts in it. If you cannot perfect the patient visits to the doctor's office, you can organize any way you want; you are not connecting with the customer. I said to Gail [Warden, CEO], 'We are the talk of the nation; I'd rather be the talk of the town.'"

Peter describes a second attempt at organization, which is now under way. In effect, most operating units have dual accountability, to their regional board and to their functional group:

> "The alternative is to take your business units as hospitals [and the affiliated physicians], the medical group, extended care, and health plan activity. Those are your four ways of measuring performance and accountability. That splits up the continuum as the building blocks as opposed to regions, and that's how you report to the board. Being the kind of institution we are, we are ending up somewhere in between. Certain parts need to be regional, including our advisory governance structure. We are still taking the boards out of all our hospitals and moving to regional governance. The regional boards should be concerned with how we are serving their particular population. What we are really recommending is to track what you are doing in each business unit in each community. The pieces are more important than the continuum at this point in time. That's why we didn't create a solid line relationship between the region and its business units, and have kept these silos, if you will.
>
> "Ambulatory care, inpatient care, and extended or special care are the silos. We went back and said, 'We have 70,000 admissions, 2.5 million physician visits, and 350,000 encounters in nursing homes and hospice. Let's make these a fairly standardized, high-class, predictable experience for our customers.' In doing that we embraced the patient-focused model across each of these entities. It's the one thing that has made a difference. Where we have organized a care team in the ambulatory setting working together, we improve customer satisfaction and performance. At Henry Ford Hospital when we did care teams we really saw it was the only way to leapfrog our numbers and break the mold.
>
> "Steve Velick, who leads the hospitals group, and the medical group leaders really focused on profit improvement within their silos. It's not that we are ignoring the continuum of care, but we are saying we'd better do well in areas where we have similar processes across 40 ambulatory sites and 6 hospitals.

We do have a team that works on the needs of continuing care."

Once the structure was understood, the opportunities for improvement began to appear. Peter notes important revisions in inpatient care and the emerging picture of ambulatory care organization for the group:

> "We've learned much more than just the clinical differentiation and pathways. In inpatient care, it's not just a grouping of homogeneous patients and bringing services to the bedside. We have many fewer job categories. It's a very different physical model, handheld cellular phones for nurses that make them accessible wherever they are, for example. There is no centralized nursing station. It's similar across all of these nursing units, irrespective of the specific disease the unit serves. A lot of people have abandoned patient-focused care nationally. I think we are one of the exceptions because we put hours and hours of training into our personnel. We built the pathways and the facilities and the way we chart. We went the whole route and stuck to it. Other people have piloted it and abandoned it.
>
> "On the ambulatory side, we are talking about somewhere between three and seven providers—doctors and extenders—taking responsibility for as many as 10,000 panel patients, supported by the appropriate information systems, and incentivized financially under a common set of standards of customer satisfaction and quality. We have four or five units like that out there now. In the end, the performance building blocks for us are down at this level. It's not at a business unit or a region. It's not at a medical group–wide level. What gets people excited and really started doing things differently is when you get down to an individual patient unit or a care team. That's where we see results. Structures have been over-emphasized, and processes have been under-emphasized. Until you can communicate down to the care team level, you are not going to get the impact.
>
> "Tom Royer [M.D., senior vice president for medical affairs] and I are glued together at the hip. With an issue like laboratories, which affects both the group and hospitals, we have the authority to centralize the service. We've done that with laboratories. Radiology has stayed local. We haven't forced the political issue unless there has been a quality issue. At the same time, some services have become decentralized. We set

certain goals, and the regions say they can't make the goals if they have to continue to spend as much downtown as they have in the past. They point out failures in services sent out from downtown—'The part-time doctors you send out here cancel half the time. That's why my access numbers are bad.'"

The implications of Peter's approach are far-reaching. He continues:

"We worked six months on franchise rules for when you must use downtown specialists. In the end we said, 'There are no such rules.' We have moved from setting rules to agreeing that the regions must do what it takes to satisfy their customers. If that means abandoning the downtown region, we have to do it, but we better have some discussions about it. I think we are finally over the hump. People wanted the rule book; there is no such thing. This is a wake-up call for the group chairs. The good ones are learning how to serve the regions; the bad ones are lagging behind.

"We are moving more decision making to regional levels as opposed to downtown. We are trying to put less emphasis on corporate staff and more on operations. Some of that has emerged by itself. People knew we are settling in on this model. Performance measurement reinforces the model."

Peter goes on to some of the governance aspects of the patient-focused approach:

"We have left regional the ability to deploy capital as a system, to plan, to measure how we are performing, and philanthropy. This creates a very collaborative, necessary relationship between the medical group and the hospitals, both those we own and those we contract with. They are very aligned on how they are going to strategically address their market. But when we revised the regional model, we said, 'From an accountability standpoint, we are worried about improving processes within hospitals and ambulatory sites. We'd rather spend time on that than the horizontal slice across the region. The continuum pieces are coming and going. We'll coordinate that in a planning sense, but the accountability will be through the business units.'

"The accountability is still a little fuzzy in some people's eyes. The regional advisory boards have just begun. We only got serious in September. We told them, 'You have a real job, we don't want you just to show up. We want you to worry about community need, how well you are serving the population, whether we are deploying capital appropriately. We are going to get pretty specific about this charge.' Some people think you should just have a system board and eliminate all these regional units. We don't believe in that. We believe that if you don't have the diverse communities represented and looking at these kinds of things, you will put yourself at risk one of these days about being a not-for-profit organization. If you want to serve 25 percent of southeast Michigan, you had better know that you have somebody behind you who does not live in downtown Detroit.

"We have not organized the region around a hospital and a set of satellite medical offices. In the western region, we do not own a hospital. We contract with St Mary's at the moment. We've learned that you do not have to own hospitals. You need a relationship that will do well on the cost side, satisfy the patients, and give good-quality care. Ownership almost messes it up. If we get our senior people entrenched in everything that's going on in an affiliated hospital, we can hit these numbers. It's similar on the ambulatory side. That's where you are really going to prove yourself, because you have two-and-a-half million visits that you are trying to make unique. In the end, I think the best we can do is someday say you'll have a predictable experience."

Tom Royer, M.D., speaking in his role as chair, medical group board of governors, talks candidly about the difficulties the group has encountered:

"There has been a lot of work across the country looking at group models versus IPA models like the HAP affiliates. For that first wave of things that needed to be done, the independent practice models did it better than the group practices. During the '80s, it was hard to say that the Henry Ford Medical Group was really bringing any value to the table.

"I'm comfortable that long term, into the next century, the group practice model will be the surviving model. Because what we are learning is that to get into the second wave of things that make us cost effective, you need to get your days down, avoid certain admissions, and integrate better with nursing homes, home health, and diversified services. Hospital care needs to be integrated with outpatient care very early on. Those require closely managed activities. Our Toledo installation, called the Medical Value Plan, is exclusively an independent practice model, and their numbers exceeded the group's for a period of time. In addition, they are growing very rapidly. Now the group's utilization, access, and quality exceed Toledo's. The Toledo plan is losing money because they can't go that next step to manage their days per 1,000 subscribers. Their days are about 20 percent higher than ours. You are going to see the group model go back to being the premier network.

"The group is losing money. There are several reasons. First, we merged the Metro Medical Group. Integrating the two cultures was difficult. Second, we supported primary care assignment, so we can understand the populations we are dealing with and each person will have a primary physician. As physicians were selected, a lot of subscribers chose the network instead of the group. We think that the sicker people chose the group. Third, the group has not had the incentives to align pay with performance. We are not as efficient or effective as we need to be.

"I see the light at the end of the tunnel. We have not been profitable, but that does not mean we can't be profitable in the future. We just haven't figured out all the pieces yet."

He goes on to identify some things the medical group can do that would be beyond the reach of a looser organization:

"The basic core competency of the group is teamwork, the ability to manage that continuum of care from birth to death, ingrown toenails to heart transplants. If it's done right, we should be able to do that better than private practice depending on a referral to another specialist. Our core competency is R&D [research and development] of clinical processes, disease management, and programs. We just looked at a pathway yesterday for radical prostatectomy. We reduced the length of stay to four days from eight, increased patient satisfaction by 32 percent, and decreased costs by almost 30 percent. We're looking at how people access the system and accept the care, how to prevent the disease and manage the hand-offs between specialists. We are looking at door-to-door time, rather than just what happens in the exam room, and using strategies like the electronic medical record and paperless radiology. They are all going to make us successful. We need to have the franchise rules well defined, so people know what's going on

> behind the blue sign [the Ford Health System logo], as they do behind the golden arches. Someone has to R&D that, and someone has to pay for the R&D.
>
> "About 50 percent of the group's business is managed care. In the suburbs it's about 70 percent. New technology has permitted a lot of that care—91 or 92 percent—to be done locally. We said we've got to let that care be done locally because people don't want to come downtown. The only referrals will be for quaternary care, sophisticated centers of excellence—transplants, brain tumors, epilepsy surgery. The referral cadre is shrinking. If you look at 1975, primary care has gone from zero to 40 percent, specialists from 100 percent to 60 percent.
>
> "We think everybody should learn to work within a capitated system. At the present time, the group primary care physicians take capitated risk, but we pay our specialists on a discounted fee basis, and our hospitals get a fixed amount for the total hospitalization. We'd like to sub-cap our specialists. We are looking at hospital prices based on competitive alternatives, rather than solely on the hospital's costs. The issue is that we are part of a system, and sometimes you have to compromise what is best for the individual pieces to generate what is best for the system as a whole."

There are three keys to making this strategy a reality. The spider diagram is the most critical. Jim Blazar, vice president for primary care and clinical services, reports to both Peter and Tom:

> "I update the spider diagrams. I worked with the leadership to determine what the measures would actually be. Staff working for me developed the definitions and collected the data. My role is to make sure people understand them and their implications, to make sure that they are accurate, to get them to the governing board and the regional leadership. We changed some measures, added some, deleted others. My role is to bring the concept to life. It's working.
>
> "One reason it's working is that it's clear to the leadership that this gets reported to the board and that there is a reaction from the board. Peter meets with people and is saying, 'Let's talk a little bit about your variance here.' People's evaluations are now based on this. You add these things up, and people are taking them seriously. There was a lot of push-back when we first started. You don't hear that anymore; you hear more about how we can improve it. Initially, I think that people

thought if they complained enough it would go away. It's not going away.

"In addition to the spider, there are back-up pages that give time trends and basic data. The regional reports have more data than the system. Some groups, like northeast, have developed their own diagram with even more measures, for people in the regions. They have some process measures. For sure, it's reviewed by the leadership team of each region. The managers who work for the leadership teams know about the measures and can talk about them. Some places, more people would know about it. It is posted in some meeting rooms, so that it is down to the supervisor level. We haven't gone down to the employee level.

"In almost every presentation I have made for the last two years, I start with the spider. When my staff starts putting together its plan, we start with 'What are we doing that's actually going to improve these measures? If there's not a value added, we'd better look carefully at what we are doing.' A lot of people are using this to pull the whole organization forward. It's been a very valuable tool."

Within the group, the problematic measure on the spider right now is patient satisfaction. Jim describes how measurement of satisfaction has been expanded, emphasized, and benchmarked:

"We have a satisfaction system that surveys 75 patients a year for each doctor in the medical group who sees ambulatory patients, so that we have satisfaction measures down to the individual physician level. Every doctor gets a report on themselves twice a year. The leadership gets an aggregate report quarterly. Any leader who has a physician they are working with to improve can get a monthly report, with oversampling to get reliable data. There is support for those physicians—there are only about ten—communications training, mentoring programs, buddy systems to help them. The survey is used by other large clinics across the country, so we can compare our performance with them. The response rate is up to 38 percent. We use a personalized letter that talks about my visit with this doctor on this date. It's signed by Doctor Royer [M.D., senior vice president for medical affairs].

"What's good about this is that we've recognized that satisfaction is important. For years we have been giving it lip service, and now we are working at making improvements. In fact, the scores have gone up for the last three quarters. But we have to do better. We are still below the mean of our peer group. There is huge momentum to do better.

"We have a serious problem with prompt access to primary care sites. One way to solve an imbalance is to tell people to work harder and schedule more appointments. The other approach is to use an analytic model that adjusts staffing to the need. Adjusting staffing means saying, 'I'm sorry, doctors. You can't all take vacation April 5 even though your kids are out of school.' That has created some problems. But it also means that some clinics are understaffed, so administration must add staff. We have tested this, and Tuesday we are meeting with the primary care clinic managers.

"We could extend the satisfaction survey to the network physicians. HAP is using a different company for its survey. I've said, 'Wouldn't it be better if we both used the same instrument?' But I can't force HAP."

Finally, the third key is the ability to restructure care, moving beyond profiles, protocols, and case management to invent new and better approaches. Jim talks about the effort to develop disease-based models, and the effort to translate from the group to the total Henry Ford System:

"Reggie Baugh [M.D., medical director of the clinical resource improvement service] and I partner on clinical improvement. We put together a regional leadership group, which is the regional medical directors, clinic and hospital administrators, physicians that represent the affiliates, and representatives of behavioral services, senior services, and some specialists from downtown. The downside is that it's a very big group, but the upside is that it has some voice. We interviewed all these individuals on what they thought were the most important clinical processes priorities. We profiled those areas by the risk, the size of the population, and the savings and quality improvements reported by others. We developed a book that profiles 12 different opportunities. Last July we came up with six areas for systemwide study this year. They included diabetes, breast care management, depression, chest pain, childbirth care, and 'abnormal results reporting.' The last isn't a single condition, but it is a major risk factor for us. We put together six systemwide teams, staffed by my department. We developed a value compass for each area. They are at different stages of evolution.

"Chest pain I think will be the first systemwide success. They decided there will be system standards for chest pain emergencies. The time delays for care and the tests and drugs you need will be standard in all our hospitals and clinics, beginning October 1. We will report the same information, measured in the same way. The chest pain group will meet periodically to see how we are doing.

"Depression has been very interesting. Behavioral services and primary care developed a protocol for treating depression in the primary setting—what you can do, when to refer. Maybe as many as 20 percent of patients coming to primary care are depressed. They are still functioning, going to work and so on, but they could be helped by counseling or medication. It costs lots of money because these patients come in for other symptoms that we treat without getting to the root cause. We have a screening device, a self-administered patient questionnaire, and protocols for the primary physician on what to ask, what to look for, what to prescribe. The team got consensus around the protocol, but the push-back has been from the primary care physicians, that the protocol takes a lot of time, makes it hard to meet the productivity requirements, and other issues. All these things sound simple, but then the next thing comes along, and the next. The primary physicians don't even want to identify these depressed people, because it's more work.

"So we will do four pilot implementations. Two pilots will use just two questions from the questionnaire on every patient. If both are positive, we will use the rest of the questionnaire. Behavioral services will work with us to see if we can use the questionnaire on site or by phone, whether we can train nurses to handle the next steps, and really get down to what would make the primary physicians more comfortable—how you integrate so it's not just another form and another burden. The other two pilots will only do higher-risk patients—seniors, chronically ill, people with some indication of depression.

"Childbirth won't start until this September, because we had a new chair of OB. The diabetes team should report protocols and a tool box for a consistent approach around the end of the year. There is a joint venture between the American Diabetic Association and NCQA on diabetic management. I'd like for every one of our sites to be certified by the ADA in the next year, including our network physicians. If they do that for their HAP patients, they will do it for all their patients.

"Breast care will have two parts. One issue is the lead time for a mammogram. In the group, that's now four to six weeks. In the network, it can be done tomorrow. The other issue is management of an abnormal diagnosis from the mammogram, the time to get a biopsy and, if necessary, do treatment. For the group, that's now six weeks, and we think that's unconscionable. We decided this project with GM's PICOS group, which runs a program to attack specific processes and redo them quickly. We'll try to do the whole job in three days' time on each issue. If it works, we'll apply the PICOS techniques on other initiatives. I suggested that one solution would be to say that these procedures could be done anywhere in the system. So women could get their mammograms wherever it's most convenient to them. There's a lot of resistance of course—quality issues, things traveling under the banner of quality issues, and revenue loss for the group. Dr. Demers, the head of the cancer program, and I have stood firm: 'Let's look at the quality issues, and if there's a problem we'll address it. But we are going to treat this as a system initiative.'

"The abnormal test results group is working on the reporting of laboratory data—which results indicate an immediate risk of death, which need reporting the same day, and so on. They are collecting data comparing the regions, identifying what the doctors think is most important. The other part is actually harder, what values can we agree upon as abnormal. There is difference of opinion on that."

Slowly, perhaps "in a drunken stagger," the strategy is coming together. Bill Conway, M.D., chief medical officer for the Detroit region, talks about some of the successes:

"We could beat anyone in southeast Michigan on referral care costs, especially if it involves hospitalization. The work Reggie Baugh [M.D., medical director of the Clinical Resource Improvement Service] has done at the main hospital, 40 care pathways, has had dramatic effect. It's not what's written down as the protocol, it's getting the thing implemented, getting the clinicians and nurses all bought into them.

"We do more things outside the hospital than you could imagine. My daughter just had her anterior cruciate ligament repaired in her knee. Two years ago it was a four-day hospital

> stay. She had it done in the ambulatory center in the north region, stayed overnight in the 23-hour unit and went home. The most radical changes probably involved the neurosurgeons and urologists. The urologists have cut their length of stay more than 50 percent, and they have hardly any patients in the hospital anymore. They have moved their patients to the 23-hour unit. The neurosurgeons have cut the length of stay for spinal surgery to a single day.
>
> "Putting a clinical evaluation unit in the emergency room has eliminated hospitalization in some diagnoses. Six to 12 hours of treatment by the ED team is all that is needed. Most of the surgeons have worked hard at moving procedures to ambulatory care. Breast biopsy technology we started two months ago. The chair of surgery is sure it will eliminate any use of the operating room. It will be done in a procedure room, with a large bore needle that leaves a smaller incision. A lot of this is movement of surgical techniques to micro technology.
>
> "You might have heard pathways described as cookbook medicine a few years ago. When you actually work with this, what you are standardizing is the routine and the repetitive. The doctors' lives are much easier. They no longer have to check a lot of things that happen automatically. We track all kinds of complications and readmissions, and I don't know of any of the pathways that have gone awry. Some have had positive quality improvements; most have stayed neutral."

By deliberate intent of the medical group board of governors, the mission and vision of Henry Ford Health System includes both teaching and research. Tom Royer, M.D., senior vice president for medical affairs, talks about the educational mission:

> "We believe that education is integral to good, high-quality patient care. Good practitioners stay on the cutting edge because they are educating the people who come after them. Research is critical in that. The research mind helps us to stay focused on everything that we are doing, why it is happening this way, and how we can do it better. Although we say we are a tricycle model, where the patient care is the front wheel and research and teaching are the back, we feel that all the wheels have to be there. The driver is patient care. We are not a three-legged stool, or a unicycle or a bicycle.
>
> "We are trying to right-size our educational programs. We said it is not right that we should be training unneeded specialists.

The reimbursement at the federal level makes it expensive to do the right thing. We intend to do the right thing, and hope the finances will follow. Right now, we lose $90,000 if we close a residency.

"We have affiliations with about 17 medical schools. Case Western Reserve, Chicago Medical School, Michigan Osteopathic are the primary ones. These are places we can work with. They are geographically nearby. They are schools that want to understand managed care better. They are willing partners. We are as nonthreatening as a system can be, and there is win/win there. We see ourselves as a virtual medical school, a medical school without walls, where the student can start basic sciences anywhere. We see ourselves doing the clinical part, and we want them here long enough that they have a Henry Ford brand—the Henry Ford kind of medicine. We understand how to bring diversity in."

Tom goes on to Henry Ford's research activities:

"One of the things that makes Henry Ford a unique place is its long-standing commitment to both basic research and clinical research. Our major endowment, the Fund for Henry Ford Hospital, is committed to funding the best science, whether it's outcome research, molecular biology, clinical research. The fund supports $8 million of research each year for the best science. Many of the specific topics have direct support in addition. Our total research budget is $40 million.

"Why should Henry Ford Health System invest this money? It's very simple. First, being a research institution you attract a better, more up-to-date clinician. An active research environment and an active education program are essential to recruiting the best people. Second, a research environment lends itself to the whole issue of inquiry. Today, medicine is in many ways a constant inquiry. We want every physician every day to try to make healthcare more effective. Third, I think it pays back to the community. All responsible citizens pay back to the community. Healthcare is where it is because of the initiative of the scientific community.

"You want to have a mixed portfolio. We include basic science, work that does not identify any immediate clinical implication. We also have a commitment to research that will pay off tomorrow. We are working in molecular epidemiology to identify genetic markers for breast cancer. We have epidemiological research in breast cancer and post-traumatic

> stress disorder. We think that has very short-term implications. And we have health outcomes, which is critical in healthcare delivery. We do transitional research, where you can see the relation between the research and actual clinical practice.
>
> "A university might have a different balance. If you think of Henry Ford as a tricycle, patient care is the big wheel, the driving wheel. Research and teaching are the small wheels. In a university, the wheels might be more equal in size."

Research will cover the range of clinical areas, but Ford's special contribution may be the understanding of disease in populations. Reginald Baugh, M.D., medical director of the clinical resource improvement service:

> "We are focusing on patient understanding, patient response. We have a registry that tells us what diseases the patient has, such as diabetes. We track them whether they are sick or not. Traditionally, if you don't come in, we assume you are well. We are trying to keep their overall health outcome as good as it can be. It's maintenance of health, rather than treatment of illness. It's a different philosophy.
>
> "The advantage at Ford is the unique combination of teaching, research, and care. If you can show us, with good data, that there is a better way, the Ford Group will go the better way. There is a willingness to change. If managed care walks away from teaching and research, it will hurt. If you don't have the constant innovation that comes from questioning—why we do it, why it is so—it will hurt. Ford has a combination of solid data and a large population. HAP has been over 250,000 people for a decade. So the combination of clinical outcomes, pharmacy, and hospitalization is a wealth of information to support innovation."

Diversification and Community Outreach

Diversification

Henry Ford differs from Legacy and Moses Cone in owning a health insurance company. Although owning (or eliminating) the health insurance functions is in many people's vision of integrated health systems, there are actually few examples, and the record for combining both functions under a common ownership is mixed. Ford is one of the success stories. Walt Douglas, trustee and chair of the Health Alliance Plan board, discusses the future for HAP:

> "I'm a Ford dealer. I came to Detroit in 1966, working for the Internal Revenue Service as assistant director of the IRS Data Center here. I decided after the riots that getting involved in urban affairs was important. So I left my job and joined New Detroit, an urban coalition that came into being as a result of the riots. I went there as a vice president and then became its president. In the late '70s, I joined the HAP board of trustees. New Detroit was continuing an effort to get diversity in healthcare. There was not very much diversity in healthcare boards at that time. I've enjoyed it. I've learned a lot. I've been chairman ever since 1984. This is my last year. When HAP merged with HFHS, in the late '80s, I joined the Ford board.
>
> "We want to grow HAP. We're pleased with the quality of care and the NCQA accreditation, so what we need to do is grow it. One of the challenges of any HMO is to live down the allegations that you can't have good service and good quality and good healthcare if you are a member of an HMO. I don't believe that's true. It doesn't have to be true, and what we're trying to do is make sure HAP measures up.
>
> "Growing it is one goal. Recognizing it is part of the system is another. HAP shouldn't be totally constrained. It should have its own life. We've set up an insurance company, Alliance Health, to make sure we have the capability to say to customers, 'Whatever you want, whether it has already been designed or it's a figment of your imagination, let us see if we can't create for you and your employees the kind of healthcare coverage you want.' We also have to make sure we do it geographically."

Walt expands on what the two goals of growth and integration imply:

> "We used to set the premium by looking at where we were and where the market was. Now, we have to look first at the competition and have a lot of dialogue with our major payors and the providers. We listen with one ear and don't listen with one ear. In the last few years, the payors have become more specific: 'We want a 5 percent reduction. We want this and we want that.' The challenge for us is to look at our costs, try and maintain the quality and service we want to provide, and take costs out of the system.
>
> "HAP needs to have a good quality committee. The board has to keep its eye on satisfaction and access. They are not quite as important as the bottom line, but they don't fall

behind by a whole lot.

"Two years ago, we looked at some disastrous re-enrollment numbers. I got on the phone and talked to Gail [Warden, CEO] and said, 'Gail, our price is too much. We got to do something about it.' That means the hospital has to do something about it. We all have to learn to live with that. We did, and we saw a turnaround last year. That's just the beginning. In the future, it will be more difficult to move ahead. We have to maintain a competitive edge. We don't have any intention of backing up. We have an advantage; we enjoy a good name, and we think we can maintain a growing market.

"We know we aren't going to make it incrementally, signing up another 2 percent. What growing means is attracting another HMO. We've had discussions from time to time. Nothing has been consummated, but we anticipate there will be some consolidation over the next five years, and we want to be a player in that."

And he speculates on the value of having HAP as part of Henry Ford:

"You have to answer the question of what HAP has contributed in the context of HFHS. The system made three decisions that have made it what it is. One was the practice model, which was done when Henry Ford set the hospital up. The second was to decide to stay in the city and then to develop an ambulatory care satellite mechanism throughout the metropolitan community; that allowed them to give outpatient service in a dispersed geographic area and, at the same time, to stay in the city. That was a key decision for them and for the city. The third was to effect the merger with HAP. It started as just a loose alliance, but Stan Nelson and Doug Peters [the previous CEO and COO] began to see what was happening and strengthened the relationship.

"It has occurred to me that HAP could be separate from Henry Ford. But by keeping them both in the same system and each having its own board gives each some protection. I would not want to separate them. I don't see any advantage to saying to HAP, 'Okay, you go out and grow, cut deals, and screw the Health System if you have to.' I don't know that that is necessary. The pressure is not so great that we have to have that.

"What do I know about the HMO market in Michigan? Even the experts can be wrong, and I'm not an expert. So, what do I know? Anything I say is said with that in mind. But I don't see any major shift in the HMO market. Everybody says the big guys [national health insurance companies] are coming. They've been saying that; the big guys haven't come. Some of the allegations of the fee-for-service doctors might be true of the big guys."

Jim Walworth, senior vice president for managed care and president, Health Alliance Plan, describes the evolution of HAP from a small group practice model quite independent of Henry Ford to its current position. Jim is retiring. His replacement, Cleve Killingsworth, was announced in December 1997. Jim describes the market issues as he sees them, beginning with employment based coverage:

"We now have 550,000 lives, and we are the major HMO in Detroit. We offer a full range of products, using our subsidiary for things that do not fit our HMO license. We sell a PPO using the HAP panel to self-insured companies and smaller companies. The employers seeking the PPO are not seeking managed care, although we can provide that if they want it. They are largely interested in cost, which often means tailoring the benefit structure and omitting benefits that are mandatory under the HMO law. There are no constraints on deductibles and copayments, so they can pretty much define a package that meets their needs. It's usually fairly inexpensive, along the lines of a major medical contract. When you talk about saving by managing more tightly, it's something they question in their minds. And, in reality, the panel is used to managing care anyway. We offer the PPO as a self-insured product or an insured product, as the buyer wishes.

"The United Auto Workers has been the market maker for health insurance in Detroit, but that's beginning to change. Ten years ago, my friends on the Coast could not believe that the major banks in Detroit provided comprehensive health benefits, with a very small employee contribution, even for family coverage. The East Coast banks maybe provided some kind of major medical approach and paid only for the employee. Dependents were on payroll deduction. As the banks have become interstate, they are no longer caught up in the same local perspective. In auto itself, the salaried people have gone to a benefit menu where the base program is major medical [a catastrophic insurance with high deductibles and copayments]. If you want more, you have to buy into it."

As Jim notes, HAP is also deeply interested in the Medicare and Medicaid managed care markets, although these introduce complications:

> "Medicare managed care is limited in this marketplace. The Medicare population mostly has access to comprehensive supplementary coverage through their retirement. We've estimated that probably no more than 20 percent of the elderly in southeast Michigan will enroll in a risk product unless we can figure out how to get it packaged into the retirement plan. That's the challenge. The unions have a whole set of established relationships, and the risk product is available only to a subset of the retiree group.
>
> "The Medicare enrollment process does not acknowledge that these people have a relationship with an employer. According to the government, the subscriber can disenroll in a month, but the employer expects them to make arrangements for a year. Medicare enrollment is individual, and the employer's contract is for a group. What happens when one person from the group chooses the risk product? What if there is a dependent child? We are getting wonderful dialogues on these issues. HAP actually has more retirees to whom we provide conventional supplementary coverage than enrollees in our risk-product. Most of the risk product people were our HMO subscribers who aged into Medicare.
>
> "We are also a Medicaid insurer. Our biggest problem has been developing primary care physician capability in areas where the Medicaid population lives."

Jim thinks the HAP opportunities are enhanced by value-oriented programs of large employers like General Motors:

> "I'm excited about the GM benchmark program not just because HAP came out well. [HAP was one step short of benchmark, and the highest scorer in southeast Michigan.] To begin with, we have made a tremendous investment in the infrastructure to measure quality indicators and to develop and implement improvements. It required going back to capture new source data. This enabled us to achieve full NCQA accreditation and be among the early HEDIS producers. Yet there was little tangible reward from the marketplace.
>
> "But the change in the GM message, to make a differential in the benefit value based on factors other than just premium cost, is remarkable and refreshing. It has three advantages for

HAP. First, employees now receive standardized comparative information on quality. Perhaps over time, the employees will come to understand quality and be willing to pay somewhat more for it, and we will directly increase our enrollment. Second, our ability to cite the importance of these measures to GM is useful with smaller purchasers. Third, it gives GM a mechanism to cease offering higher-cost, lower-quality plans without argument. [Several smaller Detroit HMOs scored badly.] That will force consolidation.

"We are still being driven by the customers to expand our network. They are not looking for exclusivity, but for competitive networks. Our network is now substantially broader than the medical group, so much so that the group is contemplating other arrangements with other health plans, including Aetna. I don't see Aetna or similar companies coming into our market in any major way. As part of their national contracts, companies like Aetna need some kind of managed care in southeast Michigan. Their entry is based on a competition model that says they can come into town and command enough presence to move the business from one provider organization to another and drive the price low. What the market is telling us right now is, 'We aren't interested in this competition stuff. Why don't you broaden the network?' I have to believe the commercial carriers are hearing the same thing.

"The other thing is that the local health plans are relatively successful, but they are provider based. A commercial HMO has to compete against an organization that is provider owned and provider dominated and won't cut any great deals. I think they said, 'This is not the market place for us.' I think their analysis is the correct one."

Jim goes on to discuss price pressures and the price outlook for the future:

"Our decision to be competitive has driven our costs. We have gone out in the last couple years with price decreases. The decision was made by a combination of the senior management, including Gail [Warden, CEO], and the board of trustees. It fit in well, too, with our quality initiative, and some of our trustees' own experience that devotion to and continuous focus on quality improvement would create greater efficiencies. We had substantial support at the board, particularly on the HAP board.

"Blue Care Network [the second largest HMO in Detroit and the largest in the state] got to be the low-premium plan by having a favorable contract with their providers. When they diminished their membership six years ago, they shrank their provider base. They lopped off the high-cost providers. They worked very well with the physician leadership that remained. In all honesty, they did not use the most prestigious providers, and they were very judicious in their utilization management. That drove a lot of providers right out of the system. They were quite a low-priced product. Then they started to add members and providers, and I now understand they will have to have a rather significant rate increase. I think up to 12 percent. That will go beyond our premium.

"A number of people are beginning to suspect that the very low prices that you hear about on the West Coast may be priced too low, with quality suffering. I worry a great deal about how accurate those numbers are. There are differences between plans in age, and a few studies that have tried to adjust for that.

"Part of the difference between us and Minneapolis is the nature of employment. Detroit industries have high fixed costs and raw materials costs; Minneapolis employers are much more service and labor intensive. In Minneapolis they have a sense of dynamism and a focus on healthcare. If you look at Rochester, New York, beginning in the early '50s, there was a concentrated planning of hospital beds and insurance prices.

"In Detroit, the consolidation of the hospitals is the major factor. We've seen them begin to align themselves in various ways, including mergers. I look at the Ford System, and we have not closed hospitals, nor have we consolidated services that we could. When that happens it could lower costs. Patient management would improve and fixed costs would be reduced."

Jim documents a theme heard before, that the large employers are not pressing vigorously for rate reductions:

"The major employers here do have an interest in bringing down the cost of healthcare, but in the context of everything, it is not their most compelling issue right now. All the major employers are making record profits and getting their labor costs down. It's difficult for them to argue that they have to make major changes, particularly when their healthcare costs have been static for several years. Instead, they are going to cafeteria approaches and encouraging the employees to participate in the decision. The new hires for the autos will have only HMO choices in their initial years. That certainly gives the HMOs an opportunity to demonstrate that they are okay, they can give satisfactory service. The negative side of that is that new hires perceive it as, 'we're going to give you something that is not as good as what you'll be able to choose later on.' I worry about that message.

> "We have a lot of ongoing dialogue with major purchasers. Even when we get into justifying our rates, there is always a recognition that we have been working together for 25 years, and we are likely to continue working together 25 more. Our board and system have tried to adhere to a strategy characterized by stability of rates, not major swings. We went to our major customers and said, 'Unless inflation really breaks loose, you should count on us for a stable premium increasing or decreasing in the 3 to 5 percent range.'"

Jim notes that one important component of managed care costs is virtually outside local control:

> "[In the near term] we will see flat to modest increases. The only exception is the prescription drug program. Most anybody who is writing that coverage has seen it accelerate dramatically in the past couple of years. Four or five years ago, we had a lot of focus on the drug industry. They pulled into their shell a little bit, but now they are back with price increases. And of course there are a lot of new drugs. They are clinically appropriate and represent good-quality care, but they are expensive.
>
> "I really don't see anything on the horizon for the next three to five years that would drive major change. The biggest thing in our market right now is a change in the Medicaid program. As it moves to more rigorous management, it will have an impact on the marginal hospitals. They are close to the edge anyway."

And finally, Jim talks about the difficulties of owning and operating an insurance company and a provider organization simultaneously:

> "I think the relationship between the HAP board and the system board is about to undergo another change. It has changed before, driven by operational relationships. There are

a couple reasons for change. One, we have had to restructure HAP to manage our new products in the Alliance Health line. We also need to play a better role of working with community physicians. We've not created PHOs at Wyandotte or Cottage Hospitals. We've expanded throughout southeast Michigan, and we've pushed the envelope. We've got to think about decentralizing into the regional communities, not just for marketing but also for provider relations. Yet we have to make the whole thing fit together, so we can do NCQA and HEDIS data and so forth. We are likely to see some HMO consolidation in the next few years. That's another major wedge between the delivery side and HAP. Somebody else is going to want to sit at the table. I think that will drive us to create a different kind of relationship.

"At a strategic level, HAP is drifting off from the provider organization. As owner, HFHS says it has to do that to be successful. If you say, 'I don't want to have anything to do with that kind of business,' you could spin HAP off or sell it, but I don't think we will do that. We have so much of our economic livelihood tied up with HAP. We are able to jointly work through many of the issues of quality improvement. We can work on opportunities together. We can also work separately. The group can work on a problem, and the affiliated physicians can work on the problem separately. We put the two of them back together and show improvements on HEDIS data measurements. The approaches are remarkably different, but both are useful. There is the issue of which is the better way to go."

Henry Ford Health System operates a broad spectrum of services, including a mental hospital, a nursing home, home services, and occupational medicine. John Polanski, vice president for diversified services, is in charge of many of these units. He describes how two of them, ambulatory pharmacy and home care, are moving to a managed care approach:

"Ambulatory pharmacy is under contract with the medical group to manage pharmacy utilization. In 13 months we can document more than $6 million of improvements. Still, our managed care drug costs are running in excess of $17 per member per month. We are really focusing on appropriateness. For instance, we have a pilot on a cholesterol-lowering drug. Seventy percent of the population should have a

> high-density cholesterol ratio of 85 or more. We were actually only 30 percent. We integrated the pharmacist and the primary care physician for a group of 20 patients and began to look at compliance. After nine months, 19 of the 20 patients are above standard. We increased our drug cost, but we can also point to specific clinical improvements. We are talking very specifically with the drug manufacturers about having them go at risk with us on specific applications. We'll develop fixed payment systems for the total need for that drug.
>
> "We have transitioned home care into a managed care agency. We stopped counting visits [that is, focusing on output rather than outcomes] to focus on a continuum of high-quality, low-cost care. We are on the leading edge of how you transition patients to improve quality and reduce costs. In some conditions, where most agencies are at 30 visits per patient, we are at 12 or 13. We began discharging patients directly from ED to home about four years ago. Now almost 100 patients a month are admitted to home care directly from ED. We are supporting more than 50 ventilator patients at home, keeping readmissions low through patient and family education.
>
> "Our home wound care program found there was a great variation and little or no standardization. We were using more than 75 different products for wound care. That kind of variation in itself causes high cost and not very good quality. The home care program was the driver to create a standardized approach to identify the physician practice, the nurse practice, and the products. We are doing a lot of things in the home I never thought we could do."

Nancy Whitelaw, Ph.D., associate director of the Center for Health System Studies, leads much of the research effort supporting care of the aged and the eventual success of the Medicare HMO product. She looks at the gaps in integrated care for the aged:

> "We are moving to team-based models. We have a training grant to have medical residents, nursing and nurse practitioner students, and social work students actually work in teams. In the last six months, we have added pharmacy. The team develops a division of labor and a continuous improvement strategy using weekly or biweekly patient conferences. In the past we said that the way to get clinical teamwork was to get good people together and they would make it work. Now we

are introducing the teams to key process training, using a model of interdisciplinary learning teams. We have an eight-month cycle on improving team skills for geriatric care.

"I think we will see more models like PACE On Lok [a nationally recognized experimental program for the aged emphasizing comprehensive social, emotional, and medical support]. We have a replication site here. A large proportion of the management of chronic disease, diseases that are being managed not cured, takes place in the home and community—whether the housing is safe, they can get support services, medication, other treatment. We have been so focused on our buildings and what goes on inside them.

"Henry Ford is developing relationships with community-based agencies. It is difficult in southeast Michigan, because the community side is highly fragmented, with numerous competing agencies. We are collaborating with health departments and other agencies, trying to get a better understanding of our patients' lives and resources. I think it's beginning to go in the right direction. We don't need to duplicate these community-based programs and services, but we need to partner with existing agencies. I don't see us ever owning a Meals on Wheels program, for example, but we will learn how to work more closely with that program."

Community outreach

Henry Ford is increasingly committed to community outreach activities. Mariam Nolan, trustee and chair of the quality committee, is a particularly knowledgeable commentator on the Detroit community:

> "I'm a novice and a newcomer, both in healthcare and on the board. I've been on the board three or four years. The rest of my life is as president of the Detroit Community Foundation. I spend most of my waking moments thinking about how to improve this region. Being a part of HFHS is an important part of that.
>
> "My view of HFHS is that it is very committed to its community and its region and has made decisions based on that commitment, balanced with wanting to provide the highest-quality, low-cost service it can, with the highest customer satisfaction. There are tough decisions being made all the time on how to balance all of those elements. I think the decision to invest heavily in the downtown campus was done with a large

realization that there is a responsibility and costs associated with it. I think the community program relates to a healthier population and it is the right thing to do.

"Ford is particularly good at paying attention to business, doing its community business well and wanting to do it better, and trying to do it in a way that we can afford to continue to do it. A piece of that is connecting to the community. We have been a good citizen in trying to partner with others, not always successfully. I don't know if I could articulate to you what our community outreach strategy is. It will be important to sharpen that, and specify why we are a charitable organization and not a for-profit institution. Commitment to place, and staying here, while trying to build a complex network that can help us afford to stay here: that's how we do our business.

"I think collaboration with other health organizations is very important. It's more than being available; it's going out there and trying to form the collaboration. It's a way of doing business that there is deep trustee support for."

Mariam points out the complexity of needs in Detroit and a slightly different perspective on the system contribution:

"The most pressing need in Detroit today is education. The skilled workforce issues can drag us down, and all the other areas are now on upward trends. That's a different answer than I would have given three years ago. Three years ago I would have said, 'Keeping the private sector hitched.' I believe it's hitched. We are going to see physical improvements and new housing downtown. Ten years from now we'll have a very different community. All of the elements you need to rebuild a vital community are happening downtown, including job creation, except a quality education system. The education system is not going to turn around quickly. We are starting to struggle with it, and it's not lack of money. It's lack of leadership, biting the bullet, making tough decisions.

"I think Ford can make a contribution by continuing to find employees in the community, and getting them the training they need—use local employees if we can. We can exercise pressure and leadership to continue to raise the quality of education. We can be a positive force in keeping the pressure up. We are a large employer, and we have a significant voice pushing for change. We probably have some employees here who can exercise leadership, getting out there and speaking up."

Gail Warden, CEO, talks about Detroit and outreach:

> "The city of Detroit has a lot of problems. We made a decision in 1993. The board was unanimous that we had to reinvest in the city. Because if the city continues to deteriorate, in the long run it will have an impact on the whole region. What is good for Detroit is good for southeast Michigan, and vice versa. We made two very big decisions that resulted in $120 million invested in the city, in capital alone: the acquisition of the system headquarters building and the decision to build the west wing of Henry Ford Hospital and reengineer the whole rest of the institution, downsize it, convert it to patient-focused care, and so on.
>
> "We were pretty isolated from the community when I came. Nobody trusted us. We still have problems to some extent. A million people live in the city, and most of them have health insurance. The patient population of Henry Ford Hospital is more African American than Caucasian. We developed housing projects around here and neighborhood programs around Mercy Hospital; we created the school-based clinic program and got a big Kellogg grant for it. We got the big grant from CDC for the immunization program. We created a new minority business program with St. Johns Health System and the Detroit Medical Center. We put a lot of emphasis on diversity in the organization. These are all things we thought we had to do to live and be successful in Detroit. Some people were opposed to the idea. Their position was that it cost a lot of money and Detroit would never come back, and the real market is in the suburbs. They are still on the board; they have gotten over it.
>
> "What I'd like to do is convince the mayor that he should contract the public health department out to us."

Bill Conway, M.D., chief medical officer for Detroit region:

> "We are doing a lot of good, in a variety of not always connected programs. The school-based program may be one of the most successful. We provide the medical staff for the clinics the city runs. We have four neighborhood clinic sites now, and we will increase that to eight in the next couple of years.
>
> "These are eight-doctor clinics, with 24 support staff, focused on primary care. They are geographically convenient centers to reach out and work with the local community groups. The facilities and staffing are similar to the small suburban clinics, but the delivery of services is different. We have a parish

nurse program. We work with the churches on screening and preventive services. We offer walk-in services, because the community doesn't take well to scheduling. The care management model isn't anything like what we want to see in the future, but a couple of chronic diseases have structured programs. Case managers screen the sickest people, based on the recent history of healthcare. If we marry that with chronic disease management, for instance a patient with chronic heart failure, we can monitor their weight and edema and keep them healthier."

Vin Sahney, senior vice president for planning and strategic development:

> "Every hospital and every large satellite has responsibility for community activities. Janiki Darity, who reports to me, collects information about community needs, evaluates requests for funds, and keeps information for systemwide reports. We give her a pool of about $200,000 to distribute, and she files a plan for its use. She also makes sure we have appropriate representation on committees and boards. When people propose ideas, like the recent Red Cross program to train nurses from the inner city, she coordinates the Ford response. She contacts the relevant departments and prepares a summary document and recommendation. She's also serving on the Detroit Area Health Council "Healthy Detroit" Committee.
>
> "Our relationship with the Detroit Health Department has an interesting history. McGregor Fund made a grant of $200,000 at the time of the Clinton health reform. Gail [Warden, CEO] convinced them that one problem would be the lack of primary care physicians in the city. The problem is not at hospitals. Once people get to hospitals, there are people more than willing to take care of them. The grant was to assess the primary care capacity of the city. We promised McGregor that we would involve all the healthcare systems in Detroit. So we created a CEO council that meets quarterly. That gives us access to the information. One of the recommendations that resulted was to agree to staff the Health Department clinics. The Health Department was unable to recruit physicians because of limits on the salary. That's been in operation about a year-and-a-half."

A possibly unique contribution of Henry Ford is its MEDTEP program for African Americans. Barbara Tilley, Ph.D., the program director, describes it:

"The Center for Medical Treatment Effectiveness program is focused on improving health outcomes for African Americans. It also tries to develop African-American researchers and to increase the interest in the problems of African Americans among other researchers. The center is responsible for both doing the research and disseminating it. It was funded by the Agency for Health Care Financing and Research [a federal agency that sponsors research]. A local foundation will be contributing to a new study of the needs of aging African Americans.

"Our question is whether the healthcare needs of African Americans are different from those of Caucasians. We started with asthma and diabetes, because they are health system concerns as well as important diseases in the African-American population.

"We used our original $400,000 to get pilot data on these issues, and used it to show grant agencies that there is a need for further work. The Henry Ford user population has a lot of middle-class African Americans, so we could adjust for socio-economic characteristics and not confound those with race.

"Asthma is the furthest along. Asthma is serious in multiple ways. For the African-American children, it results in a lot of lost time from school, which means they fall behind in their education. Also, the mortality is higher among African-American children and teenagers. In terms of our healthcare system, asthma is a major cost because of emergency department use. It also leads to repeated hospitalization.

"In asthma, the prevailing view was that African Americans are higher users of the emergency room because they lack primary care. We found a similar frequency of primary care, but patients still use more emergency services. When we looked at prescriptions filled, we found similar rates for the preferred treatment but a greater percentage of African Americans also getting an additional treatment. We got an additional grant from the NIH and the National Lung Association to study the needs of asthmatic children and found that by seven years of age, African-Americans are more hyperreactive. Our data suggest that we really need some special programs for African American asthmatics. It isn't that they can be treated just like anybody else.

"We've developed a video designed for African-American teenagers with asthma, and it is being piloted to make sure it will be acceptable to the audience. If it passes the pilot, we will go to NIH for funding for a larger evaluation of its clinical effectiveness.

"Now we are starting something similar with diabetes. We've done a little bit in cardiovascular disease, providing seed money for a study in the coronary care unit on the prescription of 'clot buster' drugs. It showed that African Americans are less likely to get those drugs because of differences in presenting symptoms. So we are trying to find out if the differences are in the way the symptoms are stated or the way they are understood by the providers.

"We did a program in some African-American churches. We found that it was successful in attracting the men back for all four sessions. Now we are seeking funding to test whether the program will change behavior in that setting.

"The basic issue is that Henry Ford is willing to look at these questions and tackle them, not shy away from them. It's easy to say, 'Well, it's just poverty, and there isn't anything we can do about it.' By looking at these problems and understanding them, we can start to do things that help outcomes up to where they should be."

Strategy

Henry Ford Health System is pursuing a strategy of deliberate growth and using cost control to achieve it. It strives to improve quality and satisfaction with service, improve illness prevention, reduce or stabilize premiums, expand its HMO, win the GM Benchmark rating, and collaborate with other organizations in the Detroit area that can help it with that goal. It has achieved an annual growth of over 10 percent in the last decade, while reducing HAP premiums in real dollars. While competitors and some consumer representatives sometimes criticize the strategy, one has to note that the result has been lower health insurance costs, improved patient service, and substantial new resources available for the poor.

Several other systems will continue to exist in southeast Michigan, but they will be forced to reckon with HFHS achievements. To the employers in the area, the strategy means lower healthcare costs. To the people, it means lower costs, lower taxes, demonstrated quality, and potentially better health. The downsides are a loss of federal funds now supporting the Medicare and Medicaid program, and transfer of employment from healthcare workers to other, unknown, economic sectors. A premium saving of $240 per person per year to the employers would be offset by a loss to the community as a whole of about $50 per person of federal funds and about 35,000 healthcare jobs. These are relatively small changes in a $50 billion, 3 million job regional economy. If the people of Detroit indicate serious dissatisfaction with this goal, the "growth" focus of Ford will cause it to change direction. Overall, the strategy is far from foolproof but hard to criticize as either business or social policy. It's also challenging to manage. Allan Gilmour, chair of the board of trustees:

> "If somebody has a chance to serve on a healthcare board, I'd tell them it probably will be a fascinating experience. Most for-profit organizations are in some degree of turmoil all the time, and always have been, because the market is changeable and unforgiving. That wasn't true for healthcare for most of this century. Now the changes are quick and big relative to the past. No one knows what the future looks like. Sitting still probably isn't the right thing to do, but going helter-skelter isn't either. It will be fun teasing your way."

Keeping focus

Walt Douglas, trustee and chair, HAP board:

> "The fact that Henry Ford Health System stayed in the city and served the metropolitan community successfully from that basis has boded well for Ford and well for the city. It's maintained a tremendous number of employees in the city. The organization has changed. I can remember when if you walked into the hospital lobby, you didn't see the diversity in either employees or patients served that you do now. They provide a lot of indigent healthcare.
>
> "Like any successful business, we have to be as ubiquitous as possible. We have be where the people are. It's one thing to maintain the center downtown for tertiary care, but for someone to have simple surgery, an outpatient situation, a baby, they don't feel, if they live in Oakland County, that they want to drive all the way downtown. We understand that. The Ford Medical Group will always be the dominant medical group that will set the standard of care and quality, but we have to figure out ways, as we grow, to accommodate other needs. The whole key is the governance structure. We have a very effective governance. We don't have these fiefdoms within our system that are always throwing up roadblocks. In any merger consideration, that's got to be an important consideration. We have to be sure that our governance structure is not

damaged. If we have a group that is always voting no, that will be a problem. We've develop consensus thinking, and I'd like to see that continue as we move ahead."

Walt addresses some of the pressures that rise within a board, or the organization itself:

"There have always been some challenges from the medical group. When Gail [Warden, CEO] came, there was an interest in a structure that favored the group over the CEO. That got shot down. The former medical officer is no longer around. I don't think that medical groups can run health systems alone. I think they have to have a major voice. All of the issues of care, quality, and access they must be involved in. Plus they must also have bottom-line P&L responsibility. But they shouldn't call the shots totally, any more than the hospital administrator. I think there's got to be a team effort with both the medical and the administrative side.

"Gail was not my first choice, but the decision was made to do a search. I learned a very valuable lesson, that you ought to make that decision against what's out there. Gail Warden is absolutely the right choice.

"The second futures committee brought us a comfort level about what was happening in America. It helped us know what options we had. We made some judgments about what the system ought to be—the pros and cons of various merger possibilities, the possibility of selling HAP, profit versus non-profit structures. We chose to not go for-profit. We don't control the mergers, but we know what's a good deal, what's an okay deal, what's a politically correct deal, and what's a bad deal.

"A good deal helps cover the geographic area. It's one where we can work out the relationship with the medical staff. It would save a lot of money. It would have to have good governance. It would have to be able to make critical decisions about the organization's future. One problem is the voice of the medical staff. It has to be balanced. When you put together two large organizations, you have to have expectations about who is going to do what, who will be the CEO. You can't just say, 'Oh, we'll work those problems out; let's just go ahead.' You have to work them out before. There's a tendency to defer things. The basics of the merger have to be put together before you get into it."

Mariam Nolan, trustee and chair of the quality committee:

"The leadership structure of Detroit is changing. I'm told it used to be driven by CEOs of major companies. I think they still have considerable impact, but there is no one single leadership force that makes it easy for things to happen fast. Detroit has an operating style where just about anyone can veto action but nobody can make it happen. It is a very, very competitive environment in every way you can think about. When I talk to my directors [at the Southeast Michigan Community Foundation] about raising money, I just say, 'Go make a deal.' The healthcare industry is like that, too. There is no common vision; everybody has their own, and one of those is surviving and getting bigger. When they get together, it's because 'we're going to come together or we won't make it.'

"I don't know that Detroit Renaissance [a panel of community leaders] has ever had a discussion on the healthcare system. The auto CEOs have a vision—lower costs. I don't know if it would transfer to the others.

"The Ford board is not a downtown broker board. That hurts us sometimes. The Ford board is a diverse board. People are brought on for different reasons than being chairmen of the major companies downtown.

"I think we need to find the right partner, get a bigger share of the market. I think we need to be very shrewd in how we do that. I think we probably need to act as fast as we can."

Gail Warden, president and CEO:

"I totally changed the governance system. Before, there wasn't a board, just a bunch of buddies Henry Ford II would convene. The former CEO would turn his chair away from the table and look out the window when they were talking. The first board meeting I attended, they asked, 'What's governance?' I said it is how trustees set the direction of the organization and evaluate the CEO. So we did a governance study on how the board should be organized. We made a strong case on why it needed to be more diverse. I said we have to have people who don't live in Grosse Pointe [one of Detroit's oldest and wealthiest suburbs]. I organized a chair's council, which was a way to bring the chairs of the advisory and hospital boards together to talk and exchange information. They discuss these with the advisory boards, and it rolls up, and we have a report on what happens. So the system board is issues-oriented.

"In one of the best meetings we ever had, I told them that they had to approve a position in this organization on assisted suicide. We had two board discussions, and it went to the quality committee where it will be approved. These are tough issues, and you have to deal with them. We worked it through the medical group, the ethics committee, and management. It went to the board the first time. They raised some issues; we refined the position. Now it will be approved. Other places would have tried to avoid the issue, because it's tough."

Henry Ford Health System can afford two operations that must be done less formally in smaller organizations. Deborah Ebers, vice president for labor and business relations, links the office of the president to local industry:

"Gail [Warden, CEO] really wanted to increase our visibility and our understanding of our customers, to bring that knowledge back here so we could incorporate it in our strategic direction. At the same time we would be creating a way to be influential with our customers, so they would understand why we are moving in the direction we are and taking the steps we are.

"I came to design a strategy to help us do better customer listening, be more responsive. I think we've been successful. The strategies we've used are straightforward. There's no magic in them other than getting them done and knowing enough about our customers to know what will work.

"We've accomplished a broader dialogue on all sorts of community issues as well as performance issues, strategic direction, fund-raising, and other topics. We have taken it a step further than just understanding customers, to using the relationships to engage our customers in opportunities to work together."

Deb describes a program that is formalized at Henry Ford but that is a part of any good CEO's job:

"We do customer listening at the CEO level. Each year, Gail [Warden, CEO] and others sit down with senior management at local companies. We try to get a CEO–CEO link that establishes Gail's credibility. We have a lot of interactions at the employee benefits level. We invite people in to tell us their health benefits strategy, and we present the Henry Ford strategies to

> companies. We try to share knowledge and expertise. I'll invite company people to join us at our educational sessions, and outside speakers. We produce a newsletter three times a year. We surveyed our customers to find out what our customers wanted to know. When we asked what they knew about us, it was very little. We've increased their understanding of what a system is and does. There's ongoing turnover and change among our customers, so it's a continuous process.
>
> "We have been very attentive to understanding employer purchasing coalitions and what they are trying to accomplish, and to be responsive. We also want to help guide that decision making where we can. I think we are more attentive than others in town, but I think the folks involved in purchasing groups are still sorting out their strategies, what will work and what won't. We try to share expertise.
>
> "Organizations have different underlying cultures. Some cultures do not lend themselves to joint or collaborative activity. In other organizations, the culture is not a risk-taking one. Banks and utilities have been unwilling to expose themselves to employee relations issues related to changes in health benefits. The need for change and the pressures for cost reduction are not yet beating out the risk of taking action. Now the larger banks and utilities are taking a much more aggressive approach. I think there have been major changes in insight among the auto companies, and maybe it is spreading.
>
> "It puzzles me, because I've worked for almost five years to push our purchaser leaders to embrace a managed care philosophy. Yet there is still a lot of comfort in the fee-for-service market. Underlying it, it's the balance: 'Is it worth the challenges to the status quo, and the leadership?' "

One of the things that will increase comfort with managed care is measured quality and satisfaction. The auto manufacturers have been particularly insistent on this. Deb explains:

> "The report cards and accountability issues are important to all employers, and we have been doing a lot of work on them. There's a commitment to a strategy of informing employees so that they can make better decisions. We have demands for information that are overwhelming us. People want hospital information, physician information; it's coming from the employer leaders, the banks and unions, the employer coalition. The pressure to create information on the performance

of the major health plans and our hospitals and doctors is incredible. It's consistent, it's urgent, and it will move however the provider community responds. Our position has been to be out in front, leading the pack.

"There's a level of sophistication in town about managed care because the history has been good. The care has been reasonable, and we don't have the horror stories that came in Florida and California. All of our efforts to create more value have been to make our processes better for patients and for everyone. There are many examples of reducing the risks to improve outcomes, not 'cut a day off and send somebody home.' We have been trying to demonstrate some of those examples with our customers, so they understand the difference between managing care for people and managing care for premium. Never at Henry Ford did anyone suggest telling doctors not to discuss treatment options with patients. It doesn't fit our culture. It doesn't fit the philosophy and commitment to group practice. Never. It would astonish."

Darlene Burgess, vice president for government affairs, describes how her office links Ford to national, state, and local government:

"My responsibility is to make sure that somebody who has the skills to read a legislative bill or a regulation and the knowledge of the needs of the system actually reviews what's proposed, identifies when an organization response is needed, gets that response from the organization, and helps convey it to Congress or the legislature or the administrative unit. Somebody who is there on behalf of the organization.

"My office also has a number of initiatives that flow from issues like the Medicare or Medicaid contracts. For example, the local Red Cross has been training low-income people to be nurse aids. The funds for that are drying up, and we need the program. So there's an opportunity for us to partner with the Red Cross. We provide the jobs and on-site training. We have a demonstration project for Medicare that involves a number of large group practices from around the country. It's designed to pay the groups on an annual rate of increase rather than cost of care. So if we have a lower rate of cost increase than our community, we would share that with the government.

"When the state announced that it would capitate Medicaid recipients by county, that's 500,000 patients. The state was talking about a single Medicaid provider for each county. I felt that my first job was to convince the state to structure a program that would allow several different providers to bid, that would improve quality, and that would last more than one bid cycle. I took several of our leaders to meet with the Medicaid administrators. Several things evolved from these meetings. One is a program for the 'special needs' children; another is a senior citizens carve-out, which recognizes the very different needs of Medicaid seniors from young families; a medical education carve-out; and a long-term care program. I tried to get the state to take a 'line of business' approach.

"Then I went to work in the system. In behavioral services, I discovered that there was no one place that someone could come and get a bid for the whole system. I got the chief of behavioral services to take that on. We are developing a general risk model for behavioral services that would be salable in HAP's commercial contracts as well. By the time the RFPs came out, we had some way to respond. We set up an oversight group chaired by Doctor Conway, the vice chair of the medical group."

Alliances with other institutions

Henry Ford Health System has an extensive network of merged, joint-ventured, and contracted arrangements that includes every county of the metropolitan area, and as Gail Warden, CEO, says, almost every other major health system:

> "The other element of our culture is the special partnership relationship between the physicians and our organization. The old approach was to go to the suburbs to fill beds downtown. My approach is, 'Now that you are in the suburbs, why don't you become part of the community? Why don't you reach out and develop relationships so people can get their care close to home?' There is no place in the region where you can't get almost all your care close at home. If you choose a Henry Ford Hospital, you can have that, too. We had to make a choice in 1988 or 1989 whether we were going to try to compete with everybody under the sun or develop some partnerships with them. It seemed to me the fastest way to do that was to partner with somebody who had activities in several locations, and that was Mercy Health Services. So we partnered. We do that because community-wide systems, and getting people to work together, are important, instead of competing with each other and duplicating resources.

"We have activities with Mercy Health Services in four sites, with the biggest osteopathic system in Michigan, with Bon Secours System, William Beaumont, Providence, Children's Hospital of the Detroit Medical Center, and with General Motors for rehab. We had negotiations with Ford Motor Company about managing their medical system within the plants. We have some small ventures with St. John's. That's all the major systems in Detroit except Oakwood. Most of them I got involved with at the beginning, and others worked out the arrangements. The Mercy arrangement was mutual. Mercy had problems in Detroit; we wanted access to the two Catholic hospitals in Macomb County. The Bon Secours discussion started with a discussion between the national system CEO and me. The Children's venture started between Dr. Rozack, their CEO, and me.

"Brenita Crawford took over Mercy Hospital [the downtown hospital of the Mercy System, which serves a particularly disadvantaged population and carries a heavy charity load] when it was losing a lot of money. She cut costs. Ford put our physicians there to strengthen the staff. There were no house physicians, and no intensivist, so we could not send patients there. They did not have consultation arrangements for most specialties. We worked those out, and it became an attractive place to bring patients. That was the big change. Brenita began reaching out, getting the community involved, making them feel it is their hospital. She's made some tough decisions—laid off people, consolidated departments, cut out levels of management. Mercy will get the American Hospital Association 'Turnaround Hospital of the Year Award.'

"I think one of the reasons we are able to do some of these things is that over a period of time we have amassed a group of talented people who can assess one of these situations accurately and quickly. One of the strengths of Henry Ford is the huge depth we have. Part of it is that we can articulate something that people can buy into. They can see how they relate to our mission and goals, and where they might go with it. Also, we are an organization that is willing to take some risks. Peter Butler and I got the stuff kicked at us for awhile because we were bringing the osteopaths into the system. Once we got beyond the fact that they are osteopaths and got our physicians to sit down with them and see what they could do, our physicians bought right into it. Even the board was that way. The board asked, 'Aren't these guys kind of just a little bit better than chiropractors?' We pointed out that osteopathic education contains all that allopathic medicine contains, and that test scores of people at osteopathic schools are as good as at University of Michigan or anywhere else."

Allan Gilmour, chair of the board of trustees, talks about the future:

"I think what Gail is doing in mergers and affiliations is right for the time. One of the things that came out of the consultant's report on a current merger discussion, and the futures committee last year, is the risk of being bypassed—of standing alone and not having enough economic power to counter very aggressive out-of-town HMOs or Columbia HCA. For survival and success we need to have horsepower. Except for the most serious illnesses, medicine is a neighborhood business. We need to cover the whole geography, with everything from storefronts to multi-million-dollar facilities. Alliances is another way. We don't have to own everything. What business calls outsourcing has a role. Whether it's cleaning or food services, or things more central, sometimes those outside companies know more than the rest of us do.

"Competition in healthcare is geographic, as opposed to head-to-head product competition. We need a bigger presence in the suburbs. The future of this area is not Detroit. We looked at merger with Beaumont, but they don't want to merge. Unfriendly takeovers don't work in not-for-profits. So we have a HAP contract with Beaumont. If we want to do something badly enough, we could make a merger with another competitor or do something ourselves. A good part of it is figuring out what our goals are, and what's possible.

"I think the medical group leadership is largely in agreement, but when we get into the group, there is some concern and worry. I think it goes back to the academic medicine concept, 'We're going to have a strong department, and there will be some less talented people in the suburbs.' If we asked the suburban [Ford] doctors, they wouldn't agree. I want both. I want high-quality and national reputations, but I believe there's more to what we're doing than that.

"I'm not sure our colleagues who are trustees of the other healthcare systems fully agree with us. I don't hear the same sense of concern about the future. I think it's true that there isn't anywhere near a unanimous sense among the leaders of

Detroit that the cost of healthcare is a pressing issue. I think the leaders believe there should be some mergers and rationalization, and cost would be a consequence of that. I don't think they come at it from the perspective, 'My premiums are too high.' They just see a number of organizations that the world tells them are going to be fewer. The leadership in Rochester and Minneapolis has come from the business community. It will be in most places."

CHAPTER

5

TOWARD 21ST CENTURY HEALTHCARE

What We Know and What We Don't

The typical community healthcare organization or voluntary hospital, in Anytown, USA, can use the case studies to improve its understanding of the problem, to set realistic local goals, and to begin implementing them. These three case studies can justify their claim to leadership. They are deliberately organized to assure value in healthcare to their communities for many years to come. Obviously, they are well ahead of the pack.

We know the case studies exist in real places not unlike the rest of America, and we know they are not the only successful healthcare institutions. Rochester, New York; Salt Lake City, Utah; Grand Rapids, Michigan; Charleston, South Carolina; Fort Worth, Texas; Seattle, Washington, and other U.S. communities can claim similar achievements in creating value in healthcare. Like the case study organizations, they are building these around existing structures, with many parallels to the cases. The case studies are not accidents, and they can be replicated.

No one would claim they have the final answer. While the progress of Moses Cone, Legacy, and Henry Ford is admirable, it has not produced a simple, easily copied solution for a typical American community. There is no McDonald's for healthcare. And if there were, the Anytowns are so different that each would face a unique job installing it.

We know as a nation that we cannot continue the status quo. Unbridled healthcare cost increases ultimately will impair America's ability to compete economically with other nations and to create jobs for all our citizens. We have decided that is too high a price to pay. Congress has frozen Medicare payments for years into the future.

Growing numbers of employers have begun to insist on value and have set up risk-sharing plans with their employees. Most states have moved to similar programs for Medicaid recipients. People across the nation have come to grips with the necessity for change.

We know that despite their limitations, the traditional structures of independent medical practices and voluntary hospitals have often served us well. All three of the case studies are using them as a foundation. The two alternative structures, using employed physicians and relying on national corporations, are not faring so well. Although the employed-physician model almost certainly has a role in the final solution, Henry Ford, Kaiser-Permanente, and others that have used it extensively are moving away from it. The continuing troubles of the largest national hospital corporation, Columbia HCA, suggest that the model has substantial dangers attached to it. Continuing with tradition also helps manage the transition. Using the community hospital and its medical staff as a starting point allows incremental change. Among other things, incremental change means that individual doctors and patients with the biggest doubts about the future can linger with the past.

So most American communities should emulate the case studies. Anytown community leaders should assemble the evidence about their situation, develop consensus, and pursue strategies that will improve the cost and quality of Anytown's healthcare. They should take those steps through and around their community hospital and its medical staff. The best we can do may be what the Henry Ford people called "a drunken stagger toward quality," but it is better than doing nothing at all.

The Third Revolution in American Healthcare

The first and most important issue in the Anytown strategies is that they involve a new philosophy of medical care. Permanent improvement in cost and quality cannot occur without rethinking and improving the basic decisions of medical practice. While this seems at first to be a drastic, frightening concept, it would not be the first time medical philosophy has shifted substantially and dramatically. Such a revolution occurred after Johns Hopkins was founded, in 1876. The shift was to diagnosing specific disease entities and to using deliberate interventions, such as aseptic surgery, based on the diagnosis. The results included closing most of the medical schools in the nation, establishing dozens of new medical schools and thousands of hospitals, and developing the modern medical specialties. It took more than half a century for all this to occur. A second shift, almost as momentous, began around World War II, with the development of a new drug armamentarium around antibiotics, and a new diagnostic capability around the clinical laboratory and improved x-ray capabilities and safety. There was a vast expansion of hospitals and medical specialties that, like the first revolution, lasted 50 years.

The third revolution will be around prevention and teamwork. As Allan Gilmour put it, "figuring out . . . how to move from some of the concepts of medical schools to more of the concepts of public health schools, population-based medicine, a much better statistical analysis of results." Doctors in every case study recognize the need.

Dale Dreiling, M.D., from Greensboro:

> "We would like to see primary care, specialists, and the hospital working to provide the best care. You do it as a group. When you put your protocols together, you are not just saying, 'Primary care, what's the best way to treat low back pain?' You get everybody in the room to look for the best protocol. 'Let's look at outcomes, and see what really is the best protocol.'"

Darrell Lockwood, M.D., in Portland:

> "In diabetes, we . . . are more likely to make a house call or a Saturday visit than we used to, if it will keep the patient out of the hospital . . . . Primary care doctors are more capable of handling diabetes because of advances in diabetic teaching programs and improved monitoring. We have a belief now to monitor consistently and frequently."

Reginald Baugh, M.D., in Detroit:

> "We try to identify the diseases where it makes a difference in the population. We know that in Michigan versus the United States, and Detroit versus Michigan, there is a higher incidence of smoking, a more sedentary lifestyle, more overweight, higher incidence of diabetes, hypertension. Other major initiatives are childbirth complications, and low birth weight. It will make a difference in the short term and the long term. For us to do well, we have to address these problems."

The issue is not the reality of the third revolution—it has already begun—but assuring its successful outcome. What guideposts have the leaders established that will help Anytown to the right conclusion? Where are the uncharted hazards, and how does Anytown avoid them? There are several of each.

Guideposts for Anytown

The guideposts tend to be the values, basic assumptions the leaders have made and now view as correct. They are saying, "Success lies in working from these principles." While they can't prove failure results from other views, they keep returning to these themes to make sure Anytown doesn't forget them.

Patient satisfaction

No solution will endure that is not acceptable to individual patients in sufficient numbers to support cost-effective care. Patient needs are determined by formal survey, which all three institutions do. Surveys are supplemented by focus groups and other direct efforts to hear what the customer really wants. It is clear that most people are seeking convenience, reassurance, and emotional support. Painful as it may be to professionals, they take quality for granted; they expect appropriate outcomes and good service.

The issue is particularly clear at Henry Ford, and they address it frequently in their remarks. People have said they are not coming to central Detroit for healthcare except in extreme circumstances. Major elements of the Ford strategy hinge on this fact. The affiliation strategy with independent physicians and the partnerships with competing healthcare organizations have their origin in patient preference.

The development of the obstetrics service in suburban Portland is a similar story. Jane Cummins described the market reality:

> "We determined that we were losing market share because the women in the suburban areas would not come downtown for care. A decision was made over great wailing and gnashing of teeth to start OB at both suburban sites. Meridian Park has been in operation for three years and it has already had an expansion. It was built at ten rooms and was completely undersized."

The results of formal surveys often reveal unexpected and unpleasant information. Success requires doing the surveys and dealing with the findings. Legacy met the women's request. There was no other realistic opportunity. There won't be in Anytown.

Quality

Although patients take quality for granted, buyers and the community cannot. When outcomes are measured, quality is surprisingly variable. Where you go and who you see does make a difference. Tom Simmer, M.D., concedes that as a whole his "rebel force" of affiliated physicians does not measure up:

> "When we actually measure quality in terms of things that are important, such as the percentage of patients with congestive heart failure on an ACE inhibitor, the percentage of two-year-olds with all their immunizations, the percentage of diabetics who've gotten what they need, there is no comparison. The medical group does a far better job."

These are not trivial matters. ACE inhibitors prevent heart attacks. Immunizations save millions of days of parent lost time—and billions of dollars in preventing the tragic complications of what used to be the "usual childhood diseases." Diabetics who get either too much insulin or too little end up in the hospital, and they have shorter lives.

Patients are saying by inference, "I can't deal with quality. I expect my community institutions to deal with it." The improvement is often from one small percentage of failures to an even smaller one, with numbers too small to be consequential to the typical patient. But the cost of fixing poor quality, which occurs in excessive treatment, lost income, reduced functional ability, and disruption to people's lives, is so high that quality improvement is essential. It is a theme that many large employers have picked up. The case study trustees have accepted the obligation.

Cost

Theoretically, any community could emulate Portland's health insurance premium structure, providing care for $110 per working adult per month, and $390 per senior citizen. (Most rural counties can expect to pay substantially less for Medicare, and a few urban areas do better than Portland. Greensboro, at $373, is one of them.) Practically, the Anytown question is how to get from here to there. Downsizing a community medical establishment means closing hospitals, laying off workers, and reducing physician income. Not unreasonably, the people whose lives are most directly affected tend to resist. The community is faced with severely penalizing some of its members in order to improve life a little for the rest. Most places will solve this problem by holding prices constant, rather than trying to cut them. All three case studies took that approach. It will take dedicated, organized will-power even to do that.

Medicare payments are actually income to the community, rather than cost. Everyone pays the same premiums for Medicare; high-cost communities collect much more on those premiums than low-cost ones. They distribute that as income to healthcare workers. The impact of payments from Medicare supplementary insurance depends on who pays the premiums. If they are paid by an employer who is not a member of the community, they too are income. Under traditional Medicare, a reduction in cost is never an unalloyed benefit to the community, and it could actually be an economic penalty. The same is true of Medicaid. Savings in Medicaid costs are split several ways rather than returning directly to the community. Finally, in communities where employee health insurance premiums are paid by a remote corporation, savings are lost income for the community and gains for the central office.

Why then should Anytown be concerned with healthcare cost? There are three practical reasons. First, non-healthcare jobs are at stake in every community. The higher the healthcare costs paid for workers and retirees, other things being equal, the fewer new jobs will be created. The number of non-healthcare jobs is 8 to 12 times the number of healthcare jobs. Second, at least part of the savings always returns directly to members of the community. Out-of-pocket payments, premiums paid by local individuals and employers, and expenses of a locally owned health insurance company (like Blue Cross Blue Shield in Portland and Health Alliance Plan in Detroit) all stay in the community. Third, remote governments and employers are moving rapidly to share the risk. Premium-sharing arrangements, copayment requirements, and benefit limitations put the responsibility back on the individual and the local community. The Medicare HMO, for example, is frequently offered at a lower premium to the beneficiary, and sometimes also with expanded benefits. With it comes the obligation to control cost.

Clinical Opportunity

Improving satisfaction, quality, and cost simultaneously requires providing care in new ways, "reengineering the hospital," as Lanty Smith puts it, but also reengineering care in the ambulatory center, the doctor's office, and the home. Reengineering must be done on a disease-by-disease basis. What helps for heart disease is irrelevant for pregnancy.

The leaders show us that new approaches to care of specific diseases can pay off with lower cost, faster recovery, and better results. Locally developed protocols and case management reduce errors, promote teamwork, and improve follow-up. They are not cookbook medicine; they are better medicine. As Tom Royer, M.D., says, "I may have to follow a protocol, but the protocols are really helping me give better care."

The case study institutions reached that conclusion some years ago. They have done the routine inpatient admissions and outpatient surgeries. They are in a second stage of development, deliberately studying complex clinical problems, the places where protocols don't fit well. Together they mentioned about 50 different clinical studies, advanced protocols, or special programs for high-risk and high-cost illness. These ranged from protocols for less common but more serious problems, like transplants and neurosurgery, to special outreach activity like Henry Ford's African-American asthma program. Teen pregnancy, high-risk pregnancy, and high-risk newborns are on all three agendas. So is management of patients in the adult intensive care units. The frontier is in outpatient management of chronic disease, like diabetes and congestive heart failure, behavioral illness (Henry Ford is just starting a program on depression), and total management of catastrophic problems like cancer, multiple sclerosis, and trauma.

These are the battlegrounds of the third revolution. The revolutionaries are showing tangible improvement in both cost and quality. Disease by disease, they are reengineering American healthcare.

Prevention

There is no healthcare as good as the absence of disease. There is no treatment for a complication as good as avoidance. But human behavior and attitudes underlie almost all of the prevention opportunities, and modifying attitudes and behavior is expensive and difficult. The prevention activity in the case studies is pioneering. Three central guidelines emerge from it.

First, prevention programs must be custom-designed to specific health problems. While constellations of problems hang together, like family violence and immunization, most problems are improved by identifying the specific people who need help, the exact behavioral change, and the precise context of their needs. Teen pregnancy is an example. Most girls are not at risk: those who are do not get pregnant by accident or from ignorance. Their needs have more to do with self-esteem and self-actualization than they do with contraception or sexuality. A community with 2,000 teens maturing each year—that is a community with three or four high schools—could spend $100 on each teen, with a general program for all. Or it could identify the 200 eleven-year-olds at risk, and spend $1,000 on each. It is now clear which program is more likely to pay off.

Second, prevention requires strategy. Greensboro's community survey and consensus on priorities is the model others should follow.

The problems that people want to attack are the ones that must be at the top of the agenda, rather than simply the ones that objectively cost the most money. This is an old lesson for advertisers and retailers. Convincing people to want your product is possible, but selling them what they already want is cheaper.

Third, the strategy requires collaboration. Many sectors of the community, including the people who are at risk themselves, are deeply involved in prevention activities and the problems related to high-risk behavior. Ignoring or competing with these efforts reduces the effectiveness of the overall effort. Kate Ahlport said it best:

> "The Moses Cone Community Health Program was established for a very specific purpose, to . . . produce measurable outcomes . . . in collaboration with other agencies in the community.
>
> "We had representatives from the medical community, from HealthServe Ministry, the African-American community, the Health Department, small business. It wasn't just to get buy-in. We did not have a preconceived mission. It really was to develop a vision of what needed to be done."

Combining specific programs and a collaborative strategy will be hard for many communities to do. Some will have a substantial burden from previous acrimony between potential partners like the hospital and the health department, and like the establishment as a whole and the disadvantaged. The difficulty cannot excuse procrastination. Almost one-fifth of all healthcare expenses are directly related to high risk health behavior. Programs of clinical improvement alone cannot reach the value goals.

Measurement

Quantitative data on outcomes quality, patient satisfaction, and cost will be routinely used to assess performance and progress. Improving the measures has been the mainspring for Moses Cone's development and Legacy's. People's psychic satisfaction with success is more important than the financial reward. Measurement is what tells them they have improved. No value oriented program can succeed without it. At another level, the measures and the spider diagram are what allow Henry Ford to exist. An organization that complex can thrive only if it identifies explicit goals and measures their achievement.

With measurement comes benchmarking, the deliberate search for the best practice on a given measure, even if it comes from another country or another industry. Often the benchmark organization will describe its procedures, helping Anytown to understand its limitations. The benchmark is rarely an immediately attainable goal, but it does reveal the relative strength of local practice. A realistic goal for next year can be set in the light of the benchmark and the work to be done.

People who prefer the status quo attack measurement. One of their most common arguments is that the measures are imperfect. The argument is inherently true. Any measure has a limit in accuracy. The things we measure routinely, like land, time, and weight, have measurement limits that are no longer of everyday importance. In healthcare, our present measurement ability often raises more questions than it answers. Costs of elements of care are imprecise estimates. Outcomes quality measures are only available on a small fraction of clinical work and must be handled with great care even then. Satisfaction surveys are expensive. Done in the most reliable way, they cost about $75 per patient surveyed, which suggests that Henry Ford is spending on the order of $10 million a year for its satisfaction data.

The point is that progress depends on accepting the best available measure at the time. The ancient traders who used the best scales ended up making the most money. The nations that measured land and time, however crudely, ended up dominating the world. The American businesses that adopted the early cost accounting ended up as leaders in growth and profits. (And modern companies that follow the quality improvement approach are reporting similar gains.) The healthcare institutions that make intelligent use of existing imperfect measures will dominate their markets, as the case studies have. The answer to the argument against measurement is simply that we must get on with it. We must make the compromises to get started and improve as we go.

Risk-sharing

The cost of healthcare is everybody's problem, and everybody is going to participate in the solution. In truth, nobody can afford to check the box that says, "None of the above." As anyone who has been through serious illness or the death of a loved one knows, the problems in healthcare are frightening and painful. They are also inescapable. Risk of the cost of illness will be explicitly shared by the government, employers, patients, and providers.

We are on a path nationally that allows great flexibility and individual variation in how we will deal with the risk. The downside of flexibility is complexity. Our health insurance risk will be carried out through a menu of hybrid plans. Health Alliance Plan's strategy to develop new products tailored to niche markets is an example.

Provider contracts will be even more "hybrid." Dale Dreiling's mind-boggling plan for compensating Greensboro Health Network physicians is inevitable. So is Tom Simmer's not much clearer one for Detroit's HAP affiliates. Complexity is a consequence of accepting the need for multiple options for buyers, patients, and providers.

The message for Anytown is clear enough. All we know today is that the solution will not be simple. The search for simplicity is an illusion, seductive but unprofitable.

Integrating outpatient and home care

Improving satisfaction, quality, and cost for most patients will mean providing continuous, seamless care where the patient needs it. The most common site for care will be the doctor's office, followed by the home, the ambulatory care facility, and the nursing home or subacute facility. The inpatient hospital will remain important financially, but it will be used by only a small fraction of the patients. At the moment, continuity is missing and "seamless" is a dream. As the patient moves from one site to another, delays mount, records get lost, work gets repeated, care gets interrupted, even philosophies and terminologies change. Expensive duplicate systems are set up to catch these errors before serious harm is done, and even they occasionally fail. The eventual solution lies in eliminating the causes.

The doctor's office is by far the most important of the various sites. Most care starts there, and often the first transfer is to another office. Doctors' offices are as Tom Simmer described them: "They don't have any infrastructure at all. Their office is often their wife or their daughter; they don't even have a nurse . . . ." Somehow we must help these people do a better job.

New information systems are one major vehicle for achieving continuity. With the hardware and software come common terminology, shared protocols, and inexpensive automated safety checks. But the hardware and software are the result, not the cause, of integration. Building and operating information systems among independent, competing entities is difficult. Common ownership or collaborative organizations make it easier to decide whose definition and whose information system will prevail. They also make it possible to train people in doctors' offices and design specific assistance.

One lesson is that seamless transfer from site to site can occur with collaboration or shared ownership in the right environment. In the various arrangements between Mercy Health Services and Henry Ford, Mercy's philosophic commitment to care of the poor was protected, and even enhanced. In the Wesley Long merger with Moses Cone, key board seats in the new corporation were assigned to Wesley Long people. As Gail Warden says:

> "We had to make a choice in 1988 or 1989 whether we were going to try to compete with everybody under the sun or develop some partnerships with them. It seemed to me the fastest way to do that was to partner . . . . So we partnered. We do that because community-wide systems, and getting people to work together, are important—instead of competing with each other and duplicating resources."

The Unknowns

If the guideposts are mostly basic values and approaches, the unknowns—the issues where the case studies reflect differences, failures, and confusion—are specifics. It is clear that there is a great deal we simply don't know how to do that we must learn to do.

Medical organization

The issue in organizing physicians is how to balance the need for self-directing, self-motivated caregivers with the need for collective financing, integrated care, and protection. Forms of organization affect how individuals work, and make them more or less effective. We have not yet discovered the appropriate form for the practice of medicine. We know that the two extremes, solo practice and employed groups, will not serve our needs, so the solution lies somewhere in between.

What is the right path for Anytown? Conservative movement away from the unsuccessful extremes toward a flexible, participative, but goal-oriented structure. Building the components of organization, such as shared-risk contracts, protocols, employee training, common terminology, and information systems allow progress without permanent commitment. They help Anytown physicians to improve value in healthcare and their own incomes simultaneously. They also establish platforms for discussing and evaluating next steps. And, perhaps most important, they allow incremental change. The reluctant can hang back, and might even win the chance to say, "I told you so." The pioneers can test the frontier.

Networks, alliances, partnerships, physician-hospital organizations all have these goals. There is no evidence to select the best as yet, and, in fact, there may be no one best form.

Physician compensation

We do not know what payment mechanism provides the best incentive to the physician. The issue is tightly tied to the question of organization. We know that the simple extremes, fee-for-service and salary, don't work. We have no shortage of proposals for complicated middle grounds. We have very limited evidence for selecting among the proposals. Anytown should move away from the extremes with limited experiments. Almost any intermediate proposal that meets the ethical and business judgment of reasonableness, appeals to a substantial group of physicians, and does not involve an irreversible commitment could be accepted for trial. After all is said and done, that is what the case studies are doing, searching carefully and pragmatically for an answer.

Behavioral and geriatric services

A large part of the cost of healthcare is tied up in mental illness, alcohol and drug abuse, and care of the infirm aged. We do not know how to organize and deliver these services to large populations at a reasonable cost. Many of the conditions lie at the limits of our effective treatment skills, at the borderline of medical and social problems, and at the limits of our ability to apply an insurance or shared-risk concept. A wise and caring community responds to the need with limited insurance benefits available to those who seek them, explicit and professional case management for the more expensive care, and encouragement for the caregivers who elect these challenging areas. Realistically, we do not have the knowledge to do more.

Reaching at-risk populations

We know more about the importance of prevention than we do about how to do it. We are learning that efforts must be targeted to people at risk. Those people are often disadvantaged in several ways beyond health. Attitudes about class and race interfere with our efforts. We have a very limited understanding of how to change self-destructive behavior in substance use, nutrition, exercise, sexuality, family life, and care seeking. But all three case studies are making substantial investments, and evidence from around the country suggests that carefully developed plans in these areas will yield at least modest returns. The cost of the failures of prevention is often borne by the healthcare providers, who take care of the uninsured and underinsured when they are critically ill. This obligation is being continued and clarified under Medicaid risk-sharing. Anytown cannot afford to ignore preventive activity. A well designed program emphasizes the continuing search for better methods and benchmarks.

Scale

We do not know whether an organization the size of Moses Cone (about 500 doctors serving about 350,000 people) is big enough. We need to know a lot more about what additional contributions and difficulties come from an organization the size of Henry Ford (about 2,000 doctors, serving over one million people). We need to understand that there are only about 15 urban areas big enough to support a Henry Ford–sized organization. We need to deal with Allan Gilmour's very legitimate concern:

> "Healthcare organizations underestimate the management problems of size and geographic spread. It isn't the same task, just four times bigger. The complexities are more than that. I think we should be able to drive to anyplace we operate in an hour."

There is probably a way to replicate the case studies in all the places as big as or bigger than Greensboro. Bigger places will have bigger organizations, more like Legacy and Henry Ford. Communities somewhere around 750,000 population and up can have at least two competing organizations. But more than half of the nation lives in places smaller than Greensboro. About 50 million people live in rural areas. Rural communities can certainly start on the Greensboro model. At some point, most of them are going to need help from larger organizations. About 100 million people live in smaller cities in metropolitan areas. The demand for geographic convenience is strong. The smaller cities will need to consider their relationships to central city organizations.

Large organizations like Henry Ford will certainly have a role. We will need a way to develop and test protocols in large populations and to transfer them to smaller ones. We will need the technical skills of Henry Ford available economically beyond an hour's drive. The smaller communities will also need the lash of competition. It is unlikely that even the best-intentioned organizations will perform as well without it.

A variety of national or regional organizations already serve the smaller communities, including for-profit management companies and hospital ownership companies, and not-for-profit hospital owners and networks. They have so far not convincingly demonstrated their ability to improve value, but they could easily have an important role in the solution.

Medical Research and Education

We need to examine how we assure continued progress on the frontier of medical knowledge and how we train new entrants to all the care-giving professions. Only a few medical schools have faced the reality of the third revolution. Most are still in the model Allan Gilmour describes:

> "They talk good old academic departments. If you are good in urology, and ophthalmology, and podiatry, and everything in between, you'll be all right."

Or in the situation Richard Zimmerman, M.D., laments:

> "They [Oregon Health Sciences University] continue to train orthopedic surgeons. Most residents are used as lesser-paid employees to increase the productivity of the professor . . . . OHSU is totally responsible for the number of orthopedic residents in Portland, and it's based on the number they need to run their trauma system. The people at the medical school are not responsive to market forces because they are not affected by market forces."

Research is in a similar state. Far more money and effort goes to finding new drugs and treatments than is spent seeking value. The research establishment is heavily committed in that direction. The evidence-based or outcomes-based medicine that the various research centers at Henry Ford work on is the exception, not the rule. The current direction is an expensive one that has contributed in part to the underlying cost problem, but it also defines the leadership of American medicine. Revising that direction will take a national effort.

Next Steps for Anytown

Taken as a whole, there is certainly room for optimism. Anytown can expect to improve the value of its healthcare if it takes the steps suggested by the case studies:

1. **Start with the notion that the healthcare institution belongs to the community.**

   It's the duty of community leaders to manage the institution effectively, and that duty may be hard work. All three of the case studies illustrate this in words as well as deeds.

   > Allan Gilmour:
   >
   > "Some outside observers believe that business people aren't forceful enough on nonprofit boards. That's true. We're not; we're scared we'll come across as the mercenaries, or mean people."

Charles Reid:

"It took us months and months to sort through [changing the mission of Moses Cone]. We went off on retreats. We had facilitators. The board took psychological tests . . . . But it happened."

Charles Heinrich:

"The business group was on the hospital boards, but for a long time they viewed it as an honorary job. Our board now is very much a working board, and people are very concerned about the wellness of the whole community."

2. **Begin a dialogue around the most serious presenting symptoms of the problem.**

   The symptoms are the cost of care, borne by employers and taxpayers, and the cost of lack of access to care for the uninsured, borne by the healthcare organizations and public services. The two problems are interrelated. The dialogue should build consensus around goals and priorities, the approximate path ahead, and the strategies and values that shape the path. A broad community consensus is desirable, but it takes many years to construct. A small, focused, and committed group on the hospital board can make substantial progress.

   The profile differs substantially from city to city. It is notable that cities with better than average records, like Rochester New York; Salt Lake City, Utah; Seattle, Washington; and Portland, Oregon began this dialogue decades ago, and that they keep it up.

3. **Move deliberately toward risk-sharing health insurance and care financing.**

   The way the commitment is actuated differs in the three communities. Moses Cone has used the need for profit and the limitations of Medicare payment to encourage cost reduction and is moving toward a broader risk-sharing environment. Legacy uses the existence of extensive risk-sharing to continue forward motion, with much more emphasis at the moment on quality than on price. Henry Ford uses a combination, aptly represented by their spider chart.

4. **Emphasize value rather than cost.**

   "Cheap healthcare" is not an acceptable goal. "Quality healthcare" is both acceptable and demonstrable, and it can be obtained at Portland prices.

   The leaders work deliberately to overcome the misconception that they might be seeking cheap healthcare. They emphasize the quality aspect of value at every opportunity.

5. **Get a chief executive who can handle the project.**

   This means either reinforcing a good executive who has been effective at the initial steps or recruiting one with a good record elsewhere.

   All three of the case studies had a renaissance event. Moses Cone changed its governing board, Legacy and Henry Ford changed their chief executives.

   Allan Gilmour:

   > "Boards don't run things in the for-profit world or the not-for-profit world. If they do, we are in real trouble. Boards listen. They bring experience and judgment, but they don't say, 'Go this way instead of the other,' because they don't know enough about it. If we see companies that are off-track, the board's only real remedy, other than selling out, is to change the players. We don't say, 'I'll give you a strategic plan. We board members will have it written down a week from Thursday.' No, we won't."

6. **Develop a culture of change—measured performance, goal setting, and reward for goal achievement.**

   The quality movement programs, CQI and TQM, have a proven record in this regard, but you can have the substance without the labels, and vice versa. The traditional healthcare organization has a tradition of the status quo.

7. **Stimulate the shift to a new medical philosophy.**

   Ask for realistic performance measures, like Charles Heinrich:

   > "Doctors are extremely smart. When you put the numbers before them, they are glad to make changes."

   Don't take no for an answer, like Lanty Smith:

   > "We have to educate the physician community that they can't check the box that says, 'None of the above.'"

   And balance their contribution with your own, like Walt Douglas:

   > "There have always been some challenges from the medical group . . . . [T]here was an interest in a structure that favored the group over the CEO. That got shot down. The former medical officer is no longer around. I don't think that medical groups can run health systems alone. I think they have to have a major voice."

8. Develop prevention and outreach to high risk groups.

Allan Gilmour:

"We are not Henry Ford Illness System or Sickness System, or Tertiary System. We are a total health system, and it is immunizations of little kids, and hospice, and working in the public schools, all of those things. When I see the "Senior Plus" program at HAP assigning patients to a panel, and then having them come in for a history and some checks right away, it is almost the principle of insurance."

9. Collaborate with other institutions and continually expand the consensus.

Identify concerns, bring them forward for debate and resolution, and make tactical concessions to achieve the strategic goal.

For the foreseeable future, the goal will be met not by several institutions operating independently or in destructive competition, or a monolithic or monopolistic one. The models emerging in Greensboro, Detroit, and Portland mix competition with collaboration to achieve their goals.

Greensboro

Despite the monopoly in the city, there is provider competition in the county and the region that could enter Greensboro. Price competition is maintained by the insurance premiums, which are set regionally. Moses Cone collaborates with the county health department and the school board. It will have to collaborate with the foundation it recently established as an independent entity. This model of a well-run local monopoly operating in a context of regional competition and local collaboration may be the best for smaller, relatively independent communities.

Portland

Overt competition between Kaiser and the other two providers has clearly paid off for Portland, giving it its enviable cost structure. Efforts to differentiate Legacy from Providence seem also to have been productive. They ensure a local voice. (Providence, Kaiser, and Blue Cross now have ties to other markets, and the other insurance companies are national.) Legacy's success must be a strong stimulus to Providence and Oregon Health Sciences University. OHSIC has already found a niche, where collaboration between the competitors has paid off, in the immunization data system. There is a good chance it will find more. It might proceed more rapidly if it had trustee-level or buyer-level participation instead of executive level.

As James Perry says:

> "We have to look at what's being done at OHSU and Sisters of Providence, and they have to look at us. I think we can get that dialogue going better—it just started. A lot of people will tell you it is going nowhere, but I don't think that is the case. OHSIC is a piece of it, but it's more than that. There is an understanding among them that there are some things they should collaborate on. We ought to collaborate in some of the really high-end things. We are collaborating in trauma and the transplant program."

Detroit

Henry Ford's inventiveness in pursuing ventures with competitors has ranged from acquisitions to mergers to joint ventures to strategic partnerships to management contracts. The examples described in the case are the survivors; several others have failed. Also of note is the deliberate use of a very large and diverse 44-member board, and 14 advisory and affiliate boards including 180 members. This structure runs counter to most thinking about governance. It is made to work by the will of its leaders, including the CEO, and by the deliberate use of measured performance. The Henry Ford vision on both governance and collaboration is distinctly different from most people's.

Allan Gilmour:

> We need to cover the whole geography, with everything from storefronts to multi-million-dollar facilities. Alliances is another way. We don't have to own everything. What business calls outsourcing has a role . . . . [T]he other trustees [in other Detroit systems] don't talk this language at all . . . . We are on a different wavelength almost."

Gail Warden:

> "We had to make a choice in 1988 or 1989 on whether we were going to try to compete with everybody under the

sun or develop some partnerships with them . . . . So we partnered. We do that because community-wide systems and getting people to work together are important—instead of competing with each other and duplicating resources."

GLOSSARY

Capitation—Fixed annual payment for each patient.

Case management—Special assistance for individual patients who have either a catastrophic illness or chronic diseases in order to maximize recovery and reduce patient discomfort.

Clinical Resource Improvement Service (CRIS)—Unit developed by the Medical Group at Henry Ford Health Systems that uses clinical pathways to exploit core competencies.

Diagnosis-related group(s) (DRG)—Categories of hospital discharges by the principle cause of admission. Used as a payment mechanism by Medicare and many insurance companies.

Emergency department (ED)—Unit of the hospital that provides urgent or emergent healthcare.

Emergency room (ER)—Unit of the hospital that provides urgent or emergent healthcare.

Full-time equivalent (FTE)—Unit used to measure the number of employees working in an organization.

Guidelines—Consensus statements of best practice or what will be done routinely for most patients. Also called pathways, clinical pathways, or protocols.

Habitat for Humanity—A volunteer-based, not-for-profit organization dedicated to reconstructing houses for the poor.

Health Plan Employer Data and Information Set (HEDIS)—Set of standardized performance measurements developed by the National Committee for Quality Assurance. The scope of HEDIS measures includes clinical effectiveness/clinical quality, access, patient satisfaction, utilization of services, costs, stability, and informed choice.

Health maintenance organization (HMO)—Insurance company that provides healthcare benefits through a prepaid payment arrangement.

Independent practice association (IPA)—Health maintenance organization that pays affiliated physicians on a basis other than a fixed salary.

Information systems (IS)—The systems within an organization used to link, store, and transfer information and data, usually electronically.

Labor, delivery, recovery, and postpartum (LDRP)—Care delivered to most new mothers in a single room.

Length of stay (LOS)—Period of time from patient admission to discharge from an inpatient facility.

MedPartners—National stock physician practice management company.

Management services organization (MSO)—Provides management services to one or more group practices.

National Committee on Quality Assurance (NCQA)—An independent not-for-profit organization that assesses the quality of managed care plans, managed behavioral healthcare organizations, credentialing verification organizations, and physician organizations.

Neonatal intensive care unit (NICU)—Unit of the hospital dedicated to critical care management of newborns.

Pathways—Consensus statements of best practice, or what will be done routinely for most patients. Also called protocols, clinical pathways, or guidelines.

Program development teams (PDT)—Clinical teams oriented around specific groups of diseases.

Perinatal—The period shortly before and after birth.

Physician-hospital organization (PHO)—A physician organization that builds bridges between primary care physicians, specialists, and hospitals.

Per member per month (PMPM)—Basis for payments to a provider by insurance companies or managed care organizations.

Preferred provider organization (PPO)—A type of managed care organization that contracts with physicians to become part of their provider network in return for reductions on reimbursement rates.

Profiling—Collection of data about clinical processes.

Protocols—Consensus statements of best practice or what will be done routinely for most patients. Also called pathways, clinical pathways, or guidelines.

Research and development (R&D)—Efforts devoted to developing and improving products.

Request for proposal (RFP)—A request from an organization to other parties (e.g., consultants) to submit a proposal in order to gain rights to work on a specific project.

Same store improvement—Improvement or growth measured within an existing organization, not through mergers or acquisition.

Total quality management (TQM)—Concept used to measure performance and determine goals in order to continuously improve value within an organization. Also called continuous quality improvement (CQI).

INDEX

ABOUT THE AUTHOR

John R. Griffith, M.B.A., FACHE, is the Andrew Pattullo Collegiate Professor, Department of Health Management and Policy, School of Public Health, The University of Michigan. A graduate of John Hopkins University and the University of Chicago, he was director of the program and Bureau of Hospital Administration at The University of Michigan from 1970 to 1982, and chair of his department from 1987 to 1991.

Professor Griffith has been at Michigan since 1960. He is an educator of graduate students and practicing healthcare executives. He has served as chair of the Association of University Programs in health Administration and as a commissioner for the Accrediting Commission on Education in Health Services Administration. He is active as a consultant to numerous private and public organizations. He was an Examiner, Malcolm Baldridge National Quality Award, 1997–1998.

He is the author of numerous publications, and his text, *The Well-Managed Health Care Organization*, is currently in its third edition. The first edition won the ACHE Hamilton Prize for book of the year in 1987.

Professor Griffith was awarded the Gold Medal of the American College of Healthcare Executives in 1992. He has also been recognized with the John Mannix Award of the Cleveland Hospital Council, the Edgar Hayhow and Dean Conley Prizes of ACHE, and citations from the Michigan Hospital Association and the Governor of Michigan.

Professor Griffith is a director of The Allegiance Corporation, a physician-hospital organization serving Ann Arbor. He is a member of the National Advisory Board of Family Road, a company devoted to improved maternal and child care. He speaks and consults widely on the development of voluntary healthcare systems.